The Singular

"He's the _guy_ I'm interested in. He's just not the _kind_ of guy I'm interested in."

The Singular Self

*An Introduction to the
Psychology of Personhood*

Rom Harré

SAGE Publications
London · Thousand Oaks · New Delhi

© Rom Harré, 1998

First Published 1998

SAGE Publications Ltd
6 Bonhill Street
London EC2A 4PU

SAGE Publications Inc.
2455 Teller Road
Thousand Oaks, California 91320

SAGE Publications India Pvt Ltd
32, M-Block Market
Greater Kailash - I
New Delhi 110 048

British Library Cataloguing in Publication data

A catalogue record for this book is available from the British Library

ISBN 07619 5738 3
ISBN 07619 5739 1 (pbk)

Library of Congress catalog card number 97-069584

Typeset by Type Study, Scarborough
Printed in Great Britain by Biddles Ltd, Guildford, Surrey

Contents

'Oh, yes, poor Victor,' said Anne. 'But he was looking for a non-psychological approach to identity,' she reminded Patrick with a wry smile.

'That always puzzled me,' he admitted. 'It seemed like insisting on an overland route from England to America.'

'If you're a philosopher, there is an overland route from England to America,' said Anne.

Edmund St. Auby, Some hope

Preface

To judge by the number of books and articles that have the word 'self' in the title, interest in this topic has hardly waned in two decades. Despite this mass of literature there still seem to be uncertainties in the way the central concept itself is understood. The aim of this study is to try to excavate a common conceptual layout, or 'grammar', with which the underlying complexity of the issues raised in writings on 'the self' can be clearly addressed. I have called this grammar 'the standard model'. 'Person' seems to me the most robust notion in a sea of uncertainty. But this very notion is itself internally complex, in that it picks out beings who are both materially embodied and enmeshed in networks of symbolic exchanges, which are, at least in part, constitutive of what they are. In the spirit of Wundt, I come to the conclusion that psychologists must accept not only that their 'science' is built on a dual ontology, molecules on the one hand and persons on the other, but that it requires two radically different methodologies. With this in mind one turns to track the ways that the word 'self' is used in contemporary writing.

It soon becomes clear that, for the most part, selves are fictions. By that I mean that certain features of the flow of activity produced by persons in interaction with one another are picked out in our ways of speaking and writing as entities, as if they had an existence of their own. However, it may be that there is no better way of talking about certain common features of human interaction than some form of 'self' talk. Not all languages use neatly translatable analogues of the notion as it appears in English, but there is a widespread parallel between versions of what I have called 'the standard model'. Peter Mühlhäusler and I explored this territory in our *Pronouns and people* of 1993, and I have taken much of the work described in that book for granted in what follows.

Though none of the chapters herein are reprinted articles, nevertheless I have freely mined a number of recent publications for material relevant to the topics at issue. I am grateful to the publishers for permission to extract parts of the following papers:

'Universals yet again: a test of the "Wierzbicka thesis"', *Language Sciences* (1993) 15: 231–8.

'Is there still a problem about the self?', *Communication Yearbook* 17, 55–73.

'Forward to Aristotle: The case for a hybrid psychology', *Journal for the Theory of Social Behaviour* (1997) 27(1): 101–19.

'Postmodernism in psychology: Insights and limits', *New Psychology* (1997) April, 21–28.

'Pathological autobiographies', *Philosophy, Psychiatry, and Psychology* (1997) 4(2): 99–113.

'Fitting the body to the mind', *American Behavioral Scientist* (1997) 40(6): 798–812.

I am grateful to several generations of undergraduates at Binghamton and Georgetown Universities, who bore, with patience, the courses on personhood I inflicted on them. And I am grateful too, for the many conversations on these matters that I have enjoyed with colleagues there and elsewhere, particularly Jim Lamiell, Ali Moghaddam, Steven Sabat, Nancy Much, John Shotter, Ken Gergen and David Crystal.

CHAPTER ONE

On Being a Person: Problems of Self

I am not merely present in my body as a sailor is present in a ship.

René Descartes, *Meditations*

It is widely agreed that a pleasant way to spend a damp and chilly Saturday afternoon in the great city of Washington is to browse the time away in Kramer's Bookstore close to Dupont Circle. Drifting from genre to genre one is struck by the number of books with 'self' in the title or subtitle. In the section where one finds the books that booksellers classify as 'psychology' there are lots. For example among the popular works are Adams's *Journal of the self* (1990), Anthony's *Total self-confidence* (1993) and Cleghorn's *The secrets of self-esteem* (1996). In a more academic vein we find Baumeister's *Self-esteem: the puzzle of low self-regard* (1984), Field's *Self-esteem for women* (1997) and Lee's *Psychological theories of the self* (1979). Books with 'consciousness' in the title or subtitle are almost as common, they map onto genres in a slightly different way. We can be sure in these too the 'self' will figure prominently. Yet neither selfhood nor consciousness are clear, univocal or straightforward notions. What is it to be a human being is what is really at issue of course, and that is the perennial question!

In putting together the modest studies that make up this book I am hoping only to bring a little clarity and order into a field which more than any other seems to me to be marked by obscurity and confusion. The terminology alone is a mass of ambiguities. No doubt human beings are individuals, but individuality is not uniqueness. We could be as alike as peas in a pod and still be ever so sharply individuated, for instance by whether we are fourth or fifth from the calyx. 'Identity' sometimes means one and the same, but ofttimes, in these days, has come to mean 'of a type or group', particularly in phrases like 'social' and 'ethnic identity' (Nicholson, 1997). 'And so on', as we shall see in what follows.

The question 'What is it to be a human being?' belongs in a great many disciplines, and it would be a happy outcome if they could be found to converge on some common answer. Or even on a view as to what sort of question this is: anthropological, biological, grammatical or what? Even in this small group of studies I will have recourse to the writings of philosophers, of psychologists (both concerning the normal ways of being a person and also some of the abnormal), of literary theorists, of linguists, and of anthropologists.

Whenever one reflects on human affairs sooner or later one is confronted by the fact of personal singularity. No two people are alike, yet all bear many resemblances to one another. There is individuality, just being a different thing from other things. But there is also uniqueness, being like no other thing. This is true of all organic beings. There are flocks of birds, obviously made of individuals, but to the unschooled human onlooker displaying no individual marks of uniqueness. One goose is more or less interchangeable for another. Farmers, of course, and goose girls, have a more discerning eye. Microbiologists do not differentiate individual bacterium from each other as unique and singular beings, not because they could not, but because individuating bacterium is of no immediate value for their projects. However in the human world it is uniqueness, personal singularity, that is the leitmotif of all our forms of life. Even in those cultures that place great emphasis on membership of a collective as the basis for personal being, the groundwork is still the singularity and ultimate uniqueness of every person.

At the same time each unique human being is a complicated patchwork of ever-changing personal attributes and relations. The problem of personhood is posed by the striking fact of the preservation of that uniqueness in the context of so many similarities to other people and shifting patterns of relations with them. There is a unity of each person in the context of so much moment by moment, situation by situation diversity. Much of the discussion of and research into these matters has been based on the use of the word 'self'. But what, if anything, does this word pick out from the complex world of human life? The study of no aspect of humanity is so marked by muddled thinking and confusion of thought as this one. The modest study that follows is an attempt to abstract a modicum of order from more than two decades of a flood of writing on the topic of 'the self'.

This exploration will take us into a variety of genres: postmodernism, feminist literature, autobiography, psychopathology and philosophical psychology. In some of these genres seemingly amazing things are said that apparently cast doubt on our common-sense ways of dealing with people. I hope to show that at least some of these assertions are chosen more for their rhetorical effect than their contribution to the psychology of personal uniqueness. However the attempt to extract a rational core from a striking metaphor should not be read as a sly way of debunking or deni-grating the merit of the social plea or political plank that the origi-nal writing expressed. A close study of some feminist writings on 'the self' will show that there are some important insights for psy-chology to be found there, though plainly the main purpose of these discourses is persuasive and even political. One does not become an anti-feminist by revealing the machinery by which a certain rhetorical effect is produced in feminist writings on the 'self'.

The picture of the human form of life which I shall be sketching in these studies is framed in a certain account of mind. What sorts of attributes are those we single out as 'mental'? It seems to me that people produce streams of actions, some private, some public. These display all sorts of properties some of which we pick out as mental. There are stabilities and repetitions that recur in these streams of action, like vortices in a swiftly running stream. The body-centred structure of perception is one such recurring stability found in all acts of perceiving. There are patterns of stability and change in the streams of cognitive and emotive acts that each person produces, usually with the engagement of other people. Some are private and others are public. The private ones tend to be taken as the mental attributes of the person. Amongst the attributes of a person there are not only those currently produced in the flow of action but psychology must also take account of the skills and dispositions needed to produce the stream of activities we call 'the mental life'. Mental states, according to this point of view, are pro-duced *ad hoc* in the course of people acting, and are nothing but attributes of the stream of action. There are no mental entities other than the public and private actions people engage in. But what of *the self*? Is it an entity that must be invoked to explain the singular-ity and unity of each human being as a person?

Singularity of self

The burden of the discussion of selfhood in this book is a thread of argument to establish that the self, as the singularity we each feel ourselves to be, is not an entity. Rather it is a site, a site from which a person perceives the world and a place from which to act. There are only persons. Selves are grammatical fictions, necessary characteristics of person-oriented discourses.

The sense of self as it has been interpreted in the Cartesian tradition seems to be an intimation an *entity* has of its own existence. That entity has been variously categorized and located by generations of philosophers. Descartes presents his logical intimations through the *cogito*[1] as revealing clearly and distinctly that there must be a substantive mind in association with the body for there to be a person at all. He goes on to argue that being embodied is neither a necessary nor a sufficient condition for human personhood. Each intimated entity has been supposedly the substantial referent of the word 'I' as used by each person.

Like others before me[2] I want to show that the 'entity' account is wrong – wrong scientifically, wrong in the way that the phlogiston theory of combustion was wrong. When coal and metallic ores are heated together phlogiston from the coal was thought to combine with the metallic ore to yield a metal, a theoretical account of a well established chemical phenomenon, based on the assumption that phlogiston, like coal, was a substance. The yield of metal weighs less than the original ore, so we can conclude that the substance, phlogiston, has negative weight, or levity. At this point our credulity is strained, just as it is when we learn from Descartes that the self or ego is an entity, an insubstantial mind which is supposed to bring about bodily movements in the material world, though it is immaterial.

I will try to show that one's sense of self is not an ego's intuition of itself. To have a sense of self is to have a sense of one's location, as a person, in each of several arrays of other beings, relevant to personhood. It is to have a sense of one's point of view, at any moment a location in space from which one perceives and acts upon the world, including that part that lies within one's own skin. But the phrase 'a sense of self' is also used for the sense one has of oneself as possessing a unique set of attributes which, though they change nevertheless remain as a whole distinctive of just the one person. These attributes include one's beliefs about one's attributes. 'The self', in this sense, is not an entity either. It is the collected attributes of a person. The word 'self' has also been used for the impression of his or her personal characteristics that one person makes on another. I shall call these respectively Self 1, Self 2 and Self 3. 'The self' in any of these senses is often treated as if it were an entity. This, I believe, is a useful fiction, but ultimately seriously misleading. In the light of arguments and demonstrations to that effect we might think that the multivocal concept of 'self' could be dispensed with. The idea of point of view from which one perceives the material environment and acts on it, the Self 1, is indispensable to the management of the human form of life. The idea of the self as the shifting totality of personal characteristics, the Self 2, is as much a feature of conscious, active human life as is the visible convergence of parallel rails. Yet one's attributes are of very diverse sorts, some fairly permanent, some evanescent; some intrinsic, others existing only in relation to aspects of the human and material environment. We can hardly dispense with the Self 3, to refer to the totalities of personal impressions we make on other people.

We seem to have three aspects of personhood in focus at the same time. Though none are really entities, that is thing-like in the manner of existence and behaviour, we have forged a way of speaking about them using nouns, the very grammatical form that entity talk takes, in our several uses of the expression 'the self'.

There are various strategies that can be adopted at such an impasse. History, it seems, rewards those who go to the heart of such matters, querying and perhaps rejecting the implicit ontology[3] that frames the discussion. 'Does phlogiston exist?' looks like a sensible question. Even the intelligibility of the answer 'No, it does not exist' presumes that it might have done. But looking deeper we can see that the question presupposes an incoherent ontology. Nothing like phlogiston could have existed so it can be found neither to exist nor not to exist. It defies the frame within which the world is made intelligible in that it is incompatible with the law of universal gravitation. Does the Cartesian ego exist? This is also a poorly formed question, since to affirm or to deny it requires that the concept of an ego or self as a substantial mind makes sense. But substantial but immaterial minds interacting with matter make no more sense in the light of causal requirements for the inducement of motion in matter than do fiery substances of negative weight. How could an unextended substance be sensitive to every part of the extended human body? And so on.

The manifestations of personhood

If selves are aspects of persons, where are selves, either as personal points of view or as dynamic totalities of personal attributes, especially clearly manifested? In these studies I shall focus on discourse, story-telling of many sorts, in which the uniqueness of persons is displayed, and established. Adopting the terminology used by

Apter (1989) I shall work within a body of assumptions that could be succinctly expressed as follows: In displays of personhood, of our singularity as psychological beings, we express 'a sense of personal *distinctness*, a sense of personal *continuity*, and a sense of personal *autonomy*' (1989: 75).

However, as we shall see, it is best not to interpret these characteristics in terms of 'identity', a concept favoured by philosophers. It has drifted right across the semantic landscape to come to mean more or less its opposite. Someone's 'identity', in much contemporary writing, is not their singularity as a unique person but the group, class or type to which they belong.

I share another thought with Apter, a thought that is perhaps very widely shared if not expressed as we would express it; that 'loss of one or more of these three aspects of the sense of identity is associated with the depersonalisation of psychotic breakdown' (1989: 76). We shall find, however, that the pathologies of self extend into the very fine grain of the expressive modes by which these three aspects of personal uniqueness are manifested (Cohen and Eisdoríer, 1986). For example, in what has come to be called 'multiple personality disorder' (MPD) the fine structure of the way people use personal pronouns to express their point of view and to take responsibility for their actions is disturbed, or at least appears different from what for long has been taken to be the normal way of using them. According to the basic psycholinguistic principle on which these studies are based, expressive displays are holistically tied into what they express. To have a sense of self is to be disposed to express oneself in particular ways. Each of Self 1, Self 2 and Self 3 has its characteristic mode of expression.

Some basic distinctions

Individuality versus uniqueness

There could be a multitude of individuals, each of which was exactly like the others, 'as like as peas in a pod'.[4] We would tend to say this when the only distinction between such individuals was either their place in some spatial array or the moment of their existence in some sequence of events. Otherwise they might resemble each other perfectly. We could imagine someone with exactly the same level of skill in tennis as another, with exactly the same vocabulary of French words, who weighed exactly the same, and so on. But we could not imagine someone who was a different individual but occupied exactly the same space–time trajectory as another. This is not because of a failure of our imaginations, but because if everything else is the same we only say there is more than one individual if they occupy different space–time trajectories. To be one and the same person one must, at least, have a unique spatio-temporal location. There are problems of what to say about personhood when one individual at some moment splits amoeba-like into two, each from then on occupying a different space–time trajectory. How is the identity of the descendent beings related to that of their common ancestor? We are not prepared for coping with this kind of situation with people, though cloning may bring us close to it, and will no doubt have an effect on concepts of personhood. At this time our ontology for people (the grammar we have for talking about them and as them) does not recognize this possibility since we use spatio-temporal criteria to pick out distinct individuals in hard cases, for example the proof of bodily continuity required to establish a claim to a fortune; cf. the struggles of Howard Hughes's heirs.

But for there to be unique beings, stronger conditions must be met. A being is unique only if it differs from every other in all of its properties. By ranking properties in some order of importance we can construct a table of degrees of uniqueness. My focus in these studies is on the ways that for most purposes for which a psychologist might be interested in people, and for all and every purpose for which the law or medicine might be interested in people, the default position is that each person is unique. Each, it is assumed, actually differs in *every* respect from every other human being. Some of these differences are gross, some scarcely discernible, and some so insignificant that we live our lives together as if they did not exist. Many are ephemeral, and most are relational, anchoring each person in a network of connections to others, and to their histories (Markus and Wurf, 1987).

Individuality, as Lamiell (1997: 128) remarks, does not entail individualism. As we work our way through the leading aspects of Self 2 we shall find that the attributes that constitute a person's selfhood, in the sense of their personal characteristics, are very largely relational. Not only are they defined in terms of relations to other people, and to the characteristics of those others reciprocally, but they are in constant flux as the relations to the social and material environment shift and change. One's attitudes, for example, are rarely a stable configuration of dispositions, but appear now in one form and now another. They are, for the most part, what one believes in this context and that. Individuality, I shall argue, is primarily a matter of those aspects of selfhood that are tightly tied to our singular embodiment, Self 1 and its characteristic forms of expression.

Individuality and singularity

However, though each person's selfhood is a shifting and changing pattern of modulating dispositions and powers, coupled moment by moment to ephemeral manifestations of those powers in public and private actions, each person is also a singularity. By that I mean that everyone has a sense of themselves as occupying a point of view from which they perceive the world around them and the states of their own bodies. As a singularity a person has no attributes other than a position in space and time. I shall try to show that the sense of self as a singularity (Self 1) is a basic feature of human life. It can be traced to the fact of our singular embodiments. Part of the difficulty that attends getting clear about the use of the first person pronoun and equivalent expressions is that among their functions is that of indexing what someone says or thinks about a great many topics with this singularity of point of view. It stems from the unique trajectory that each person carves out in space and time. Each person has just one body. Our uniqueness as distinct individuals is then a product of *two* identifying features of personhood. There are our unique attributes and our unique points of view. It seems reasonable to say that a person is a human being with a sense of self – but that can refer either to my sense of my make-up as a person or to the singular point of view from which I perceive and act. Sometimes in referring to their sense of self people mean the one and sometimes the other. Every one of us must have both. Perhaps we should move away from common parlance a mite and talk of a person's *senses* of self. This ambiguity in the use of the word 'self' makes the task of understanding some of the literature on the self difficult. North American writers favour Self 2, the totality of personal attributes, as 'the self', while other writers of English tend to favour Self 1, the singularity of point of view, as 'the self'.

To a first approximation personhood presents a duality that runs right through our lives as conscious beings in intimate contact with one another. There is 'the self' as the attributes of a person, including a more or less stable physical make-up and the highly labile patterns of thoughts and actions of the active person. This must also include individual repertoires of powers, abilities, skills, liabilities and so on. Then there is 'the self' as the centre of action and experience. I shall be presenting an elaborated and differentiated version of this duality in what follows. It will serve as the stable frame within which the labile and dynamic flux of thought and action is presented. I shall call it 'the standard model'. It is an attempt to capture the main outlines of the grammar of our ways of talking as and about persons. Adding in Self 3, the way we seem as persons to others, we have a structure something like the following:

Person {Self 1, Self 2, Self 3}

where Person is the robust existent and the three bracketed concepts refer to aspects of and conditions for the flow of personal action.

Expressions of uniqueness, singularity and unity

The royal route to an understanding of the sense of self and the unity of experience must be through the analysis of the ways these aspects of personhood are publicly expressed in both speech and action.

The self as an expression of the singularity of the point of view of the embodied person in perception, the unity and structured pattern of the contents of consciousness, is always singular for every human being, in all cultures. If there are exceptions they are in the realm of myth and mysticism, for instance out-of-body experiences. Even if we were to allow people who seem to have more than one personality (MPD sufferers) and those whose conscious lives are divided by fugue and those who have blind sight even after commissurotomy to be the embodiment successively or simultaneously of more than one person, each of these 'persons' perceives the world, visually, auditorily, tactually and so on, from the spatial location of that body. Descriptions of the world and of the body as itself a territory are from a spatial point of view. The grammar of perception reports will occupy us in due course, since in them Self 1 finds its characteristic expression.

Autobiography expresses the sense one has of one's life as a unity in time. It is tied into a skein by the use of 'I' in such a way that every incident so indexed belongs to the life of the speaker, as an embodied person. There are many stories that could be told by each person about his or her life, each expressing the then current perspective from which that life was being viewed by the one and only person living it. These are contributions to or 'parts' of the beliefs people have about themselves. So while each human being has a robust sense of living a singular life in time, the incidents that are offered to oneself and to others as constitutive of that life are usually multiple. One person has many possible autobiographies (Elbaz, 1988). Again there is a penumbra of pathology, since a sufferer from fugue may have one autobiography for one section of their life and another for another. These are versions of a life but the telling of them belongs to the one singular life course. These are our beliefs about Self 2, expressed, very often, to others as Self 3.

Discourse genres for talking about people

In our time there are two main kinds of stories told about human beings. There are those told by novelists, preachers, politicians and neighbours. In these stories the irreducible, elementary being is the individual person. Narrative conventions for this sort of discourse are often centuries old. Then there are those told by doctors, biochemists, anatomists and grave diggers. In these stories there are a variety of ways in which human bodies are discussed, classified and taken apart. Several different catalogues of fundamental parts are in use: organs and limbs, cell systems, genes and so on. Perhaps in the future other kinds of stories will be told, just as there were other kinds in the past.

Lawyers, like psychiatrists, tell sometimes the one kind of story, sometimes the other. In his first trial O.J. Simpson was presented both as a person and as the alleged origin of genetic material. Counsel generally know very well what they are about. They know when the accused should be presented as a person within a traditional moralistic story, and when presented as an organism, in a biological and molecular story. Psychologists tell both kinds of stories, but it is evident that their grasp on the genres is not always secure, and their applications are less confident than those of the legal profession.

This study is an exploration of the ways that human beings appear both singular and unique and of the story-lines that present such themes to others and to themselves. It is not just an investigation of personhood within some possible psychology, but also one of 'selves', the existence of which has come to be seen by many as the core of personhood but which I am intent to show are useful fictions. I hope to do justice to both kinds of stories, the moralistic and the molecular, and to the evident plausibility, in the appropriate contexts, of each. I hope to erect some provisional signposts through an unnecessarily obscure territory, marking some of the bypaths that have proved unprofitable. The enterprise is undertaken in the spirit in which Wittgenstein undertook similar studies.

I cannot hope to emulate the profundity of his insights, but at least some modest overviews of the territory can be achieved.

I have suggested the study of pronoun grammar will reveal one way each person experiences the singularity of personhood. The sense of self, it is suggested, is a complex matter involving a singular point of view and a unique but ever-shifting pattern of personal attributes. The singularity of point of view comes from a sense of being located as an individual in two manifolds: a manifold of things, some of which are persons; and a manifold of events, some of which are actions by myself and other persons. For the most part we are related to other persons in so far as they are embodied, so we can treat the manifold of persons as part of the mani-fold of things. But this condition is sometimes suspended. For Christians the sense of self is partly a sense of being related to a supernatural being who is not embodied. Some people see themselves as distinct only as having a certain place within a genealogy, most of the members of which have either ceased to be embodied or are yet to take bodily form. But these variations are off-shoots of the root idea that in general there is or was only one body per person. We must also reflect on whether there can be more than one person per body.

Becoming a person, acquiring the senses of self

According to Vygotsky's conception of human development the higher cognitive capacities, including the ability to think about oneself, come into being during the course of interactions with others. At some point one realizes one has a point of view, and that one is a being with all sorts of attributes. In the interactions most important for human development a child's immature efforts at various tasks, both manipulative and cognitive, are supplemented by the help of more skilled performers, usually for a while, at least, the parents. At this time a cognitive or motor skill is, in Vygotsky's (1962) phrase, 'in the zone of proximal development'. Development occurs when the child takes over and does for itself the supplementing action offered by the parent. The child can then complete the task for itself. Vygotsky's original studies have been amplified by extensive work reported in Bruner and Watson (1983) on the development of cognitive capacities. Learning one's mother tongue and other practices characteristic of one's culture shapes and modulates the structure of cognition. The manifolds of things, some of which are persons, and of events, some of which are human actions, in which we have a sense of location are the grounds for the structure of major aspects of human cognition, perception, intentional action and memory. The application of the lessons learned from the study of developmental psychology and the grammar of the language of self-reference to the psychology of consciousness, agency and autobiography follows naturally.

The most general thesis concerning the development of a sense of self can be expressed as follows:

> The biological endowment of a human being with an active brain and nervous system is manifested at first in relatively[5] undifferentiated and unordered mental activities that are then shaped and modulated by the acquisition of discursive and practical skills which facilitate display of the centred organization we recognize in our own experience. This pattern of development could be thought of as the transition from the characteristics by which we would recognize any animate being capable of mental activity to the characteristics definitive of what it is to be a person, that is to be a human being with both senses of self.

Each of these characteristics is complex and is differentiated along various dimensions. For example consciousness is not only an awareness of the environment and of the state of one's body, but also, somehow, an awareness of being aware. We are not only conscious but self-conscious. Agency is the capacity not only to act without immediate external stimuli, but to manage and monitor our own actions. There is not only acting to achieve a goal but also goal setting. Fantasy not only is the capacity to imagine what is not the case, for example to imagine something not given immediately in perception, but becomes differentiated into thoughts about the past, recollections, and thoughts about the future, anticipations. In recollection and in anticipation one's sense of self is involved in different ways.

In knowing myself to be a unique being (and indeed as a unique being) the sense of self acquires a third dimension. But what exactly is this third dimension? We have learned, from the failures of introspectionists and phenomenologists to find the ego as an observable entity at the core of being, and the paradox pointed out by philosophers that the self that seeks is the self that is sought, *not* to think of the dimension of self-awareness as an awareness of self. In accordance with the principles of discursive psychology I shall argue that the third dimension of self-consciousness and self-monitoring is none other than the capacity we have to give discursive accounts of and commentaries upon what we perceive, how we act and what we remember. Of course we have to pay attention to these matters, but that requires no higher order and miraculous perceptual or cognitive capacity. The 'I' that introduces such accounts, I will argue, is the very same 'I' that introduces perception reports, declarations of intent and claims to recollect. The singularity that is the public person and that is expressed in first order conversation by first person devices is identical with the private self that is expressed in second order 'conversation' by the very same devices. The public conversation of the cultural group and the private thoughts of the members of the group form a continuous conversational web (Markova and Foppa, 1990). These strong claims stand in need of support and demonstration by the analysis of the three patterns of discourse they implicate: perceptual reports and commentaries upon them, declarations of intent and commentaries upon them, and ordered narratives recollecting the past and anticipating the future.

Phenomenologically there is only one centring of experience. Points of view and points of action are not doubled up. There is no reflexive consciousness, if by that is meant consciousness of con- sciousness, but there are iterated uses of the expressions provided by our languages to comment on what we have seen, what we have done and what we can remember.

But for all this to become established in the repertoires of young- sters entering into the human form of life as fully as they may, there must be a minimal native endowment of expressive activities and the ability to imitate the actions of the symbiotic partner. Vygotsky (1962) emphasizes the former in his critical discussion of Stern's (1938) account of the infant's discovery of the words-to-objects relation. It presupposes a complex of motoric and cognitive activity that cannot be partitioned into one or the other. Metzoff's (1997)[6] startling demonstration of the imitative powers of new-borns establishes that the necessary ability to imitate the actions and expressions of other people is a biological endowment.

It is the acquisition of a *point* of view that is the matter of interest for the theorist of personhood, since that is one of the singularities of self expressed in personal discourses.

Movement becomes transformed into action by the acquisition of intention and *point* of action, that is action is movement directed to something from the situation of the actor. Again that situation is a spatio-temporal singularity again expressed in the use of first and second person pronouns and grammatically similar constructions. From this arises the sense of personal responsibility for action. Because we have only one body with which to perceive and act these singularities are also one.

Finally, images detached from current environmental interac- tions become organized into a complex hierarchy, in which the distinction between images of what has happened and images of what might happen become distinguished, so set up a sense of a *line* of life. Out of that further distinctions develop between memories and fantasies of the past, and anticipations of the future.

For psychologists of personhood the most fundamental question must be the relation between point of view, point of action and line of life. The studies to follow are based on the hypotheses that line of life incorporates point of action and point of view and that point of action itself incorporates point of view. So the singularities of selfhood form a hierarchy.

With each singularity goes an ability and it is through the exploitation of that ability that a discursive psychologist can find an entry into the subjectivity of another human being. We have the ability to report how things are from our point of view, to take or repudiate responsibility from our point of action and to tell our stories as evolving lines of life. Each of these skills is discursive. It is in the study of the conditions for the possibility of the acquisition and display of such skills that we can enter into the sense of selfhood of other people.

Towards a cognitive psychology shorn of mentalism

A deep parallel between psychology and physics

Though their methods of enquiry are very different there are some valuable insights to be gained by comparing the underlying ontologies of new paradigm psychology and modern physics. In each science we ground our explanations in powerful particulars, active beings, and their dispositions. In physics the powerful particulars are charges and their dispositions are distributed in space and time as fields. In psychology the powerful particulars are people and their dispositions are their skills and capacities. But whereas the domain of physics and chemistry has turned out to be hierarchical, with layers of unobserved and even unobservable potent entities, one behind the other, so to speak, there is no such hierarchy in the domain of psychology. Our skills and capacities are not grounded in unobservable psychological levels, but in the neurophysiology of our bodies. It is as if at the surface we are already at the depths. One of the great merits of the psychologies of Aristotle in the ancient world (Robinson, 1989), of Thomas Reid (1788) in the eighteenth century, and of Wittgenstein's later period is a clear grasp of this fundamental point.

The person has no psychological attributes other than his or her powers to produce psychological phenomena in the flow of private and public actions, both symbolic and practical. Memories are created in remembering, attitudes in declaring or displaying judgements, beliefs in answering questions and so on. The 'selves', an account of which we are trying to construct, are a *mélange* of attributes of the flow of action, brought about often by the exercise of rather disparate personal powers, in interaction with the productive capacities of others engaged in producing psychological phenomena from their own points of view.

From the point of view of a science of psychology, the basic entities are persons. People, for the purposes of psychology, are not internally complex. They have no parts. Each person, however, has many powers, capacities, abilities and dispositions. There is no place in psychology for questions about the origin or grounding of such powers, except in the historical sense of what led to this or that person being endowed with a certain ability, or what led to the local people valuing certain abilities and training their children in them.

There are no mental states other than the private thoughts and feelings people are aware of from time to time. There are no mental mechanisms by which a person's powers and skills are implemented except the occasional private rehearsals for action in which we sometimes engage. The whole top heavy apparatus of psychodynamics and cognitive psychology is at worst a fantasy and at best a metaphor. People produce a flow of action, some public and some private, some symbolic and some practical. In one sense people are for ever producing and reproducing their own minds and the societies in which they live. The urge to base psychology on something that is occurrent, observable in its fullness here and now, and that is also persistent, constant in its nature through space and time, has to be resisted. These demands are incompatible. What is occurrent is ephemeral. What is pantemporal and more or less invariant over the multitudinous situations of everyday life can be nothing but powers and dispositions.

Of course our individual powers, skills and abilities are grounded in something continuing, and their implementation requires the working of causal mechanisms. But none of this is psychological. The instruments for personal and collective action are bodies and their organs, especially brains and central nervous systems. The illusion of a mental realm is perhaps to be accounted for by the fact that we tend to classify the parts of the body that we use as instruments by the psychological function we think they help us to perform. Even in the most PET scan driven investigations of the brain as thinking instrument the salient structures are picked out by reference to the psychological work they are involved in.

Neuropsychology would make no sense unless the taxonomy of structures and processes was based on psychological functions.

From this point of view the various ways our identities and singularities as social beings are manifested to ourselves and others, our 'selves', are complex interweavings of dispositions and powers with the momentary psychological attributes discernible in the flow of private and public action. I have called this 'Self 2', what the person *is*. I have used the term 'Self 1' for the structural singularity of individual experience and action, ordered by reference to our individual bodies. 'Self 3' refers to the multiple and shifting pattern of the complex groupings of dispositions, skills and abilities ascribed to us by other persons (Jones and Pittman, 1982). Of course these nominal expressions are fictions. They do not pick out sub-personal parts of people.

Muddles are endemic in psychology largely because of the urge to find occurrent psychological properties of persons to explain what they think and do. But there are none. The occurrent psychological attributes of people are ephemeral. Psychology is like physics at the frontiers of knowledge, working with entities that are characterized only by their powers and capacities. It is not like the many higher order layers of physical and chemical phenomena for which explanations are to be found in hypotheses of deeper layers of physical phenomena. There are no deeper layers of psychological phenomena than those with which we are all acquainted.

What will a scientific psychology look like, if we really take on board Wittgenstein's admonitions about where the foundations of a form of life are, right in front of our eyes? Where in the methodological layout of the natural sciences would a well founded psychology fit? We will be looking for powers, skills and abilities, and those liabilities and vulnerabilities. Some are invariant through different situations while others are sensitive to the environment, both human and non-human. We will be looking for patterns of similarity and difference in what is produced by active people as their psychological skills are exercised and their vulnerabilities touched.

It cannot be emphasized enough that the use of expressions like Self 1, Self 2 and Self 3, with their air of permanence and substantiality, is no more than a rhetorical convenience. The psychological products of human activity are ephemeral existents and structures. They come into being and pass away in a dynamic flux. The stabilizing influences on the structures and centres and nodes in networks of relations which are presented in the course of this study can best be thought of as norms or ideals to which the ephemeral products of our deployment of our skills and abilities approximate.

Language analysis as a research technique for psychology

The arguments deployed in this book depend heavily on a linguistic analysis that will be directed to showing that 'I', as an exemplary first person device, is not a referring expression like a proper name or an unambiguous description. The only referring expressions in the language games of self-attribution and description are proper names and their equivalents and they are used to refer to actually, formerly or potentially embodied persons.

To substantiate these bold claims two jobs need to be done:

1 to make out a case for the methodological thesis that the empirical study of grammar is the route by which the relevant forms of human experience can best be revealed;
2 to show that the grammatical function of the first person is indexical and not referential – and to analyse its very complex and culturally diverse indexical forces, which express aspects of the sense of self.

I propose to tackle the first task by illustrating its value by an example of the second. The use of grammatical analysis as a research strategy in psychology has been amply illustrated by the work of Sabat (Sabat & Harré, 1995). By attending to the grammar of first person usage in the speech of Alzheimer sufferers he has shown that there is an intact sense of self disclosed in their continued ability to manage indexical pronouns. The person marking devices of all languages fall into four classes: proper names and related words such as nicknames, definite descriptions that are satisfied by only one of a possible array of persons, anaphoric pronouns whose person marking capacities are tied to names and identifying descriptions, and finally indexicals. The sense of self as a singularity is achieved synthetically, by the tying together of definite personal locations in three manifolds – things, persons and events. These manifolds are revealed by attending to the structure of perception, to the pattern of interpersonal commitments, expectations and hierarchies of respect, and to cause–effect and other consequential sequences within which the events of a life are presented. The indexical force of the first person is nothing other than incorporating the locations of speaker and act of speaking in the manifolds presupposed in perception, action and memory in discourse. These claims will be supported in later chapters.

Since there is but one person marking device in the grammar of which a person's locations in all three manifolds are expressed, namely 'I', it is that device that pins together the otherwise disparate locations into the one person that each of us is. The psycholinguistic thesis of the social construction of selfhood is simply that in acquiring the grammatical capacity to use the first person devices the singularities of self are brought into coordination as the sense I have of my own person being as a singularity, my continuous point of view.

Social constructionism

The general position that encompasses discursive approaches to psychology, and that supports cultural anthropology (Cole, 1996) and socio-linguistics (Tannen, 1989), needs to be stated very carefully, to avoid slipping into a wholesale relativism. There are really two doctrines that comprise the constructionist thesis, as follows.

DOCTRINE 1   Human beings acquire their typically human psychological characteristics, powers and tendencies in 'symbiotic' interactions with other human beings, the necessary conditions for which are to be found in human ethology. Here we have the authority of Aristotle, Vygotsky and Wittgenstein to support this view of the matter. The essential ethological basis, the human form of life, imposes a measure of universality on what a human being can become, while the essentially cultural nature of the processes by which a merely animate being becomes a person opens a measure of diversity on what any human being actually becomes.

DOCTRINE 2   The psychological processes of mature human beings are essentially collective, and contingently privatized and individualized. The essential linguistic basis for all human practices imposes a measure of universality on what a human being can meaningfully do, since there are moral and material conditions for the very possibility of language, while the essentially cultural nature of the semantics and syntax of linguistic and other symbolic systems imposes a measure of diversity on what a human being actually does.

Carefully thought out, the social constructionist position entails that there are both universal and local aspects of the human condition and so both universal and local forms of 'senses of self'. The conditions for developing a language rich enough to construct local diversity are universal!

Nor is social constructionism at odds with at least some versions of scientific realism. There are some conditions that stand outside any discourse whatever that make discourse possible. For instance there is the set of conditions that make language itself possible, including those natural expressions of feeling, of perceptual point of view and so on without which no symbolic system of any degree of sophistication could even begin. Not only is an ethological foundation necessary but also a quite particular kind of moral order must be in place. There could be no discourse, no conversation at all, unless there were in place all sorts of practices in which certain reciprocal grantings of rights were immanent. Finally there is another realist theme, the extension of discourse, of the human conversation beyond the grasp of any participant. Just as the affordances of the material world exceed anything that people can capture in symbolic systems and tap with humanly built apparatus, so too there are aspects of the long and broad human conversation that cannot be captured in any metalinguistic discourse, or tapped by any local method of enquiry. And all methods of enquiry are local.

Conclusion

Among the many concepts that cluster round personhood there are some which pick up the ways that each of us is like others, our social identities, for instance (Breakwell, 1992). But there are others that highlight our personal uniqueness and singularity. We shall be making use of three of these, borne in different ways by pronouns and other person referring devices. Our experience of the world and of ourselves as part of that world has a 'point of origin', a singularity, which is differentiated from every other, especially as a world-line of locations in space and time. Our personal attributes, including our memories, taken together make up a unique cluster of stories different from the clusters of anyone else. Finally there is unity: the lives, experiences, thoughts and memories of most people somehow hold together as just one person. The unities of real lives are complex and ever-changing structures, but when compromised the very existence of a human being as a person is under threat.

Unless we take the greatest care in how we interpret ways of expressing ourselves as persons we can easily begin a multiplication of sub-personal entities, homunculi of various sorts, for instance 'self as mental mover' or 'self as mental contents'. As Roy Schafer remarks, we need 'to think more plainly in terms of persons constructing and revising their various experiential selves of everyday life and ordinary language. Then each person is taken to be a narrator of selves rather than a non-Euclidean container of self entities' (1992: 25). Though actions are individual, for the most part acts are accomplished jointly. The temptation to make invariances in the stream of life into subpersonal entities seems to be almost irresistible. So we have the various 'selves' of which the human person is composed. I shall use the nominative terminology throughout, pausing to remind the reader from time to time that this is intended as an ironic commentary on the way most 'self' psychology is currently presented.

In the two chapters immediately following I shall be developing, in detail, the methodologies needed to undertake the task of describing and understanding what it is to be a person, a human being with a complex psychology, through which it is, at the same time, both singular and multiple.

Notes

1 He reasoned that he must exist if he could doubt that he existed. But it does not follow from that observation that he is, in essence, a purely mental being, detachable from his body as if he were of a different substance.

2 Hasn't this metaphysical demolition already been done? Didn't Ryle (1947) dispose of the ghost in the machine, once and for all? He certainly showed that many mental attribute words were not used to ascribe properties to a Cartesian ego. But he left the sense of self, of one's own singularity, largely unexplored. Many philosophers, for instance Parfitt (1984) still play a predominantly Cartesian game, moving and splitting a mental entity among bodies, ontologically distinct from it.

3 By an 'ontology' I mean the presumptions one makes about the kinds of things that make up the region of the world one is studying or thinking about. It is more often than not implicit in the grammar that one uses to describe that region of the world.

4 The distinction between individuality and uniqueness, so often overlooked by psychologists, especially in the field of personality psychology, has been well presented by J. Lamiell (1987; 1997) in a number of publications.

5 Recent studies in infant perception have shown that even very young babies have sophisticated perceptual capacities. Perception does not occur by virtue of the synthesis of sensations.

6 Contributing to a lecture series at Georgetown University (Spring 1997) Metzoff showed a video recording of a baby less than an hour old, imitating the facial expressions of an adult.

CHAPTER TWO

Which Psychology? The Turn to Discourse

> It is but a short step from starting psychological analysis with
> people's engagement in purposeful activity to the idea that
> psychological processes do not stand apart from activity, but,
> rather, are constituted by the activities of which they are a part.
>
> Michael Cole, *Cultural psychology*

The brief introductory analyses offered in Chapter One move from
a study of aspects of discourse to claims about the psychological
role and cognitive status of the cluster of real and fictional entities,
person and selves, as laid out in the grammatical sketch I have
called the 'standard model'. This approach to a fundamental
psychological problem, the nature of mature human individuality,
is based on the assumption of the priority of language use over all
other forms of human cognition. This assumption needs to be
spelled out in more detail. It forces us to confront the fundamental
question: what is a truly scientific psychology to be like? From
where shall it derive its methods? Let us start from the obvious,
from the fact that we are language-using beings.

Language games and forms of life

Human beings think, act and speak within forms of life. I choose
the Wittgensteinian way of expressing this insight and all that
follows from it. The more or less equivalent expressions to be found
in the writings of Heidegger and the phenomenologists are
expressed in ways that make their application in psychology very
difficult, a rough sketch of which I gave in the last chapter. For
example, the metaphor 'thrown into a life-world' is offered instead
of the mundane 'born into a particular culture'. One of the more
puzzling of Heidegger's (1962: 91ff) usages is 'Being' in the sense
of the life-world outside of which nothing exists (for us?). Perhaps
this concept corresponds to Wittgenstein's thought that there is no

meaning outside the reach of grammars. In a way very similar to that of Wittgenstein, Heidegger points out that people, so thrown, inherit a language, with which they give meaning to the 'life-world'.[1] Unlike the Heideggerian linguistic innovations the details of Wittgenstein's scheme, certainly for me, lead more or less directly to usable methodological proposals. In particular there is the idea of a hierarchy of forms of life, each framed by a grammar or loosely organized set of rules and customs, according to which the correctness and propriety of what we think, do and say can be assessed. In so far as people are trained into acting according to the rules that define their form of life they reproduce it. It is in language games that a form of life takes concrete form, that is in mainly inter-personal activities, frequently involving the use of material skills, in which language plays a variety of indispensable parts. The normative constraints on these activities are only as stringent as the circumstances and the task demand. From this point of view 'a psychology' will consist of a description of the explicit and implicit rules and conventions of a culture, coupled as appropriate to a catalogue of the skills and personal powers required to accomplish such projects as and when they are called for.[2] This is very much again in the same line of thought as Heidegger. For instance Heelan (1988) sees the life-world as derived from the everyday world of skilled practical and social action including conversation. Our studies of the life-world then display the grounding conditions for our lives.

Yet another way of describing 'life-world' and 'frame' has been used by Bourdieu (1977). Pointing to much the same thing as Wittgenstein and Heidegger he uses the expression 'habitus'. This is:

> a system of lasting, transposable dispositions which, integrating past experiences, functions at every moment as a *matrix of perceptions, appreciations and actions* and makes possible the achievement of infinitely diversified tasks. (1977: 82)

However the status of 'habitus' in relation to the actions people perform, and the meanings they intend them to have, is not clear. Bourdieu uses causal language to describe this relation.

> The habitus is the universalising mediation which causes an individual agent's practices, without either explicit reason or signifying intent, to be none the less 'sensible' and 'reasonable'. (1977: 79)

Habitus seems to have drifted into a Platonic realm as a potent 'something' over and above the life forms it animates. But of course there is no habitus beyond the practices of actively engaged people. Bourdieu himself notes that practices are neither mechanical reactions to antecedent conditions, nor themselves agentive. The only agents in the human form of life are people and material things. Somehow, habitus is 'the basis of perception and appreciation of all subsequent experience' (Bourdieu and Wacquant, 1992: 54). Despite these disclaimers it still sounds as if Bourdieu assumes that habitus exists in some way other than immanent in normative practices.

Frames, life-worlds and the habitus are, as Heidegger gnomically asserts, the product of the work of 'philosophers', students of human activities, who seek to express the norms they notice are embedded in the multitudinous practices of everyday life. The same point needs to be made about the grander notions of frame etc. as needs to be made about rules. In most cases we act in accordance with rules, but that is not to follow them unconsciously. 'Rules' in such a case are what students of such normative practices write down to express what has struck them about what people do. That people do such and such is not explained by reference to frames or the habitus. Explanations would have to do with training, imitation, coping with the situation, and so on. These grand concepts are surely taxonomic. They serve to classify practices into hierarchical groupings, institution by institution, family by family and tribe by tribe. The acquisition of the skills to carry on the life of the tribe involves all sorts of matters, but dominating those concerned with personhood is the learning of the local language.

The most specific form that the influence of language has on thought ought to be visible in studies of linguistic cultures other than our own. The conclusions drawn by Sapir (1959) and Whorf (1956) are generally condensed into the so-called 'Sapir–Whorf' hypothesis, that language forms influence or (in a common misreading of the writings of both men) determine the possibilities of thought. If there are aspects of our language that are deeply embedded in our thought patterns they will be very difficult to discern. Since every aspect of our culture will display them, from family life to law to religion, we will have no contrasts with which to make them visible. For example the radical individualism of much of American life and its realization in a very rule-bound culture escapes the attention of most Americans. In just the same way the subtleties of class in Britain escape the attention of those who live by them. How can we make ourselves strangers to our own culture, the first step in devising a methodology by which the rules that express the basic patterns of cognition in our culture can be discerned? One way is to turn to linguistic and cognitive anthropology, the study of language games other than our own. Of course these studies are themselves language games, indicative of a culture, the culture of cultural and discursive psychology. This culture has its own changing norms and conventions.

Different languages, different psychologies?

In giving a central place to language in human forms of life, Wittgenstein neither endorsed nor disputed the thesis that language shapes our ways of thinking. That we do think with language and other symbolic systems that are language-like can hardly be disputed. But it has been held that linguistic differences are only superficial 'dressings' on an underlying common species-wide system with which all human cognition is accomplished, the fanciful 'central processing mechanism' properly castigated by Shweder (1991). There is often more passion than reason in the debates on this point, though it is hard to see why this should be so. Flying in the face of the facts, Pinker asserts dogmatically that 'there is no scientific evidence that languages dramatically shape their speakers' ways of thinking' (1994: 57–8). According to him the thesis of the relativity of thought to language is 'wrong, all wrong'. This dogmatic dismissal of anthropological linguistics is in marked contrast to the measured and judicious summing up of the actual evidence by Lakoff (1987: 327–37). To this I now turn.

According to Lakoff there are five criteria for deciding whether in any particular case a culture makes use of a *cognitively* distinctive conceptual system. The nub of Lakoff's discussion is that dogmatic universalists like Pinker fail to make the quite essential distinction between use and truth. 'Whorf was right in observing that concepts that have been made part of the grammar of a language are used *in* thought, not just as *objects of* thought, and that they are used spontaneously, unconsciously and effortlessly' (1987: 335).

Generally speaking it is possible to translate statements descriptive of material states of affairs in one language into statements in another, in such a way that truth is preserved. The evidence suggests that for psychological matters this possibility is strictly limited since there are many psychological words in other languages for which no equivalents exist in the criterial language, say English. The dogmatic universalist then goes on to claim that the concepts of the exotic language can be described without remainder in the criterion language. Of course, as Goddard and Wierzbicka (1995) point out, this is neither here nor there for the question of alternative conceptual systems. A conceptual system is not a catalogue of signs, it is a system *in use*. A strikingly powerful account of the use of the words 'mind' and 'soul' in English and of the word *dusa* in Russian is to be found in Goddard and Wierzbicka (1995: 44–9). These authors offer a detailed use analysis of the words in their cultural contexts.

Given the relevant experiences one can come to understand, though I would argue always *ceteris paribus*, the conceptual system of another culture in the sense of the use to which a local repertoire of linguistic tools is put. After all these are human beings with whom we share a generic form of life, based upon regularities in which the very possibility of psychologically important aspects of language depend. The point was made forcefully by Shylock in Shakespeare's *Merchant of Venice*. However there are deep cognitive differences in the way resources are used. In so far as the tools of a common human culture are used differently from those of another culture the psychologies of these cultures differ. As Cole (1996: Chapter 3) found in Liberia, there are local tool kits for local problems. We can discover and discuss exotic psychologies in just the way that we can come to understand our own, namely by discerning the normative background within which people set themselves tasks and the means they adopt to fulfil them. The short statement of all this is 'find the rules', or write some out, as expressions of how our conceptual tools are supposed to be used.

Grammar or lexicon

Whorf made an important distinction between differences in thought patterns that are embodied in grammar and those that arise only from differences in vocabulary, very relevant to the work of psychologists. Modes of thought are robustly realized in grammaticalized concepts. Pronoun grammars carry local modes of thinking about people. Tenses and other temporal markers carry local modes of thinking about events, and so on. The core of our own psychology is to be found in the grammars of our intentional practices rather than in vocabulary, though semantic resources do have some facilitating and constraining influence.

Lakoff's critical assessment of the Sapir–Whorf hypothesis makes use of a distinction between the role of a local lexicon in constraining thought and the influence of grammaticalized distinctions. From this he extracts a plausible working hypothesis about the relation between language and cognition. Though he does not refer to Wittgenstein the result of his reflections is pretty much like Wittgenstein's distinction between the framework that makes the use of certain distinctions possible and concrete episodes in which the available distinctions are actually used. The available vocabulary facilitates some cognitive activities while rendering others difficult, but surely not impossible. Miss Smilla's feeling for snow can hardly be divorced from her having to learn all those Scandinavian words for different types of frozen precipitation. But then as Pinker (1994) has pointed out, neither can mine from learning all those English words for the same sort of stuff! But Miss Smilla could instruct me in distinctions I do not presently know how to draw which it might be useful for me to make. This is a quite weak constraint on thinking. But the constraints exerted by grammar are of an altogether different cast. The normativity of grammar is such that leeway in violating its principles is narrow on several fronts. There is evidence for at least a correlation between the availability of complex tenses and patterns of temporal reasoning. But in the case of the self the grammar of pronouns clearly exerts a potent constraining force. If I open my mouth in Spain I must choose between the formal and the informal grammatical forms, for instance *usted* and *tú* in addressing you. If I suppress the pronouns the verb inflexions require the same choice in expression of the social relations presumed to obtain between us. It is not that having *tú* and *usted* in the language creates a contrast between two kinds of interpersonal relation. Rather having to make that distinction forces me to think in terms of asymmetrical social hierarchies. Whichever form I choose I cannot but express a social attitude to you. If I don't use one or the other I can't speak.

Recently, at a wedding feast in Sabadell in Catalonia, I found myself next to a well known singer from the Barcelona opera. Exchanging professional autobiographies I confessed to having an interest in the role of personal pronouns in the expression of self. In response she told me about her pronominal plight in her family circle. She is the wife of the eldest of three brothers. When visiting her mother-in-law alone conversation works smoothly with *tú–tú*, since daughters-in-law are *tú* to mothers-in-law and lay relatives are *tú* to well known opera singers. But at a family party my informant's mother-in-law ought to be *usted* to all the daughters-in-law, while the famous opera singer ought to be *usted* to all, regardless of familial relations. 'Well, what do you say?', I asked. To which she replied, 'We don't say anything.'

Vygotsky's confluence thesis

Any account of selfhood includes a genetic element. If selves are grammatical fictions, how is the grammar for accomplishing these fictions acquired? Let us turn to a more detailed account of the developmental psychology of L.S. Vygotsky (1962) than the introductory sketch in Chapter One. His developmental psychology rests on two principles:

1 For each individual person thought and language have independent origins. Thought begins in the native activity of the nervous system, while language begins in social interaction.
2 The structure of the developed human mind comes about through the acquisition of skills in psychological symbiosis with others.

According to Vygotsky (1962; 1978) individual human beings acquire a repertoire of discursive skills in symbiosis with those already skilled in speaking (and in other forms of intentional, norm-bound activity). An unskilled infant attempts or seems to attempt some intentional act and an adult supplements its efforts. In the course of this supplementation the adult or some more skilful child interprets the infant's actions as incipient cognitive or practical or expressive acts. Vygotsky gave many convincing proofs that this kind of partnership between infant and adult shaped the unordered mental activity with which new-born human beings are endowed by virtue of their inherited neurophysiology into the structured patterns of mature minds. By the age of three a human being is beginning to develop the capacity for private discourse, and is thus enabled to perform complex cognitive acts for itself. This skill facilitates higher level cognition by making possible retrospective and anticipatory commentary first upon the overt acts of public life and then on its own discursive practices, modelled on the commentaries to which its speaking and acting have been subjected by others. For our purposes the crucial step is the acquisition of powers of self-expression and self-reference.

The relation between pronoun grammar and selfhood was well understood by both Stern (1938) and Vygotsky, though neither developed a fully discursive account of the various 'selves' that I am arguing appear as attributes of the flow of personal and interpersonal action. In Vygotsky's discussion of Stern's observation that a child seems to *discover* the relation between its speech and material things, the intentional relation, he comments on Stern's 'translation' of his child Hilde's use of the word 'Mama' as in 'Mama, give me.' Vygotsky remarks that Stern seems to think that the grasp of the 'intentional tendency' is something that 'appears from nowhere' and presupposes an 'already formed intellect'. Vygotsky points out that it is not a sudden discovery, but a genetic development. It grows out of all sorts of manipulative practices, such as reaching and grasping, a point rediscovered by Bruner and Watson (1983) in his study of the genesis of requests in reaching for things. Vygotsky (1962: 30) argues that the word 'Mama' has a meaning as a request only in 'the child's whole behaviour of the moment . . . pointing is a precursor of the "intentional tendency"' (1962: 31). From the point of view of the discursive psychologist the step from reaching to asking, in which pronouns begin to displace gestures, is when the sense of Self 1, having a location as a person at a point in space and time, expressible with the newly acquired pronouns, begins to crystallize out of the growing repertoire of manipulative and verbal skills. During the same period of transition the sense of having one's own attributes also begins to appear. But in line with the realization that one is a being like other people the linguistic phase is the acquisition of proper names, including one's own. This is the origin of the self-concept, that is of beliefs about one's personal attributes, one's Self 2, as a discursive phenomenon.

To follow this transition we can draw on the Stern inspired studies of Deutsch et al. (1997), involving a repetition and extension of Stern's observations of his own children, in whose development both patterns of referring acts appeared. As Deutsch et al. note, 'the correct identification of other persons in pictures precedes the correct self-identification in development.' . . . Children growing up in various cultures and languages use nominal forms of self-reference like proper names or nicknames when they successfully recognize themselves in photographs, drawings and mirror images. At this point Self 2, 'I am a person with attributes', is established. The construction type 'proper name + object name' is used to characterize oneself as owner of an object, an attribute. This fits with the Peevers and Secord (1972) study that showed that young children tend to identify other people in terms of their possessions. But 'wishes and requests, i.e. the volitional function, are expressed by the construction type "my + object name".' The pronoun is indexing the request with the embodied person, a being located at a place and moment in the space and time of everyday life. And this is the origin of Self 1 as a discursive phenomenon. It must be emphasized that neither Self 1 nor Self 2 could become established as expressive features of person talk without the prior manipulative practices with which the child in symbiosis with others begins to make contact with the material world and in it other people.

While it may be conceded, except by those too deeply committed to modularity theories to be able to appreciate counter-evidence, that thought is shaped and constrained by language, it does not follow that cognition and language use are one and the same, or that they have the same origin. The work of the younger generation of developmental psychologists has strongly supported Vygotsky's famous thesis that thought and language have different origins. Cognitive powers are pre-linguistic and, as Metzoff (1997) has so elegantly shown, present from birth. In particular there is the capacity to act intentionally, to try to achieve a goal, and there is the capacity to imitate. New-born infants can imitate facial expressions of adults, but not by comparison between the adult expression and some part of themselves that they can see. There is 'cross-modal imitation'. What is seen can be expressed in muscular movements. Intentionality and imitation are bound up with one another in that wanting to act like another person is part of what it is to imitate them.

Metzoff's work vindicates Vygotsky's insights in a more specific way. According to Vygotsky the main development moment is when a child has been trying to do something, and the task is completed by an adult supplying the missing step. At this point the cognitive or manipulative capacity is in 'the zone of proximal development'. The child imitates the adult's contribution and so acquires, step by step, the full complement of actions or cognitive practices needed to accomplish the tasks of everyday life. Language has its source in the social and material practices of the culture that surrounds the child from birth. As it is acquired it begins to transform and reshape the patterns of thought that have emerged from the individual. For example Lewis and Ramsay's (1997) demonstration that the emergence of self-oriented emotions, such as embarrassment, is closely correlated with the achievement of mastery of the first and second person pronouns (in English) is a striking vindication both of the general Vygotskian thesis of confluence and of the particular claim that I am presenting in this study. It seems to show that a large chunk of what it is to be a person comes with the learning of the local language. At the same time work such as that of Metzoff supports Wittgenstein's insight that the sophisticated skills that constitute a culture could only have been acquired if there were already some natural regularities and natural expressions which the culture could seize and build upon. Taken together the insights of Vygotsky and Wittgenstein, with the supporting work of Metzoff and human ethologists, provide us with a foundation upon which a psychology as a study of human beings engaged in tasks, using cultural tools bound in their uses by local rules and conventions to accomplish them, has a natural and essential place.

The natural science model

For many psychologists the transition from the first cognitive revolution – the legitimizing of hypotheses about cognitive processes explicative of patterns of behaviour – to the second – the rediscovery of Wundt's insight that psychology is a metaphysical and methodological double science – has been difficult to accept. It has looked as if the discursive psychologists were abandoning hard won 'scientific method'. Despite Wundt's warnings, and decades of methodological criticisms and the establishment of a broad corpus of empirical studies based on different methods of enquiry from the prevailing methodological behaviourism, the natural science model for what a science should be still exerts a fascination. In point of fact it is often not the real methods of natural science but some imitation of some of their superficial features that is followed, a tragic waste of lives and resources. We must look very closely at the natural sciences. The key issue is the status of unobservables.

The role of unobservables

The natural sciences have alternated between two main ways of conceiving of an enquiry into nature – positivism and realism. For the former only observable phenomena are to be accounted real, and the role of theory is reduced to a logical auxiliary to prediction. Causality is a mere regularity of patterns of observable events. For the latter, theory not only serves a logical role but can also be a description of underlying, unobservable processes that bring about observed regularities. Causality is the exercise of the powers of potent entities. The attitude of each of these traditions to the entities and processes postulated by theory is quite different. Positivists deny the right of theoreticians to make existence claims for the 'hidden' beings they postulate. Realists insist that there is a well founded distinction between those hypothetical entities the conceptions or images of which are merely psychological aids to thought, and those that we are justified in believing really exist.

Behaviourism and its descendent, sometimes called methodological behaviourism or experimental empiricism, were textbook examples of a positivist science of human behaviour. The first cognitive revolution, and its contemporary offspring such as 'cognitive science', are formed within the general pattern of scientific realism. According to behaviourism, mental states, even if they exist, are irrelevant to a science of behaviour. According to cognitive psychology, mental states do exist, and they exist unobserved, just as do the quarks and intermediate vector bosons of physics. Hypotheses about unconscious mental states are invoked to account for the mental activities, both private and public, of *isolated* human beings. Behaviourism and its most rigorous opponent, cognitive psychology, are approaches to a science of behaviour both of which exemplify differing interpretations of natural science. Whether there was a direct influence from the philosophy of natural science on the architects of these two approaches to psychology I cannot say. But the parallels do suggest an interesting problem for historians of ideas.

The first cognitive revolution saw the displacement of positivistic behaviourism by realist cognitive psychology. This pattern of reasoning has a familiar ring. It is more or less exactly that which we encounter in the natural sciences. The plausibility of cognitive psychology must be assessed by reference to the status of its models of unobserved processes, in relation to the type hierarchies that embody our general assumptions about what there is. The second cognitive revolution, still in progress, involves a radical departure from *both* natural science models, turning to other explanatory paradigms and modes of enquiry. The drive behind this development is a general scepticism about the plausibility of the claims that such and such hidden cognitive mechanisms exist and explain thought and action. Of course the invention of models of human functioning using the concepts of overt mental activity could hardly be objected to. It is the elevation of such models to the status of a real inner world of causal mechanisms that is in question. As I have argued in many contexts in which psychological matters are being explored, in particular the contexts around personhood and self, the causal paradigm must give way to the normative.

If we find the idea of unobservable mental states uncongenial or even, as some philosophers have argued, unintelligible (Searle, 1995), we might ask, 'What unobservables could there be in the human sciences?' Only two types of entities seem to have the requisite standing. There could be unobservable aspects or domains of the vast network of interpersonal communicative acts that constitutes the lived reality of human existence, with its multiple storylines and diverse readings of intentionality. And there could be unobservable material states and processes of the organismic aspect of human existence. The ontological basis of the hybrid psychology advocated in this chapter comes from the insight that both are needed for an adequate science of human life. What is not needed is a neo-Cartesian mental realm of cognitive states and processes behind the public and private cognitive activities of real people. In

the task and tool metaphor, to be deployed below, I shall try to show
how this can be achieved.

To clinch the point I would like to draw on two short passages
from a recent work by Searle. Commenting on the basic 'rule'
account of social life, Searle draws attention to much the same point
as Wittgenstein made in distinguishing 'following a rule' from
'acting in accordance with a rule'. As Searle puts it:

> he [sic] doesn't need to know the rules of the institution and to follow
> them in order to conform to the rules; rather he is just disposed to
> behave in a certain way, but he has acquired those unconscious dispo-
> sitions and capacities in a way that is sensitive to the rule structure of
> the institution. (1995: 144)

And in relation to the oft-repeated point by Shweder (1991) apropos
of mysterious 'mechanisms' Searle says:

> a person who behaves in a skilful way within an institution behaves as
> if he were following the rules, but not because he is following the rules
> unconsciously or because his behaviour is caused by an undifferenti-
> ated mechanism that happens to look as if it were rule structured, but
> rather because the mechanism has evolved precisely so that it will be
> sensitive to the rules . . . the mechanism need not itself be a system of
> rules. (1995: 146)

One could hardly hope for a clearer statement of the position that
many of us have been arguing for years.

Escaping the natural science paradigm

Wittgenstein's philosophy of psychology bears upon this question.
For him cognition is a discursive process conforming, context by
context, to many different standards of correctness and propriety.
Logic, in the formal sense, is only one among many 'grammars' that
we use to give order to discourses. Bruner's (1993) work has
emphasized the important part played by story-telling and its conventions in everyday life. In his studies of the role of narrative conventions in the shaping of people's actions and attitudes, Bruner
(1991) has shown how a body of knowledge, stored, somehow, as
shared narrative conventions, is to be discerned in the way people
manage their lives. Narrative conventions can be expressed as
rules.

However there is a duality in the use of the notion of rule emphasized in the last section in Searle's strictures on assuming that there
is unconscious rule-following in all cases of normative practices in
which rules are not explicitly followed. There is an ambiguity in the

use of the word 'rule'. In cases of rule-following the rule is an instruction explicitly formulated and used in the management of action. In cases of acting in accordance with a rule people behave in an orderly way because they have acquired a habit of so doing. A psychologist might express this orderliness by writing out a system of rules. But, following Searle's warning, we must be careful not to assume that when there is no conscious rule-following there is really unconscious rule-following going on. This duality in the use of the word 'rule' and similar notions raises tricky philosophical problems about the status of those rules which are available to their users only in so far as they are immanent in a practice. Are they no more than part of the discursive repertoire psychologists use to express orderliness, or do they have a sort of independent existence, if not quite like that of rules which are explicitly formulated and knowingly followed? In my view the basic work must be done by the concept of 'practice', one of the metaphors for which is 'action according to a rule'.

Underlying most of the arguments for a radical distinction in methods of enquiry in the natural and the human sciences lie two features of human behaviour which have no counterpart in the behaviour of inorganic materials. Human behaviour displays or seems to display intentionality, that is human actions are what they are by virtue of their meaning, point or aim. And human behaviour also displays normativity, that is it is generally subject to appraisal as correct, proper, appropriate or as incorrect, improper, inappropriate. It can be right or wrong.

Bruner's emphasis on the role of narrative in the structuring of ordinary life, and also in our efforts at understanding it, forces us to pay attention to both these characteristic features of human behaviour. This emphasis also draws our attention to the role of context in the explanation of the fine details of how human beings think and act. Both intentionality and normativity are sensitive to context. The same movement, in the physical sense, can have different meanings or points in different contexts. The same action, even when its identity is fixed by common intentional criteria, that is it does seem to have the same meaning in two contexts, can be judged correct in one context and incorrect in another.

The arguments in favour of a normative, rule-based account of human life, and so for a psychology based on the study of goal-directed action according to local standards of correct procedures, depend in part on showing how only in that framework can certain deep problems with the still popular causal approach be resolved. One of these concerns the vexed question of the determinacy of private cognitive processes and public conversational interactions. Both, I believe, are indeterminate unless made to some degree determinate for some purpose or other. Much the same point has been made in a rather different way by Shotter (1993), drawing on ideas of Bakhtin (1986). What are the conditions for a cognitive process to be determinate?

By a process or a state being 'determinate' I mean that it has a sufficiently definite meaning for the actors in a certain situation to successfully accomplish joint actions. To put the point another way, for people to bring off a social act the actions they perform must have the same meaning, *ceteris paribus*, for everyone in that cultural matrix who takes part in the action and/or who pays attention to it. It should also be sufficiently well specified to have an outcome, as an intended *act*, that is sharply enough defined for the question of its being the proper or correct outcome in the relevant circumstances to be settled, at least in principle. Social life is full of devices for ensuring this requirement, even so drastic as the ordering of a retrial by an appellate court. If we cannot make out what someone meant by their actions then the issue of their correctness, *as the performance of the contextually required act*, cannot arise. We would not know how to apply a rule or standard to it. These are general conditions or constraints on the intentionality and normativity of human actions. However in real life it is rare that issues of determinateness of either actions or acts are pushed to extremes. But at whatever degree of determinateness an act-creating sequence of actions is left unchallenged there is an intimate relationship between context and meaning.

To require that cognition be relevantly determinate, within the paradigm defining the first cognitive revolution, is to raise the well known 'frame problem'. A cognitive process is determinate, to whatever degree the situation is taken to call for, only relative to a set of framing assumptions, which reduce the ambiguity and spread of the possible meanings of a cognitive act. Putting this another way, every cognitive act must have some relevant degree of determinateness and this presumes certain background assumptions, which are not specified in the description of the cognitive act itself. This is the distinction Wittgenstein drew between frame and picture, or in another well known image, between grammatical and descriptive propositions. Since there are indefinitely many such assumptions or background framing conditions, some selection from among these assumptions must be implicit in any cognitive process, in order for the two requirements of intentionality and normativity to be met in a sufficiently determinate way. The selected assumptions or conditions constitute the 'frame' or grammar within which the cognitive process is intentionally and normatively determinate, relative to the task in hand.

In real human cognition, such as remembering or problem solving, these abstractions from the indefinitely complex background are *ad hoc* and only locally valid abstractions. They are both spatially and temporally idiographic. It is only in *this* place and at *this* time that *this* selection from among the conditions is relevant to a locally valid pattern of cognitive acts. Rules for the admissibility of evidence, as they are administered by a particular judge, in a particular trial, are a case in point. Each trial is managed by a unique 'frame'. In the absence of such abstractions the background is both huge and indeterminate, each assumption within it dependent for meaning upon other, as yet unspecified assumptions. Cognition is possible only if the proliferation of conditions is either deliberately constrained as in the trial of O. J. Simpson, or implicitly constrained as in everyday encounters, for all practical purposes. However we can never tell whether some other, unacknowledged assumptions are at work, that will appear only when some seemingly novel and surprising decision, inference and so forth has been made in the light of a particular frame constraint, or some well established discursive convention is successfully challenged. Some recent challenges to established discursive practices have been mounted by feminists on the ground that they wish to change certain features of traditional culture, features hitherto unnoticed or simply taken for granted as if they were natural.

Discursive psychology and its founding insights

The ubiquitous role of discourse

It is important to remind ourselves that not only the telling of the stories of a life but many of the most characteristic human psychological phenomena are discursive, brought into being through the public and private use of symbols under all sorts of normative constraints. Remembering (recollecting the past correctly), deciding (making up one's mind to the best effect), reasoning (drawing a conclusion rationally), persuading (getting someone to change their mind successfully) and so on generally either are performed wholly discursively or make use of discourse in important ways. This is the insight that lies behind the recent trend to use discourse analysis as the methodology of a thoroughgoing discursive psychology.

Conversation as an exemplar and as a working model

In setting up a scientific paradigm one chooses an ideal type as the exemplar for the kinds of phenomena one believes the field for research covers, in our case the nature and expression of that many faceted but central aspect of human life we call 'self'. The main exemplar for discursive psychology is the conversation in which two or more people carry out some cognitive task in the course of speaking (or sometimes writing) to one another. Real conversations are exceedingly complex phenomena, ordered according to multiple levels of conventions and realizing ever-shifting personal intentions, consensual agreements and patterns of mutual positioning with respect to rights to speak and obligations to listen and/or respond. In the course of conversing people create, maintain, transform and abrogate social relations. In the course of conversing people adjudicate disputes, arrive at decisions, confirm or disconfirm claims to remember, and display the sense of self as a singular responsible being in accordance with which they engage in all these activities.

For discursive psychologists, not only are the interchanges of interpersonal conversation the sites of much mental activity, but the general notion of a conversation is also a fruitful model with which to analyse, interpret and understand other human activities which are not overtly linguistic.[3] The most striking example of the extension of the conversational model is to the understanding of public and private displays of emotion (Harré and Parrott, 1996). For example a display of jealousy, whether in public behaviour or as a private feeling, is interpreted as the performance of a complex discursive act, expressing a judgement concerning the rights and wrongs of a certain state of affairs, and, at the same time, the performance of an 'illocutionary act', a protest or complaint about the violation of one's rights.

If we adopt the principle that psychological phenomena are characterized by intentionality and normativity, then we have, in a sense, pre-selected the type of model or analogue which will be most enlightening in the analysis and explanation of patterns of human behaviour. The most obvious though not the only model that a discursive psychologist might take for a public and collective cognitive process would be *conversation*. A conversation consists of an exchange, in which the performances of each participant are relevant in so far as they are meaningful in terms of the particular conversation going forward. They must also be proper or correct in so far as they conform to the rules and conventions of conversations of that sort. While a great deal of cognition is literally conversation, for example in many cases remembering and deciding are accomplished conversationally, sometimes with others and sometimes with oneself, there are some performances which are not conversational in the sense of exchanges of things said. It is a central insight of discursive psychology that we can usefully use conversation as a model or analogue for studying other complex forms of social interaction. For example the growth and confirmation of a friendship, or for that matter a game of tennis, are not conversations, though they often include conversational episodes, but can be illuminated by being considered as if they were conversation-like.

The use of the term 'discursive' for a psychology which is grounded in intentionality and normativity serves to highlight the dominant role of the idea of a conversation in the analysis and explanation of much human behaviour. Bearing this in mind we can see that, to a first approximation, there are three major categories into which regular patterns of human action and interaction can be classified, as follows.

CAUSAL Exhibiting a fixed action pattern, say smiling, as a neuromuscular spasm, in response to someone else's smile, as stimulus, can be exhaustively described in physiological terms. The stimulus triggers an inherited, genetically sustained, neurological mechanism that produces the effect. If attended to at all a causal process is experienced by the person in whose body it occurs as if he or she were a spectator.

HABITUAL Once fully trained a person's habits, such as depressing a certain pattern of keys on a clarinet to produce middle C, are similar in appearance to causal patterns. In some of the early presentations of the discursive point of view these were called 'enigmatic', since it would not be clear from a mere description of the phenomenon whether it was causal or habitual, inborn or engrained. Habits are the prime case for the application of the concept 'acting according to rule', rather than 'rule-following'. There are rules in the background of habits, since habits are acquired by training. But once trained habitual behaviour is rather like causal behaviour. Indeed in training we are building micromechanisms in the brain and nervous system. The experienced player feels the fingers move towards a new key pattern, almost like a spectator.

MONITORED Some patterns of action, such as performances in job interviews, and especially what we do in the course of acquiring or improving a skill, are self-consciously managed by the actor or actors, by reference to a conversation about a conversation in which meanings and rules are considered, 'on line', so to say. Here we have a paradigm case of rule-following as discussed in an earlier part of this chapter.

I believe that the whole of psychology, as a discipline, hinges on whether and to what degree we should assimilate habits to causes or to monitored actions. It seems so obvious as to be scarcely worth reiterating that nothing but confusion can arise from so extending the application of the notion of cause that it covers every regular temporal pattern of action without further qualification. Since monitored actions absolutely require the concepts of 'meaning' and 'rule' as explanatory devices, the question is sharpened to this: should we use these concepts for understanding habitual actions in preference to the causal concepts that would recommend themselves if we assimilated the habitual fully to the causal?

One of the reasons that psychology has proved so difficult to found on a stable base of an agreed ontology and methodology is, I believe, that there is no simple answer to the question just posed. Habits partake of the causal and they partake of the monitored, in different circumstances in different ways. In the origins in some individual's life they are tied closely to rules, explicit as instructions or immanent in the practices in which one has been trained. In their immediate activation their basis in the brain and central nervous system may be very like the instigation of an inherited fixed action pattern, a paradigm for behaviour which is caused. This is quite a different question from the evergreen 'Are reasons causes?' It is not a question of how to classify the antecedents of discernible instances of human behaviour, but rather one of whether they involve different modes of the bringing about of joint action.

Wittgenstein's (1953) observations on psychology may seem at first reading to push us towards the assimilation of the habitual to the monitored, and so to the use of the concept of 'rule' as the most powerful and basic analytical and explanatory concept. But this would be a superficial interpretation. To see how this concept can play a role in both habitual and monitored patterns of action we need to emphasize the distinction already sketched out between two main applications of the notion:

1 Following a rule: the rule is explicit and the action is managed by a conversation about a conversation, be it private or public, in which the rule is attended to as such.

2 Acting in accordance with a rule: the rule is implicit and the action is habitual.

At this stage of the argument the distinction in the application of the notion of 'rule' is still somewhat crude, and we shall come to it again below. It suffices I hope to make clear the way that discursive psychology differs from 'mainstream', in that the latter has been built up on a largely unexamined assumption that habits should be assimilated to the domain of mechanistic causes. This has tended to obscure the cultural relativity of habits, leading to unjustified claims for the existence of universal psychological laws on the basis of locally observed regularities in patterns of human thought and action. The distinction between mechanistic cause/effect patterns and sequences of thoughts and feelings ordered semantically, by meanings, is clear enough to attempt a preliminary characterization of the task of a scientific psychology as the making explicit of the implicit rules of human action, and the structures of meaning that they sustain and that sustain them. We shall be studying the expressive presentation of self in its various forms and uses in the grammars of personal discourses.

Expressive and descriptive uses of language

My analysis of the sense of self relies very heavily on there being a robust distinction between expressive and descriptive uses of language, especially in psychological discourse. The distinction, in the form I want to make use of it, comes from Wittgenstein's (1953: 241–315) private language argument (PLA). The 'argument' involves two interwoven and mutually supporting strands that are relevant to the distinction between descriptive and expressive uses of language as I wish to use that distinction. There is a demonstration that the traditional account of learning a meaning, in situations in which the mentor points to an exemplar of what the word being taught stands for, cannot be the only way meanings, that is knowledge of how words are to be used, are acquired. Meaningful words for sensations and bodily feelings could not be learned that way. This demonstration depends upon a common-sense but fundamental observation. Since feelings are private, itches, pains, and so forth are experienced only by the person who feels them. Private feelings could not be exemplars with the help of which an infant learns words for sensations and feelings, such as 'itch'. Exemplars must be public. Yet these words of our 'feeling' vocabulary are seemingly learned with ease.

In addition to the assumption about exemplars the denotational account of meaning is based on the assumption that meaningful words denote objects. The second strand of the PLA shows that feelings are not objects in the sense that the material things that are pointed to in ordinary situations of learning words like 'spoon', 'cat' and 'potato' from an exemplar are objects. Itches occur at definite places and times, as do potatoes. But we must not be misled by this similarity to take it for granted that material objects and feelings are alike in all respects. We must ask how we decide questions of sameness. There are two such questions. Is this the very same thing that was at some other place and time? Is this thing the same as that? As philosophers say, there are questions about numerical identity and about qualitative identity. If we try to analyse the concept of 'same feeling' in similar contexts, in one's personal experience and in comparison between the experiences of others, we will realize that it cannot be analysed along the same lines as we analyse concepts of sameness for material things.

Wittgenstein shows in some detail that the criteria for making identity judgements of things have no place in language games in which we make such judgements as 'This is the same feeling I had yesterday' or 'I know just what you are feeling, I felt the same myself once.' Since I cannot juxta-pose my past feelings with those I presently experience, or my feelings with yours, similarity judgements about feelings must be based on criteria different from those for things, where identity is decided by some sort of comparison. Yet everyone makes lots of everyday unproblematic judgements of sameness and difference of their own and other people's feelings. Since they do not meet the relevant criteria for 'sameness' and 'difference' as material things, bodily feelings are not objects in the relevant sense. But even if they were their privacy precludes their use as exemplars for denotational learning.

How to resolve this seemingly intractable problem? We use feeling words perfectly well, yet it seems that we are never in a position to learn them. The impasse comes about because we took *two* things for granted. We assumed that all word learning is by a 'baptismal' procedure, by pointing to an exemplar of the kind of object talked about. We also assumed that feelings were a special sort of object or entity, for which the usual, thing-related criteria of identity were appropriate. But feelings are not thing-like. So we have two gaps to fill in understanding how it is possible to discuss our private feelings with others and to reflect on what we felt in the past. How is it that words for feelings do get their proper meanings? And what do we mean by 'same feeling' in both intra- and interpersonal contexts?

How do words *refer* to sensations? – There does not seem to be any problem here; don't we talk about sensations every day, and give them names? This question is the same as: how does a human being learn the meaning of the names for sensations? – of the word 'pain' for example. Here is one possibility: words are connected with the primitive, the natural, expressions of the sensation and used in their place. A child has hurt himself and he cries; and then adults talk to him and teach him exclamations and, later, sentences. They teach the children new pain behaviour.

'So you are saying that the word "pain" really means crying?' – On the contrary: the verbal expression of pain replaces crying and does not describe it. (Wittgenstein, 1953: 244)

In this well known paragraph both questions get the same answer, in effect. What are the language games in which feeling words are actually learned? A child grazes its knees and sobs. A punter chortles with satisfaction as he picks up his winnings. A weight-lifter groans with effort. These are natural expressions of how one is feeling. Words for feelings are learned as alternatives to natural ways of expressing feelings. Instead of groaning we learn to say 'I am in pain.' So here we have the essential move in a resolution of the problem of how it is possible to learn a feeling word. And it is in just these sorts of language games that we can find a place for the judgements of 'same and different feeling'. They are not made by a comparison between your feelings and mine, or between my feeling of yesterday and my feeling of today. They are made by attention to parallel patterns in the language games in which our feelings are expressed.

Wittgenstein goes on to develop a thoroughgoing distinction between describing something, say a state of mind, or a mental image, and expressing 'how it is with me', for example how I am feeling. In the former case there is room for evidence, and error. In the latter there is no gap between the groan and the feeling, as if the feeling were evidence on which the tendency to groan were based. The groan expresses the feeling. It does not describe it. Feeling and the disposition or tendency to groan, sigh, rub the spot, weep and so on are integral parts of the same phenomenon. Abstract any of them and the phenomenon is no longer what it was. If we have no tendency to groan then whatever the feeling is, it cannot be pain. Expressive ways of using language depend on a pre-existing etho-logical repertoire of natural expressions of the ways we are feeling – sad, in pain, happy, and so on. This is part of the natural history of humankind. But the point is a subtle one. Wittgenstein's account of an individual acquiring the 'pain' language game cannot be generalized to an account of humankind acquiring it. The 'pain' language game must already be in place in the culture as a necessary condition for the substituting of these words for the expressive behaviour to become part of the local form of life. In summary the PLA establishes:

1 that meaning is not always and necessarily established by reference to an object signified;
2 that there are both expressive and descriptive uses of language involved in telling about myself;
3 that having an experience and the tendency to act out a certain kind of expression are two sides of the same, unitary phenomenon, introducing Wittgenstein's 'ethological holism';
4 that private feelings are not mental *things*.

Points 2, 3 and 4 contribute to point 1.

Wittgenstein's suggestion that uses of words for feelings are established as verbal substitutes for natural expressions has a very important corollary. We must enlarge our conception of the role of language in life. Sometimes we do use words for describing things. Descriptions can be right or wrong. We cite evidence for or against a putative description. But this picture of language use will not do for the expression of private experience. To be in pain is a complex but integrated and unitary state, including the having of an unpleasant feeling and the tendency to groan. The groan is not a description of the feeling but an expression of it. So when we have discursively transformed the groan into a verbal avowal the same grammar applies. To be in pain is to experience an unpleasant feeling and to be disposed to say such things as 'I'm in pain.' When someone pretends to be in pain we should not say that they are speaking falsely, but that they are acting insincerely. To pretend to be in pain is a moral fault not an epistemological prevarication. The unpleasant feeling is not evidence for a right or wrong judgement, but the occasion for an appropriate expression. From a discursive point of view the private experience of a human being is shaped and ordered in learning to speak and write and in acquiring the know-how of other social and material practices. This was Vygotsky's great insight. That ordering is expressed in the use of language and other intentional, norm governed practices. This was Wittgenstein's great insight. Discursive psychology has focused on the role of linguistic practices in the formation and expression of mind, though the acquisition and exercise of bodily skills are also important. In many cases we can treat practical action within the 'conversational' model.

According to this point of view our sense of our own identity also originates in Vygotskian appropriations of the structure of public discourse between particular and singular persons, for the ordering of private experience and the expression of our personal identities as singularities in public space. What would be the characteristic expression of a person's sense of self? It will surely be in the uses of personal pronouns and other self-expressive devices. As I shall try to show, the pronoun 'I' is used not to refer to oneself but to express oneself as a singular, responsible being. Personal identity finds one of its most characteristic expressions in autobiographical discourse. The sense one has of one's own identity is an essential ingredient in the conditions that make autobiographical telling possible. In terms of the concept of a 'frame', introduced above, we have something like the following: I fall asleep, wake up as myself, without having to look for evidence that I am the same person. That I am is part of the frame of the human form of life, and it shows itself in the grammar of the personal pronouns and other such devices. Thus 'I know I am the same person today as I was yesterday' is a misleading way of speaking about my sense of myself as a continuously existing being. But when I see you again after a break, I do, maybe implicitly (and explicitly in hard cases), gather evidence that the person there is indeed you. In that case I can properly say 'I know you are the same person as you were a decade ago.' But that is possible only if my life story is part of the frame within which I live my life.

According to Vygotsky everything occurs twice, once in interpersonal interactions and once in an individual mind. The inchoate and unstructured mental activity of neonates becomes 'the mind of a person', including that person's sense of self, as a synthetic unity, by virtue of acquiring cognitive and practical skills, prominent amongst which are the skills of speaking. Vygotskian appropriation of the structure of public person-to-person discourse results in a reproduction of that structure in private discourse, that is in thought. Wittgenstein's distinction between descriptive and expressive uses of words suggests that we research the private sense of self by studying the public expression of selfhood in such devices as the personal pronouns. The concept of 'self' is many sided. The first step towards a systematic analysis of the tellings of lives will be to look closely at the field of uses of the very word 'self'. We owe to Wittgenstein an all-important insight for a methodology for psychological research, that the ontological distinction between thought (ineffable and meaningful) and language (audible, visible, tangible and meaningful) does not matter in certain key cases, because in the expressive mode there is a holistic unity. Part of the art of psychological method is to be right in distinguishing those psychological phenomena for which the holistic principle holds and those for which it does not. There is no epistemological gap between a feeling and the expressions of a feeling. I shall be arguing that there is no epistemological gap between a sense of self and the expression of that sense in one's use of pronouns and other index-ical devices.

Using words to refer to things is part of the language game of describing. If self-talk is expressive rather than descriptive then 'I' need have no referential function, and there need be no object reference to which guarantees that the first person is meaningful. In the next chapter we will look closely at the grammar of the first and second person, to show that it is not a special case of the grammar of referential expressions. 'I' and 'you' are not a special class of names. They are not used to refer to people. Their tie to the lives of those who use them comes about in a quite different way.

Integrating the two psychologies

The tool/task distinction

Without racquets, balls, a court, an agreed set of rules and so on it would not be possible to play tennis. Yet the playing of tennis cannot be reduced to a function of these impedimenta. Tennis is a performance, an activity that is *done by people,* in so far as they have the necessary basic skills to take part. The actions of tennis players are provided with meanings and judged for correctness by refer-ence to a socially maintained system of customs and rules. To play tennis people use an array of *tools.* Should we include their bodies and brains amongst these tools? Racquets behave according to the laws of physics and brains according to the laws of biochemistry and neurophysiology. Having the tools enables the playing of tennis. But the rules of tennis are not some conjunction of the laws of physics and neurology.

The brain and the central nervous system are also 'tools'

The basic structure of a *psychological* investigation of some aspect of human life, such as consciousness or the emotions, as these enquiries would be practised within the framework of hybrid psy-chology, would take the following form:

1 Every psychological process or phenomenon is made possible by virtue of a certain condition or state of the brain and nervous systems of those engaged in the activity. Following well established tradition I shall call the neurological foundation the 'enabling condition' for the activity. Some enabling conditions exist by nature, so to say, while others are established by training and practice. A useful model for neurological enabling conditions is expressed in artificial intelligence.

2 Every psychological process or phenomenon is a skilled performance by a person or persons. A performance is skilled if it is intentional, that is directed to some end, and is subject to criteria of correctness, propriety, in short is normatively constrained. A useful model for skilled action, that is action that is intentional and normatively constrained, is conversation. From this insight and some of its methodological consequences comes the generic title of 'discursive psychology'.

Amongst the psychological phenomena so characterized are perceivings, doings and sayings. Discursive psychology is focused on activity and process, and is sceptical of entity-style ways of conceiving mentality. For example playing a musical instrument is a psychological phenomenon, made possible by the changes that have occurred in the brain and nervous system of someone who has acquired the skill. The action of playing is indeed psychological, since it is intentional, that is the player is trying to play something, and it is normative, that is the performance is subject to a variety of standards. Just in the same way performing an arithmetical calculation, making a decision, displaying an emotion, forming a friendship, and so on are all to be construed within the basic framework of enabling conditions and skilled action.

Enabling conditions are somewhat more complex than the brief introductory sketch above would suggest. Not only do they include the neural state of the human organisms involved, but also there are environmental conditions that must obtain for a skilled performance to be possible. One cannot display one's skills as a mountaineer unless there is some rockface (or artificial surrogate) to climb. One cannot be jealous unless there is someone whose rights to a good are thought by you to be inadequate relative to yours, and so on. One cannot read without some text to follow. In what follows, for example, a discussion of consciousness in the discursive frame, the environmental conditions will play a minor though essential part, since it is only in a certain kind of discursive environment that consciousness, as we know it, can come into existence.

The very idea of a skilled performance forces us to take account of the social conditions under which the performance is assessed. In many cases the criteria of such assessments are immanent in the relevant community, only becoming overt when someone has to be corrected or reprimanded, or when training is going on. Many skills are picked up with overt training and normatively constrained without overt judgements of correctness being offered. Sometimes the standards of performance are embodied in experts and legitimated judges, sometimes they are embodied only in the reactions of others. Sometimes they are embodied in manuals of etiquette or instructions. My ability to play a backhand passing shot is embedded in the state of my nervous system, but the standards by which that shot is judged for style are part of the normative background of tennis, while the question of whether I gain or lose a point by it is determined by the socially maintained rules for the game and the ability of the line judges to apply them.

A dual ontology for a double science

Molecular clusters and active people

Taken separately each pillar of discursive psychology rests on an ontology. Roughly speaking we could say that the basic particulars of neurophysiology are molecules and their structured interactions, while those of skilled performances are people and their intentional and normatively constrained actions. It is people who play tennis, display emotions, make decisions and so on. It is people who are conscious.

However we do not know what are the biomolecular constraints on the range of intentional systems the human body can sustain. We do know at least that there must be a certain ethological foundation in some fixed action patterns, those that sustain the natural expression of feeling and intention on which Wittgenstein's account of the acquisition of linguistic and other higher functions depends. We also know that the perceptual systems must be so structured as to identify the higher order invariants that Gibson has identified and that make perception of material things possible. Without that capacity a self-system built around the embodied person could not come into play.

We might be tempted to ask 'What *are* people?' when confronted with the grammatical duality above. We might be hoping for the setting up of a set of necessary and sufficient conditions for picking them out from the diversity of the world. We might even be wanting an analytical account in terms of internal parts and structures. But if we were hankering for the latter, 'person' would not be the word for the basic particulars of our scheme. If you want to know, with the 'persons' grammar, the 'persons' ontology, which beings are people, we can only gesture to some examples of creatures who are and to some who are not. But there will be lots about which we are not *fully decided*.

Choosing an ontology

Ontologies are, in effect, grammars. They are specifications, some explicit, some implicit, of ways of identifying and marking the boundaries of particulars for some purpose or other. Sciences are created by choosing an ontology – or, what is more likely, finding oneself already committed to one in the way one has been thinking and acting – through the use of which phenomena are to be identified and ordered and explanations are to be constructed. Ontologies, as expressed in grammars, loosely fix the forms of discourse appropriate to this or that human project, including laying out the project. Ontologies also fix methods. Since ontologies are prior to phenomena there is always a choice. In the case of psychology the twofold schema above permits a choice between founding the science of human thought and action on molecules as the basic particulars, and founding it on people as the basic particulars. In the end the choice of ontology is largely justified pragmatically: how many of the phenomena of interest does it enable us to comprehend in a fruitful and constructive way?

However we cannot adequately describe a grammar without an account of the practices that go along with it. Wittgenstein insisted that speaking is at its most characteristic as a human activity as part of some practice or procedure. Words are more often used to instruct than they are used to describe. Each grammar with its associated practices makes available a different aspect of the indefinitely complex world we inhabit, either by highlighting it or by creating it, or sometimes by both.

Discursive psychology is created by choosing 'person' as the elementary being or basic particular for a psychological science. Constrained by that choice, brains become tools for persons to use in accomplishing certain tasks. Most cognitive tasks are set culturally. For instance the task of tallying a flock of sheep (in a cultural milieu in which an 'exact numerical count' makes sense) can be accomplished by notching a tally stick or by using one's brain, or by some combination of the two. Someone who wished to play tennis needs a racquet, arms, a court, a suitably modified nervous system, an opponent and so on. Neurophysiology slots into psychology as the study of some of the tools that people use for accomplishing their projects according to locally valid norms and standards. The troubles that ensue from choosing some anatomical or neurophysiological entity as the basic particular for psychology have been nicely set out by Coulter (1983), but they are evident in a glance at the 'mainstream' journals. Physics slots into psychology as the study of some of the tools in use, for instance the tennis racquet, or as part of the requirements for the study of the eye and visual system as a tool that people use to see things with. The study of that organ system becomes relevant to psychology just in so far as people make use of it for various purposes.

Our culture is pretty much dominated by the two grammars sketched above. But our discourses are also shot through with fragments and residues of other grammars, once dominant, and perhaps intimations of others yet to come. In popular discourse some of the discursive tropes of soul talk survive. More people follow the astrological pages in the papers than would confess it. Fragments of early Christian discursive practices survive along with odds and ends of Buddhism. Could a third dominant grammar appear that would heal the rift that is so obvious in our current ways of speaking? Perhaps.

Colonization

Is it conceivable that we might simply short circuit all this tedious debate and colonize the territory of one of our contemporary ontologies with the grammar of the other? There is a nice observation by Herbert Spencer (1896) which sums up one of the problems, clearly formulated long since by John Locke:

> Can the oscillation of a molecule be represented side by side with a nervous shock, and the two be recognised as one? No effort enables us to assimilate them. That a unit of feeling has nothing in common with a unit of motion becomes more than ever manifest when we bring the two into juxtaposition.

We might try inserting the word 'person' into the molecular grammar. In finding a place there it loses its moral connotations, and can mean no more than 'human being'. Goffman has remarked on the rituals of depersonalization that prepare a person for surgery, during which they exist socially only as a body. There are complementary rituals of repersonalization in the recovery room.

But try inserting 'brain' or 'hand' into the person grammar. These words now take on the character of words for tools or instruments, figuring amongst the means by which our multitudinous practices are carried on. Or to put in yet another idiom, in the molecular world things happen, while in the world of persons things are done.

The analysis offered here does indeed support a dualism, but not a Cartesian dualism of substances. Everything in the universe can be seen (and, if the resources are there, described) in itself, maybe in causal relations to other things. It can also be seen and described as standing for something else. In the latter case the relation it bears to what it stands for is semantic and conventional, not causal. Potentially everything has a dual aspect. But only human beings, so far as we know, are capable of this cognitive trick of constructing meanings, of creating discursive tools. Everything that is characteristic of human life stems from the exercise of this capacity. What is it that is seen when a material thing or state of affairs is seen as a symbol? Is it an additional property to which the uninitiated are blind? It is no more but no less than realizing to what uses the sign can be put. Of course the first uses we make of a sign do not foreclose on what we may later do with it.

The threat of behaviourism

Once again we come upon the idea that mind is created by people *ad hoc* in the activities of everyday life, including private acts of thinking as well as public and collective cognitive performances. Mind is nothing but meaningful action. Why is this not a return to behaviourism? Both Ryle and Wittgenstein have been called 'behaviourists' just on the grounds that they insist that meanings can only be learned publicly. Behaviourists tried to identify the elements of behaviour by essentially material or physical criteria. What counted as the same or different behaviours was so defined. 'The rat presses the bar in the Skinner box so many times.' Methodological behaviourism takes note of a wider range of behaviours, particularly answers to questionnaires, but the seemingly wilful avoidance of reference to the intentionality of human action remains firm. Discursive psychologists share with behaviourists a distaste for imagined and invisible cognitive processes, but it is in the identification and classification of actions that the *huge* differences emerge. Actions are functional in practices, complex patterns of action through which tasks and projects are accomplished. Actions serve in this way only in so far as they are meaningful, that is accomplish acts. Sameness and difference among actions are determined by reference to the acts performed. Actions accomplish acts only in this or that form of life. Anthropologists sometimes use the contrast 'etic/emic' to make the same distinction. An action would be recognized as intended in almost all human groups, and so would be distinguished by an etic criterion, whereas acts are recognizable only locally, by emic criteria. A person organizing their actions to display their selfhood (Self 1, Self 2 and Self 3 in our methodologically reified terminology) must needs adopt the local practices in performing the necessary acts. But above all the force of this psychology is to place great emphasis on the priority of joint action for the capacities and skills of individual members of tribes. Social life is not an *ad hoc* coming together of individuals, hazardously trading hypotheses as to what each one is thinking and doing. The minds of individuals are privatized practices condensing like fog out of the public conversation onto material nuclei, their bodies.

Conclusion

The more extreme advocates of a postmodern interpretation of science, though certainly in the same camp as the practitioners of discursive psychology, have claimed that each and every psychology, say mainstream American, is just one story amongst a slew of others, all of which have claims to our attention. Of course, as I have been arguing for decades, in a sense that is true. Conforming to the discursive conventions of 'science' may not be the best strategy for certain purposes and for the performance of certain tasks. If you want to know about the human heart and subtleties of misery and happiness you would be better to read Tolstoy than Argyle. But radical relativism does not follow from the postmodern insight. It does not follow that *relative to the task in hand*, stories cannot be ranked according to rational criteria. They are not of equal value when judged in the light of some project. I think we have to see people as engaging in joint tasks and projects, adopting positions in the local moral order, and guided in what they do, publicly or privately, by the story-lines that are appropriate to the task. Sometimes this takes the form of explicit rule-following, sometimes it can be best described as imitating and so reproducing a practice. The natural sciences are not just one genre of stories among others with respect to the task of comprehending the material world, when what is in question is building bridges, synthesizing useful chemicals and explaining the array of products in an atom smashing machine. But with respect to the task of finding our place, as human beings, in that world then indeed they are one amongst other genres and less compelling than some. Once we take up the task-oriented approach then stories can be ranked. If I want to send a space probe to the vicinity of a Jovian moon, Galileo's discovery of the parabolic path of projectiles would be the story to adopt. But if I wanted to think through my attitude to an elderly relative suffering from Alzheimer's condition, the chemotherapy story that governs some treatments of those whose word-finding difficulties lead to their being diagnosed as psychologically confused would be one to eschew.

There could be a *preferred* scientific psychology, provided that the honorifics 'scientific' and 'psychology' are detached from too heavy a dependence on the methods and strategies of the natural sciences. For example, calling questionnaires 'instruments' and the results of answering them 'measures' to which statistical analysis is applied does not make the practice a science. As we shall see, in looking at some of the ways that such personal attributes as 'self-esteem' have been studied, the ontological question 'What is the referent of the expression "self-esteem"?' cannot be ignored. The natural science model tempts us to think of such concepts as referring to causally potent inner states of people. A closer look shows that the expression makes sense only as a feature of discourse. The irony is that studying the answers people give to questions is a possible scientific method, provided that it is seen for what it is, a study of some of the discursive conventions for answering certain kinds of questions. Modelling some of this in a computer can give us a ready method of testing whether we have a reasonable grip on the rules for conversing on this subject matter in this context. Discursive psychology has a natural ally in a modest style of artificial intelligence methods for modelling rule systems. It does not give us access to an abstract model of unobserved cognitive processes. It may give us access to the neurophysiological bases of the relevant skills, that is to the bodily mechanisms a skilled performer uses to accomplish tasks. But that is when we pass to another ontology and exchange one frame for another.

In relation to the problems discussed in this book, the basic point about the discursive method is that in the different uses of 'I' different senses of 'self' are manifested. As Young-Eisendrath and Hall put it: there are different 'ways of speaking of self' (1987: 439–61).

CHAPTER THREE

Which Grammar? Indexicals and Names

> 'I' is not the name of a person, nor 'here' of a place, and 'this' is
> not a name. But they are connected to names. Names are
> explained by means of them.
>
> Ludwig Wittgenstein, *Philosophical investigations*

Throughout these studies I am comparing and contrasting the sense
of self as a singularity with the self-concept, those things we believe
or know about ourselves. While the former is necessarily private,
the latter, at least in principle, could be, and often is, public. In the
techniques and devices referring to persons the distinction is
immediately prominent in the two main person referring devices,
names and pronouns. Names could be substituted for first person
pronouns in self-descriptions, though it might sound odd. My
beliefs about myself are beliefs held by this person about him or
herself and others could hold them too. But names could never be
successfully substituted for pronouns in expressions of the sense of
self as a singularity, as the one and only one being from the location
of which all else is viewed, because the name would have to be
accomapanied by a contingent spatio-temporal reference. Nor
could the implication that the speaker is the person taking responsibility for what is said be captured by the use of a proper name. In
this chapter the informal analyses of some discourses of self-expression, briefly sketched in Chapter One, are developed in a more systematic way.

The three domains of the expression of selfhood are those of Self
1, expressed in the first person pronouns and inflexions, of Self 2,
beliefs about which are expressed in personal stories and self-
descriptions, the self-concept, and Self 3, which is expressed in social
action, in the personality and character I display in my dealings with
real and imagined others. I shall look first at the role of pronouns
in the expression of that singularity of self that comes from
each person's unique embodiment providing a spatio-temporally

grounded point of view. Then I will turn to the role of proper names in the expression of each person's public personhood. I shall be bringing to light the linguistic devices by which the standard model, Person {Self 1, Self 2, Self 3} is expressed. I shall begin with its expression in English.

At the heart of the dual science of psychology is the active person, creating their own mentality as they use the tools provided by their biological endowment and by their culture to pursue their projects, plans and intentions, with each other. I will show how the expression of the person as agent appears particularly in the way in which first person accounts are used to establish the actor as a centre of power and efficacy.

It cannot be emphasized too often that within the standard model both Self 2, one's personal attributes, and Self 3, how one's character and personality are expressed in public speech and action, are ephemeral, transitory constructions. What holds firm day by day, moment by moment, are one's powers, capacities, liabilities, vulnerabilities, skills and abilities. Even these develop, change and decline in the long run. A person could never be individuated by reference to their skills and talents. Using these a person creates a flow of symbolic and practical action, within which certain invariants appear. What we *call* our selves can never be more than invariants in the flux of action, private and public. Our skills and abilities change too, but they do tend to show a long-term stability, once they are established. A person then is both more than and less than the sum of his or her selves: more than in that a person exists continuously in space and time; less than in that a person, as the singular locus of powers, liabilities and skills, is but the spatio-temporal location of the personal repertoire of resources evident in action.

I must also reiterate that much of our cognitive activities are joint and collectively produced. It may be that no one engaged in a joint production of some mental process or ephemeral attribute is aware of or pays attention to constructions that come about without anyone specifically intending them. Shotter (1993) has drawn our attention to the importance of the 'third realm' of cognition, into which we enter only in so far as we can find ways of making this 'hurly- burly' intelligible to ourselves. Many of our constructive activities are taken for granted in the flow of action, for example, our bringing into being accounts of the past.

The expression of Self 1

The Jamesian grammatical account

Where would we expect to find expression of the sense one has of one's own singularity? The obvious place to look is in the grammar of the personal pronouns, particularly the first person and to a lesser degree the second. The grammar of the third person has little relevance to the question of expression of singularity, though it is important in discussions of the recognition of other beings as persons. Interestingly first and second person pronouns fall into one group grammatically while those of the third person are in another. A third person pronoun is literally a pro-noun, and can, with preservation of sense, be substituted for and by a proper name or other referring expression. Such pronouns are said to be anaphoric. In 'Jim skidded and he fell off his bike and he broke his collar bone' the successive he's and his's carry forward the same reference initiated by the proper name 'Jim'. However first and second person pronouns belong to a different word class. They are indexicals, having grammatical properties like 'this', 'here', 'now' and so on. I shall try to show that they are used to express one's sense of the singularity of oneself, as a person, in several dimensions, but particularly with respect to the singularity of one's material embodiment. No lesser person that William James presented a highly finished account of indexical aspects of the verbal expression of Self 1 in an unjustly neglected passage:

> The individuated self, which I believe to be the only thing properly called self, is a part of the content of the world experienced. The world experienced (otherwise called the 'field of consciousness') comes at all times with our body at its center, center of vision, center of action, center of interest. Where the body is, is 'here'; when the body acts is 'now'; what the body touches is 'this'; all other things are 'there' and 'then' and 'that'. These words of emphasized position imply a systematization of things with reference to the focus of action and interest which lies in the body . . . The body is the storm-center, the origin of coordinates, the constant place of stress in all that experience strain. Everything circles round it and is experienced from its point of view. The word 'I', then, is primarily a noun of position, just like 'this' and 'here' . . . the word 'my' designates the kind of emphasis. (James, 1977: 187)[1]

I have been at pains to point out that the use of 'I' to index the content of a report with the point of view of the speaker implies a centring among material things in the environment and also among the parts of one's body as territory within the larger territory. This has been remarked by many authors, for instance:

The personal world of every individual thus becomes centred around himself [*sic*], as William Stern (1938) has pointed out ... in making judgements of 'space' and 'time' the individual inevitably uses himself as a central point of reference. This holds for what we regard as 'inside' and 'outside' ourselves. (Sherif and Cantril, 1947: 92)

The grammar of 'I' and 'you'

By setting out a kind of generic grammar of the first person I hope to make clear some of the ways that particular grammars differ from one another. The key notion is that of indexicality. That 'I' is not a device for referring to oneself has taken a surprisingly long time to be accepted by philosophers and linguists. Something of the story of this struggle can be read in Glock and Hacker (1996).

The indexicality of a word can be looked at either as the fact that its meaning is completed on each occasion of use by some knowledge of the conditions of each particular utterance[2] or as indexing the descriptive content or the social force of an utterance with the place or moment of its utterance. Since the place of an utterance is generally and primordially the location of the embodied speaker, the singularity of the indexical reference of the first person and the uniqueness of human embodiment are intimately related. In what follows I shall be emphasizing the latter aspect of indexical expressions. For example the meaning of 'I' is completed on an occasion of use by local knowledge of the location of the body of the speaker. By virtue of that fact about its usage the situated use of 'I' indexes the empirical content of a descriptive statement with the spatial location of the embodied speaker. Similarly the grammar of 'you' is also indexical, indexing the empirical or social content of a statement with the spatial location, moral standing and so on of the person to whom it is addressed. For all sorts of historical reasons the English pronoun system is impoverished in expressive capacities, particularly in the second person and the first person plural. For instance English does not express the difference between 'we' = 'us two' and the 'we' of indefinite number, nor is there a grammatical expression of the difference between 'we' as referring to those present and 'we' referring to some such group as family or professional association, the members of which do not need to be present on the occasion of the use of the word. The grammar I shall be describing is an abstraction from the grammars of many different languages, each of which includes some but not all of the indexical properties we know from comparative studies to be possible.

An indexical expression marks the sense of an utterance with the relevant location of the speaker and the act of uttering in some array of entities within which some speaking occurs. There are two major arrays involved in first person grammar, as well as in the grammar of such in-dexical expressions as 'here', 'now', 'this' and so on.[3] There is the spatial array of material things amongst which the body of the speaker has a place. And there is the temporal array[4] of events amongst which the act of uttering is located. The structures of these arrays, as they underpin particular conversations, need not be New-tonian. For example in Yucatan Maya the demonstratives, elabora-tions on 'this' and 'that', index the content of an utterance with the location of speaker, addressee and object spoken about in an array of things, structured around a principle of 'line of sight'. 'That seen by both of us' and 'that seen by you and not by me' are referred to by different indexicals, though the thing is, in a sense, in the same place.

The array of material things includes a subarray of embodied persons. This subarray is invoked in two further indexical placings. The person array is structured not only by the spatial locations of bodies, but by such moral relations as mutual duty and obligation and by multiple patterns of status relations. I shall call locations in the former 'positions', following recent writings on the subject (van Langenhove and Harré, 1991), and locations in the latter 'standings'.

Drawing on a wide range of languages we can assemble the following generic grammar of the first person as an indexical (reminding ourselves that the main indexical expression in some language may not be a pronoun but an inflexion of the verb):

1 The descriptive content of a first person utterance is indexed with the spatial location of the embodied speaker as a thing amongst things. If someone uses the first person in a report of what they can see, feel, hear and so on we understand that what is reported is from the spatial location of the speaker at that moment, and (when qualified by tense) it gives us notional retrospective and prospective indexings of point of view. 'I will visit the gallery' places the embodied speaker in a particular material setting in the future, while 'I saw Fred at the dog races' locates my embod-ied self at a former moment at a certain place in the city. The use of demonstratives is, in a certain sense, also a first person use, since the sense of 'this' and 'that' or 'here' and 'there' depends on the location of the speaker on the occasion of utterance. Percep-tual reports express the organization of perceptual experience relative to the embodied location of the speaker.

2 First and second person pronouns index the social force of an
   utterance with the 'position' of the speaker and interlocutor in
   the local moral order, an array of persons ordered by relations of
   obligation, duty and trust. For instance the use of 'I' commits the
   speaker to whatever the utterance implies, for instance a promise
   commits one to fulfilling it. This commitment is understood by
   others by reference to their knowledge of the speaker's moral
   character (reliable, dishonest and so on) with respect to the
   matter in hand. When someone has said 'I'll do the dishes', we
   generally expect that the dishes will get done. Similarly when an
   order, request or exhortation is addressed to a second person,
   singular or plural, the efficacy of the order is determined by the
   indexicality of the pronoun with respect to the local moral order.
   Most people live their lives in many moral orders, so the
   phenomenon of positioning is both complex and ephemeral.
3 First and second person pronouns of many oriental languages
   index the social force of an utterance with the 'standing' of the
   speaker and interlocutor in the local social order, the array of
   persons ordered by relations of social class, respect and so on.
   English pronouns do not serve this indexical function, but in
   most European languages it is strongly present in second person
   uses (the *tu/vous* distinction in its various manifestations, in both
   pronoun use and verb inflexions: Brown and Gillman, 1970). In
   addressing someone in French one must choose between *tu* and
   vous and so one must display one's assessment of the mutual
   standings of oneself and the one addressed in the local social
   order. The Japanese first person forms have strong indexical
   implications for the relative standings of speakers and
   addressees in local social orders. For example in Japanese the
   choice of *watakushi* rather than *watashi* as the first person expression indexes the social force of the utterance with the respect due
   to the addressee and at the same time expresses the high standing of both. The pronoun not only picks out a person, but
   expresses a social relation.
4 Indo-European languages use verb inflexions rather than
   pronoun variants to index the content of speech acts with the
   relation of the events narrated or referred to, to the event of the
   utterance of the speech act. In some Indonesian languages,
   notably Kawi, the classical language of the region (Becker and
   Oka, 1974), the forms of pronouns, including first and second
   person, are sensitive to temporal indexicality. For example the
   locative particle 'Nga-' when prefixed to the deictic formative '-
   k-' and to one of the person particles '-i', '-a' or '-u', yields *Nga-k-i,*

meaning 'I-at-some-past-time'. English uses of tense and the temporal indexicals 'now' and 'then' (the latter indexing the content only with a time other than the present) leave the 'I' as indexical of a continuing and self-identical person throughout a narrative. Kawi story-telling is not under the constraint that tends to constrain much story-telling in Indo-European languages to a picaresque unfolding of events in the order of their occurrence. An Indonesian story can be ordered by virtue of the importance of the events narrated, since the broad temporal structure is expressed by the tense of the indexical pronouns.

English is capable of expressing, by choice of pronoun, only the first two of these indexical possibilities. Japanese does not inflect the first person for tense as does Kawi, only for relative social standing. Generally speaking, while the English 'I' indexes the social force of an utterance with the commitment and location of the speaker, other indexical aspects of speaking must be borne by other grammatical devices, such as titles, forms of address and tenses.

Where would one look for an expression of the seemingly elusive sense of self? Presumably, as James thought, in the uses of the first person, in pronouns and verb inflexions, demonstratives and tenses. Somewhere in the grammar of these devices the nature of the sense of self might be found.

Indexicality and the description/expression distinction

The thesis of this chapter borrows from Wittgenstein's distinction between description and expression, worked out in detail in the private language argument (Wittgenstein, 1953: 240–315). It also invokes his distinction between the 'frame' of a discourse, its grammar, and the 'picture' that is painted within that frame. There is a certain structure to each and every person's perceptual field, centred around a point; the same point centres our perceptions of the things in the world around us as centres our perceptions of the extended body, the location of which fixes our place in the world. This centredness is one of the singularities that enter into my sense of self. When I describe what I can see, feel, touch and so on I express, in those descriptions, the centredness of my experience. That expression is carried by the indexical devices in the description of what is perceived. There are the demonstratives, 'this', 'that', 'here', 'there', 'now' and 'then', by which reference to the ordered array of things and events in my perceptual environment is expressed, with respect to my bodily location. Then there is the first person grammar that indexes perceptual discourse with my singular point of view as a being embodied in some spatial location, as a thing among things. Some of the subtle differences in viewpoint that distinguish the life-worlds of the blind and the sighted have been quite thoroughly explored. However the explanations of the typical 'delay in the acquisition of "I" as a stable pronoun' (Fraiberg and Adelson, 1973: 539) are not always satisfactory. For instance the authors just quoted go on to say that 'the blind child's delay in the acquisition of "I" as a concept and a stable form appears to be related to the extraordinary problems of constructing a self-image in the absence of vision.' This must surely be wrong. Rather it must have to do with the kind of Self 1, the sense of singularity of location in space and time, which is triangulated with respect to the spatial location of embodied people and other things.[5]

By analysing the grammar of these indexical devices we can enter into the structure of personal experience. In describing what I see I am describing not some state of myself, as phenomenologists and sense-datum theorists would have it, but some state of the world, indexed with the point of view from which it is seen, heard, felt and so on, and that is the location of my body. There are both implicit and explicit indexings with the locations of embodiment. When someone says 'There's a bittern!' or 'The snow has started again' or 'The horn playing in Mahler 5 was marvellous', we understand these descriptions and evaluations of what is being and has been perceived as implicitly indexed with the spatial point of view of the embodied speaker. We do not need to ask 'Were you there?' and similar questions. By bringing together the distinction between descriptive and expressive discourse and that between referring to something and indexing the content of a statement with the point of view of the speaker, we arrive at an analysis of the grammar of perception statements:

1 'There's a bittern' is about the material environment and is implicitly indexed with the location in that environment of the speaker and with the perceptual modality by which the speaker has become aware of the bird. The default modality is vision.
2 'I can see a bittern' is also about the material environment but is explicitly indexed with the spatial location of the speaker, namely where his/her body is, and with the perceptual modality by which the speaker has become aware of the bird, namely visual.

The above examples are identical in empirical content but differ in 'grammar', the latter being the explicit form of the former. Both are expressive, neither is self-descriptive. That is, the latter no more ascribes a property to an entity denoted by 'I' than does

'Washington, DC is at 39°N 77°W' ascribe a Washingtonness to something denoted by an expression that has a place in the grid of latitude and longitude. The expression '39°N 77°W' does not denote an entity other than that which is located by means of it. It is an indexical that marks the content of an utterance with a spatial location.

Introducing perceptual statements, descriptions of how things look, sound, feel and taste, with an explicit 'I' does not change the essential features of reporting how things seem to me. In particular it does not transform them from reports about the world to reports about the mental states of the perceiver. The 'I' is an explicit indexical, expressing the point of view of the embodied speaker. So 'I can feel a lump in the mattress' is a description of the mattress, in the perceptual modality of tactile experience, indexed with the location of my body, as the position in space from which the lump can be perceived. I describe the mattress, I express my point of view. To put this point in another way, favoured by Wittgenstein: I need evidence to back up my claim about the lump, such as a certain feeling in my back that you too can experience if you take my place in the bed. But I need no evidence to index the experience as mine. I do not need a second fact, that might have been otherwise, namely that it is me feeling the lump. There is no empirical gap between my use of the indexical and my experience, as there is between my claim about a lump and my feeling. It might not be a lump in the mattress at all, merely a crinkle in the sheet, but it makes no sense to suppose that it might not have been me feeling it. 'I' is part of the grammatical machinery by which I express my point of view, not a device for referring to a subject to which properties and states are being ascribed.

The iterated 'I'

This analysis becomes even more to the point when we consider more complex statements, in which 'I' is used in a qualifying clause within which a perceptual claim is embedded. Thus to the question 'Are you sure it's a bittern?' I might reply 'Well, I think I can see it' or something of the sort. Is the way now open for the reappearance of the 'ego', as the referent of the embedded 'I'? To reach a proper understanding of the grammar of those statements in which a first person description of how the world looks from the speaker's point of view is embedded in an outer sentence frame also in the first person, we need to remind ourselves of the double indexical force of the English 'I'. It indexes content with the spatial location of the speaker and it also indexes the social force of the same utterance with the moral position or standing of the speaker. In speaking in the first person I am committing myself to the veracity, accuracy and so on of what I am reporting. In short a descriptive statement is also a performative utterance, the social force of which is something like 'Trust me . . .' or 'I guarantee . . .'. The degree to which others will give credence to what *I* report is evidently tied up with my 'moral' reputation as a reliable or reckless person.

Generally a factual, perceptual statement in the first person is indexed both with the spatial location of the speaker's body and with the moral position of the speaker as a person. The point of making the first person implications of that sort of statement overt is to *strengthen* both indexes. If we compare 'There's a bittern' with 'I can see a bittern' we can see that the latter emphasizes the spatial location of the speaker as the point of view from which this rare bird can be seen, as well as committing the speaker more firmly to the reliability of the identification.

However we often embed one statement introduced by 'I' within another statement, also introduced by the first person. 'I expect I will have another slice of Tin Roof Fudge Pie' expresses my resignation to the forces of greed and self-indulgence. 'I think I saw a bittern' expresses a more cautious commitment to the identification than the simple claim 'I saw a bittern.' What is the relation between the two occurrences of 'I'? There is a grammatical model waiting to entice us. I could also say, on observing the look on the face of my fellow diner, 'I expect he will have another slice of Tin Roof Fudge Pie' and many other statements like it, in which a variety of third person comments are embedded in the outer first person frame. Since 'he' is anaphoric and refers to a person, perhaps the embedded 'I' is also referential, picking out a person and ascribing a mental state to him or her, contrary to our analysis of first person grammar according to which 'I' is always indexical.

But reflection on the role of the iterated 'I' in everyday discourse makes clear that the outer 'I' which frames the unqualified statement weakens or strengthens its 'I' commitment. Thus if I say 'I think I can see a bittern' my claim is still that there is a bittern out there on the edge of the swamp, but the embedding frame serves to qualify the strength of my assertion. It backs off from the full force of 'Trust me: it's a bittern!' Many statements we make have this double aspect: stating a fact or making a prediction, the empirical content of what is said, *and* committing *myself* to the trustworthiness of what has been said. In all these cases in which the iterated 'I' frames the simple assertion, promise and so on, the double indexicality of 'I' is evident.

Consider the statement:

I am going to be sick

It could be read empirically as a prediction, and the 'I' indexes the prediction with the location of the speaker's body. Read this way one might reply 'Run to the bathroom' or 'Put your head out of the window', picking up the spatial indexing of the prediction to the speaker's bodily location. Suppose the speaker embedded the original statement as follows:

I think I'm going to be sick
I'm sure I'm going to be sick

If the inner statement is read as a prediction the iterated 'I' serves to qualify its social force, the degree of commitment of the speaker to the prediction, weakening it in the first case and strengthening it in the second. The original utterance could also be heard as a threat. Interpreted thus the double indexical force of the first person is even clearer. In these sorts of cases the iterated statements would weaken or strengthen the social force of the threat. In either case the grammar is the same. Inner 'I' is indexical of the spatial location of the possible catastrophe, and of the moral standing of the speaker with respect to the social force of that statement. Is he or she reliable? Does the speaker carry out their threats? The outer 'I' is indexical only of the moral standing of the speaker, and qualifies only the force of the embedded statement.

By no means all performative utterances can be qualified this way. For example if I say 'I order you to move forward', statements like 'I hope I order you to move forward' or 'I think I order you to move forward' make little sense. Qualifying the social force of a command is achieved by changing the verb. 'I hope you will move forward' is weaker and 'I insist you move forward' perhaps is stronger than just 'Go forward.' In these cases the explicit use of the 'I' is indexical of the speaker's moral standing *vis-à-vis* the act required and the person who is being told to do it. We shall study locutions of this type when we come to consider the singularity of persons as agents. Our agentive powers are manifested not only in what we do but also in what we say. This is particularly true when those powers are exercised over other people and certain animals. People are held to be responsible not only for their bodily actions, but also for their speech acts.

However one must be careful not to over-generalize the agentive implications of the indexing of responsibility which we take so

much for granted. In her study of the role of the first person in
Indonesia and its indexical forces Berman notes 'the tendency in
many Asian countries to de-emphasize agency . . . [as] symbolic of
possible definitions of person as something other than the responsible unique individual' (1992: 5). In everyday talk 'I' may be
omitted, and 'we' favoured, while time, place and responsibility are
de-emphasized. However Berman's studies do tend to show that
with 'I' in place, there is a tendency to read the speech act so qualified as a commitment. Only thus is the omission of 'I' a significant
act.

Other persons: the anaphoric pronouns 'he' and 'she'

The way that Indo-European languages inflect the third person
singular pronouns and the past and present participles for gender
has not gone unremarked by psycholinguists with an interest in
feminism. In accordance with Lakoff's emphasis on the importance
of grammaticalization of distinctions in shaping thought and
conduct this very robust gender distinction is surely of some significance for the self-concept. The use of 'he' for the inclusive
male/female has been shown to be frequently misread, as a privi-
leging of the male sex in the discourses in which it is so used. As
Elaine Morgan has remarked, statements like 'Man evolved on the
savannah' suggest to the modern ear that human evolution took
place entirely via the interaction between the males of the species
and their environment. Be that as it may, English and most other
languages, with the exception of the Ural-Altaic group, have this
grammar. It also serves a locative function, placing the person
talked about in one or other location in a two-place gender space.
Interestingly biological sex may not be the only item of a person's
Self 2, reflected in the self-concept, expressed in action and opinion
or not, as a relevant distinction that ought to be expressible in the
third person.

In recent discussions of 'gays in the military' American politicians and commentators were presented with the problem of
expressing locations in a four-place space, the space needed to deal
with the cross-product of biological sex and what is now called
'sexual orientation'. The four locations in the space are 'men who
prefer women', 'men who prefer men', 'women who prefer women'
and 'women who prefer men'. 'He' and 'she' are tied to a two-place
gender manifold. At present there does not seem to be any sign of
a fourfold third person singular developing to express location in

the four-place manifold. However it may emerge in the appearance of words borrowed from other registers for the work of third person singular expressions of location in the cross-product manifold.

Other cross-product manifolds are also possible if any of the manifolds of the four main indexicals become salient in certain special situations, for instance gerontology. For example 'old/ young' could be multiplied into 'he/she' to yield another four-place manifold.

Names: proper and improper

In every culture we know of, to be a person is, amongst other things, to have a name. The giving and sometimes the rescinding of names is an important matter, frequently given ceremonial form, but not always. Ways of acquiring names are complex and various. Exploring them would add another dimension to the diversity of the many concrete versions of personhood our species displays. The crucial point is that proper names are used to pick out persons as publicly identifiable individuals and refer to none of the discursively constructed pseudo-entities, Self 1, Self 2 or Self 3.

Personal and family names

Patterns of naming differ widely. In some there is a strong emphasis on genealogy. For example in Spain the custom is for everyone to have their own personal name, usually that of a saint, then the family name of the father, followed by the family name of the mother. But since there are many Maria-Teresas, Pablos, and Pedros, Spanish is rich in nicknames. Among the Chinese, naming traditionally leaned towards sympathetic magic, in that a name for a virtue or a beautiful or pleasing object might serve as an exemplar in life, so I have been told. Was there a serious psychological theory to go along with this? It would make a nice study to find out. We do know that nicknames affect character and personality (Morgan et al., 1977). Among some cultures there is a rapid turnover of names, for instance the adults in a Land Dyak village take a name derived from the personal name of the youngest child, something like 'Father of X' and 'Grandmother of Y' and so on. All of these names are the identifying marks of persons. They are, in principle, the marks of personal identity, and also, in principle, the marks of the tribe, family or clan (even profession or religion) to which a person belongs, of identity in the sense of 'type' or 'group'.

For intuitions as to the work names do in the context of self concepts, as the kind of person one is, one must go to the autobiographies of those for whom their birth name is a mark of humiliation.
Some black Americans feel that their 'official' names, often derived
from the surname of the plantation owner by whom their forebears
were enslaved, are demeaning. They seek others, often drawn from
Islamic culture, but sometimes from incidents in their lives that
display them as they would like to be. Sanyika Shakur (1993) offers
the following account of how he came to his new name 'Monster':
'I stomped him [my victim] for twenty minutes . . . [he] was disfig-
ured from my stomping. The police told bystanders that the person
responsible for this was a "monster". The name stuck, and I took
that as a moniker over my birth name [Kody Scott].' Later Scott
changed his name to Sanyika Shakur, under which he published his
autobiography from which the above quotation is taken.

'Official' names

What do our masters do when faced with the 'ingratiating chaos'
of the everyday traditions of personal naming? They invent a
nomenclature that assigns one mark uniquely to each embodied
person. In the US6 it is the Social Security Number, in the UK there
are various identifying numbers, though the nomenclature is
tending towards the unified American style. Again, the work is
person identification, rather than the expression of any of the main
aspects of selfhood. One's social security number, as a personal
attribute, is part of Self 2, and in so far as one knows what it is,
forms part of one's self-concept.

Nicknames

If unique embodiment is the crux of proper naming then personal
characteristics and history provides the dominant motivation in
nicknaming (Morgan et al., 1977). Traditional British nicknames like
'Fatty', 'Skinny', 'Lofty', 'Four-eyes', 'Bugalugs' and so on pick out
characteristics of physical appearance that diverge from local
norms. *Ad hoc* constructions turn out to be mostly motivated by
incidents in the recipient's life. Thus someone was called 'Coop'
because in reading a passage from French aloud, his voice broke on
the word *coupable*. Other cultures focus similarly on deviations from
normal appearances and from 'right' courses of action. So
nicknames tend to highlight biography and self-presentation,
aspects of selfhood that are defined, so to say, in the public domain,

qualifications of the individual as *person*. Nicknames enter quite deeply into the content of Self 2.

Conclusion

The ways people express themselves as themselves and the ways people talk about other people draw on quite different word classes. I have tried to show that the grammar of indexical pronouns, the devices by which we express our selfhood in its three-fold aspects, is not a special case of the grammar of proper names. The latter play an essential role in describing people other than oneself. They are like anaphoric, third person pronouns. The next step in our investigations will be to begin an overview of the many ways that the word 'self' is used in psychology, both lay and professional, extending and refining the brief sketch in Chapter One.

Notes

1 In this and other quotations from American sources I have retained the local spelling conventions.

2 For this reason first person pronouns were called 'shifters' by Jakobson (1957), in that their object of reference 'shifts'. It will be evident that I do not accept the underlying assumption that first person devices refer to their users.

3 For an elegant short treatment of the indexicality of 'I', see Glover (1988: 66).

4 We tend to take for granted the temporal sequences imposed on life events by the almost ubiquitous clock. Premodern cultures may treat temporality in other ways: one example we shall see later in the discussion of indexicality in Kawi.

5 I owe this reference to my colleague W. ver Eecke (1989).

6 In principle there could be only 999,000,000 Americans. SS numbers do not go back into a pool when a holder is deceased, so I am informed. In this respect they are unlike phone numbers and car licence plates.

CHAPTER FOUR

Persons and Selves: A Surview of some Current Concepts

I am nothing but who I am to other people

Maxine Kingston Hong, *The woman warrior*

The startling paradox expressed in the above quotation is typical of much postmodernist writing on personhood. It cannot be both true and intelligible, at least taken without further interpretation. That one adjusts one's actions and opinions to the human context in which one happens to find oneself is a truism. That one adjusts one's beliefs about oneself to such contexts is also true, but a matter of greater import. However there is just one person whose life Maxine Hong is telling. And that is Maxine Hong. Some distinctions in what work 'I' is doing in our discourses are very much needed. There is the embodied person. There is the author of his or her actions including what is said and what is otherwise done. There is that complex of relational attributes that constitute that being, and more.

I shall be trying to show that what people have called 'selves' are, by and large, produced discursively, that is in dialogue and other forms of joint action with real and imaged others. Selves are not entities, but evanescent properties of the flow of public and private action. I turn now to survey the many ways the word 'self' is used in current talk.

The complexities of personhood and the self

In Chapter One we have seen how complex is the field of concepts in play in discourses of personhood. Since there is my discourse directed to and about other people, and my discourse directed to and about myself, there must be a double rank of 'person' concepts in use. Or putting the point phenomenologically there is how I experience others, how I experience myself, and how I display or express myself to others and they to me. In the stripped down categories of logic we can express some of this in the distinction between numerical (one and the same) and qualitative (similarity) identity. But this allows only the individuality of human beings to be expressed. There is need for concepts to express the experience and the expression of uniqueness. Each individual is different from every other in two ways. As a singularity each person has a unique viewpoint on the world, and this is closely tied up with the spatio-temporal uniqueness of personal embodiment. And each person exercises their powers to display a unique set of attributes. Human beings never strictly fulfil the requirements of qualitative identity. With each of these goes a specific sense of self. With point of view goes a sense of the self as perceiver and actor, having a place in the world of things and events. With unique attributes goes a sense of the self as the totality of those attributes, at least as that person believes them to be. Thus there is a complex of concepts for discussing how I am to myself, while there is another complex for discussing how I am to you and how you are to me. The former invokes the concept of personhood and the reflexive experience of it. The latter invokes the concept of personhood and the interpersonal experience of it.

Despite the seemingly simple vocabulary, which in the everyday vernacular is limited to 'person' and 'self', there is a subtle variety of concepts in play in discussions of the singularity, uniqueness and identity of human beings, taken one by one. Some of the difficulties that we encounter in trying to give an account of human uniqueness come from the fact that, in English, the word 'self' is used to express several of them. In what follows I shall try to create a vocabulary that is not too far from ordinary usage yet which remedies the ambiguities that the current broad use of the word 'self' and its partial overlap with the word 'person' leads to. In this way the preliminary sketch of the layout of 'person' concepts in Chapter One will be expanded into a scheme adequate to discuss some at least of the psychological phenomena around the person.

Drawing on the basic analysis of Chapter One, the frame in which selfhood will be analysed looks something like this. Each human being is a centre of powers and capacities, refined, developed and modulated into a repertoire of skills. Each human being is thereby a person. Exercising these skills, people bring psychological phenomena into being, privately and publicly. The primary psychological reality is the public domain of interpersonal interaction, some of which becomes privatized in the course of development. The flow of action has certain characteristics, some of which are highlighted as referents for various uses of the word 'self'. In analysing the field of family resemblances of the use of this vocabulary, three will stand out. There is the centred organization of personal action, the centre point of which we have called Self 1. There is the totality of the actions a person produces including beliefs about those actions, and when this is bundled up with the skills and capacities a person has and believes they have, we have a loose knit cluster we have called Self 2. Finally there are the attributes of the public actions of a person which can give rise to opinions and beliefs of others, and each such manifestation we have called Self 3. It is not generally true that each person has but one Self 2 and one Self 3. The maintenance of the singularity of Self 1 takes us to the borders of pathology.

There are only persons as powerful particulars, exercising their skills in the production of psychological phenomena. The flow of psychologically relevant actions has certain characteristics, readily misinterpreted as if they were entities. We have such expressions as '*The* saturated self', '*The* protean self' and so on. There are no such entities. They are only persons and what they do. Part of my task in this set of studies is to dispel these misinterpretations and restore the 'self' characteristics of personal action to their proper place in the domain of human affairs.

As this study unfolds I hope it will become increasingly clear that personal singularity is a product of social processes, while the very attributes that characterize the seeming 'free-standing' person are through and through relational, having their terms in other people and other features of the environment.

Locke and the traditional agenda

The contrast between the public individual, the *man* in Locke's terminology, and the private sense of individuality that Locke refers to as what someone 'calls *self*', is not perhaps wholly due to Locke, but much of the agenda for the next three hundred years was set by it. As Locke says, 'it is not the *idea* [perhaps in modern terminology "concept"] of a thinking . . . being alone that makes the *idea* of a *man* . . . but [that] of a body . . . the same successive body, as well as the same immaterial spirit, go to the making of the same *man*' (1686: Book II, Chapter XXVII). Here we have the linking of the concept of personal identity as an interpersonal concept with the criteria for deciding whether some being is self-identical by reference to embodiment.

The same pattern characterizes Locke's account of the private sense of identity that each person has of themselves: 'it is [consciousness] that makes everyone be what he calls *self*, and thereby distinguishes himself from all other thinking things. . . . As far as this consciousness can be extended backwards to any past action or thought, so far reaches the identity of that *person*.' And this has proved to be the fatal move, the linking of the concept of personal identity as an intrapersonal concept with the criteria for deciding it. It has made it seem as if one needs criteria to determine whether one is unique and singular. And that present consciousness including memory of the past establishes it. As we shall see the simplest riposte is just to point out that for something to be a memory it must be a thought about *my* thoughts and actions, thus presupposing the very continuous self it was offered as a criterion to determine. Of course if I want to know whether I did something, trying to remember it or looking it up in my diary or asking someone else is the way to proceed. But none of that makes any sense unless it is against a background or frame of personal identity.

One might defend Locke's use of the twinned concepts 'person' and 'self' by interpreting 'self' in his usage as more or less the Self 2 of the standard model. Then what I can know of myself is largely contributed by what I remember of my life. If my Lockean 'self' is what I now know of myself, then it is identical neither with myself as a person nor with my sense of a singular spatio-temporal location.

People

'Person'

Dominating the lexicon is the concept of 'person'. Each person is a unique embodied being, rich in attributes and powers of many kinds, having a distinct history and, importantly, being morally protected and liable to be called to account as a morally responsible actor (Taylor, 1989). By 'moral protection' I mean something like the Kantian principle that people should be treated not just as means to ends but as ends in themselves. In a more modern idiom that principle amounts to the declaration that people have certain inalienable rights, in so far as they are persons. This is a conceptual truth about the concept 'person' and neither an empirical discovery made by anthropologists nor a legislative fiat created by law makers. Complementary to rights there are duties. Again this aspect of personhood is neither an empirical fact about persons nor yet created by a legislative act. Duties and rights can be assigned in so far as the concept of 'person' involves powers and capacities on the one hand and vulnerabilities and liabilities on the other. A person is a publicly identifiable individual whose origin and existence depend on there being other persons. A person has, by virtue of their community status, rights and duties with respect to other persons, as they have to them.

Persons, as Strawson (1959) has eloquently argued, are the basic particulars of the human world. It is as persons that human beings belong in that world, not as organisms. But the fact of embodiment is not an accidental feature of what it is to be a person. The concepts of identity, singularity and uniqueness are logically tied up with the embodiment of a human being as a thing among things in a world laid out in space and time.

I have used the Wittgenstein metaphor of 'frame and picture' to call attention to the difference between kinds of seemingly similar statements. 'I am here' and 'The cow is in the vegetable garden' have a superficial resemblance. Both seem to locate a being in a place. But now consider 'I am not here' and 'The cow is not in the vegetable garden.' While the latter may be false it makes sense. But the former seems to be nonsensical. Why is that? It is because the affirmative assertion, 'I am here', expresses a grammatical fact about 'I', that it does some of the work of 'here'. If the statement tells us anything it displays something about how the first person pronoun is used, that is displays an aspect of its 'grammar'. It shows us something of how we frame our thoughts and actions in a world of persons. The concept of 'person' belongs to the frame. The truisms we might want to assert about persons are best thought of as framing (or as aspects of our conceptual system) within which our lives as persons are lived. It is in terms of this concept that all else that pertains to the psychology of human beings is made thinkable, and discursively expressible. I shall be trying to show that the cluster of person concepts that characterize discourses of self play the role of a grammar, the rules that make a discourse of persons possible. They are not the result of empirical abstractions from experience. They are what make experience, as we have it, possible. In particular the grammar of first and second person pronouns and other devices for drawing attention to the personhood of people in dialogue reveals important aspects of the 'frames' of our human forms of life.

However our organic being, as material bodies in a material environment, is not only part of the frame or life-world within which we live, but also part of the 'picture'. Throughout this investigation I shall be working with the principle that bodies and their organs serve the people not only necessarily, as sustainers of their identity and singularity, but also contingently, in that they serve as a set of tools and instruments for the performance of all sorts of tasks. Some of these are material, such as opening doors; others are cognitive, such as remembering the family birthdays. For some there are surrogate or prosthetic devices which will perform the same function.

'Person' belongs to the grammar of psychological discourse. It does not delineate a topic for empirical study.

Persons are subject to criteria of numerical and of qualitative identity. We make use of the idea of the persistence in being of one and the same person, interwoven with the idea of people of the same sort. Philosophers are familiar with and especially sensitive to the fact that there are two kinds of sameness, sometimes lexically marked, as in Spanish *igual* and *mismo*, sometimes, as in English, not differentiated verbally. In both singularity, being one and the same person, and 'identity', being a person of a certain type, the characteristics of the human body play a part. That persons are embodied is no more an empirical discovery we make about ourselves than is the principle that persons are morally protected. It is part of what it is to be a person. It is a feature of the frame or grammar within which we live our lives as persons. These remarks will no doubt seem dogmatic at this point. However their appropriateness to the topic of the singularities of self will show itself as our investigations proceed in this direction and that.

The psychological literature does not offer a clear guide to extracting a repertoire of concepts for describing human beings in their particularity. Sometimes the word 'self' is used as a synonym for 'person'. For example Gaines explicitly links the two expressions in declaring 'we can assume that some concept of person, that of the self, is a universal, a particular conception or set of conceptions need not exist cross-culturally' (1996: 177). Just where splitting would seem to be called for, Gaines lumps. In what follows I shall try to keep to the usage of 'person' as a word for a human being as a social and psychological being, as a human organism having a sense of its place among others of its kind, a sense of its own history and beliefs about at least some of its attributes. The word 'self', variously qualified, will do duty for the many aspects of personal being that appear in personal and private regard.

'Self'

'Person' is a rich and powerful concept, yet to do justice to all that we need to say about the singularity of persons and the many dimensions of diversity within that singularity we seem also to need some further concepts for a comprehensive enough discourse of which we ourselves are the main topic. These concepts are immanent in our discourse of persons. For all of them the word 'self' has been appropriated from time to time and by this author or that in the English language discourse of persons. This is a situation guaranteed to cause confusion. We do need a word for persons as seen by themselves. The word in use for this job is 'self', in reflexive pronouns such as 'myself'. 'I did it myself' simply means the person who did whatever it was is the same person as the speaker. But detached from its pronominal locus it is used in several quite different ways.

Psychologists have used the word 'self' in such phrases as 'self-concept', to refer to what persons know or believe about themselves. Of course any attribute or power that a person could believe they[1] have, could also be an attribute or power of someone else. One's personal identity under the 'self-concept' is to be the possessor of a unique set of distinctive attributes, taken as a whole. The descriptions of these, person by person, will be different; and each such description, as made by or able to be made by each person, is their self-concept. Each of us has at any moment and over the life course a unique ensemble of attributes that has come to be called our 'self' by many authors. In this usage 'the self' is what a person is. These attributes are partially and to some extent inaccurately reflected in our self-concepts. The self as the totality of a person's attributes is Self 2. This concept has been well established in the literature. For instance Kohut introduces his psychology as based on the 'conceptual separation of the self from the ego' (1977: xiii). He goes on to explicate 'self' as follows:

> While it is . . . not an agency of the mind, it is a structure within the mind
> . . . The self, then, quite analogous to the representations of objects, is a
> content of the mental apparatus. (1977: xv)

What is evidently not part of Kohut's version of this concept is its dynamic, ephemeral and constructed character.

But there is something else we need to find a word for. Each of us has a sense of personal being, not just as the possessor of a unique set of attributes, but as a singularity, that is neither that of being a publicly identifiable person nor yet that of being a mere cluster of attributes. In G.H. Mead's (1934) terminology there is need for an 'I' as well as a 'me' in the conceptual resources needed to express personal experience. It is not too far from the usage of everyday to adopt the phrase a 'sense of self' to express our experience of our personal being as a singularity. I have called this Self 1. But we must be careful not to slip into the Cartesian fallacy of supposing that this is something to which the attributes of personhood belong, the centre to which all that is personal is related. It is the centre from which all that is perceived is viewed, but is not for that reason a thing, any more than is the North Pole or the Equator. There are only persons. Unfortunately the expression 'sense of self' has also been used for the beliefs I have about my Self 2, that is about my attributes as a person. In this way of speaking 'sense of self' is then roughly my self-concept, as a kind of summing up of what I think I am.

The equivocation in the use of 'self' between singularity of point of view and totality of personal attributes, and the interaction of both usages with the use of 'person', induce a continual uncertainty and instability in our readings of writings on the topic of 'the self', particularly when the author is of a postmodern orientation. The main problem is brought about by the transfer of aspects of the Self 2, the shifting pattern of attributes of a person, to the Self 1, the person as one experiences oneself as having a point of view, as a singularity in space and time.

To illustrate what I mean I offer some instances. There are many examples of this indeterminateness in recent writings on the topic of human individuality. In Grodin and Lindlof we have phrases such as 'destabilization of self', 'the self becomes multivocal', 'individuals may find that they no longer have a central core with which to evaluate and act, but instead find themselves "decentred"' (1996: 4). Here is a clutch of diverse metaphors crying out for deconstruction. What does 'destabilized' mean, in a concrete situation? What does the metaphor of 'becoming multivocal' mean *exactly*, with examples? How can *individuals* find *themselves* decentred? The 'that' which finds itself decentred is necessarily already a centre! Here are some suggestions for interpreting these opaque phrases. For 'destabilizing of the self' read ' the changing beliefs a person can have about his or her own history, abilities, and so on'. For 'the self becomes multivocal' read 'the differences in authority with which I speak *qua* gardener, parent, inhabitant of Oxfordshire and so on may come to seem important to me and to my friends and acquaintances.' The core referred to in the third opaque observation cannot be one's sense of self as a singularity, since that is presumed to be intact in the whole remark. It might refer to some set of beliefs and opinions that I, as a

continuing, stable, uninterrupted personal being, change from
context to context, sometimes presuming one set in what I say and
do, sometimes another. The self as singularity, the 'I' of Mead and
James, is never in question – only personal attributes, Self 2.

That there is a slippage from one use of 'self' to another in this kind
of text is confirmed throughout the book from which the above
quotes have been drawn. For example, in explaining the notion of
'nomadic subjectivity' Brown writes about 'a subject position, a way
of reading and re-creating one's social relationships' (1996: 56) which
is created only temporally and changes with 'cultural location', by
which is presumably meant something like 'socio-linguistic context'.

Again in Brown we have 'the self is constructed of what one says
about oneself and what is said about one' (1996: 57). Here we have
the confusion between Self 1 and self-concept in exemplary form.
Who is the *one who says* and who is *the one about whom others say
things*? It cannot be the self that is being constructed since it is just
those very things that are being said that constitute 'it'.

Finally an example of a common account of the sense of self, as
in the distinction between personal singularity and self-concept, is
given by Anderson and Schoenig:

> Identity – inward looking . . . provides a consideration of the existence
> of a unity, a coherence that extends across time and situation. This unity
> can be the 'essence of the individual' that serves as the core of all par-
> ticular manifestations. Outward looking, identity is that constellation of
> characteristics and performances that manifest the self in meaningful
> action. (1996: 207)

It should be clear that these aspects of personhood cannot be the
same!

The confounding of Self 1 with Self 2 is fairly easily remedied
when attention is paid to the means by which selfhood is expressed
in personal discourses. Self 1 is expressed in personal pronouns and
functionally equivalent devices, while Self 2 is expressed, however
inaccurately, in the content of confessions, self-descriptions, autobiographies and other reflexive discourses. My beliefs about
myself, my self-concept, may not be an accurate rendition of the Self
2. But, it must be remembered, that very set of beliefs is among the
attributes of the person who holds them.

The genius of William Stern

The position taken in these studies has already been anticipated in
several particulars by Stern (1938), the unjustly neglected proponent

of 'personalism'.[2] For Stern persons are the basic particulars of the human world. He defines this concept as follows:

> The 'person' is an individual, unique whole, striving towards goals, self-contained and yet open to the world; capable of having experience. (1938: 70)[3]

Commenting on his definition Stern observes that 'except for the criterion of "experiencing", which was purposely placed at the end, the specifications throughout are *psychophysically neutral*. Into the totality of the person are woven both his physical and psychical aspects' (1938: 70).

But in what does this uniqueness consist for Stern? Bodily identity seems to play a predominant part, in that Stern glosses the general definition as follows:

> A living being is of such a character that its total *nature* is continually being actualized through its activity while likewise remaining a whole in its incessant intercourse with its environment. (1938: 71)

This seems to refer to organic individuality and self-identity over time of the self we have identified as a person's attributes. This impression is confirmed in Stern's distinction between 'experience' (*Erlebnis*) and 'consciousness' (*Bewusstsein*). He wants to get away from the implication of the latter expression that personhood is manifested in knowing, which is the root meaning of 'consciousness'. But he also wants to repudiate the idea that personhood is manifested in awareness, the common meaning of 'consciousness'. Like the discursive psychologists Stern insists that 'experience' is intentional, that it has *objects*, and is normatively constrained, by the taking up of 'values' in a process he calls 'introception'. Psychology is, for him, the study of experience. The study of introception belongs to another science, 'personalistics'.

In what does the uniqueness of an individual person consist? Stern's account of this is more or less a declaration rather than an analysis:

> The person is a totality, that is, a *unitas multiplex* . . . All the multiplicity included in the person . . . is *integral* to the totality . . . it is the *consonance* of multiplicity with the personal whole and of the person with the world that makes human life possible. (1938: 73)

In other words the biological, experiential and introceptive attributes of a person are the necessary characteristics of one entity – without any of which it would not exist as such – but that entity is logically prior to and not the mere aggregate of these three sets of characteristics. Every person has both a Self 1 and a Self 2, that is a continuous point of view on the world, from which he or she acts both on themselves and on their environment, and a set of attributes including amongst them their own beliefs about those attributes. Neither are entities.

The root concept of 'person' is further refined by Stern in the thesis that persons are *sources* of activity: 'the person is not here regarded as a mere go-between or passive theater of psychophysical events, but as the true generator and carrier, governor and regulator' (1938: 85). The body is among the instruments people can use for realizing their projects.

Extending individuality into social life

Even the threefold distinction between persons, each of whom has a self-concept, a set of ever-changing beliefs about the ever-changing 'self', Self 2, and a sense of itself as a singularity, is not enough to provide a grammar for all that we want to say about people. There is a third use of the word 'self', which I have called Self 3, popularized by Erving Goffman in his famous work *The presentation of self in everyday life* (1959). This notion of 'self' requires two further concepts to do justice to the identity within variety that so characterizes the way persons appear to one another in the everyday human world. The word 'personality' is usually used to refer to the style of the public and private way of being of a person, while 'character' is used, as Goffman does, to refer to the opinions others hold about the nature of a person, particularly with respect to his or her likely ways of acting in relation to them. Goffman's concept is even a little richer than the mere conjunction of 'personality' with 'character', since part of what he had in mind was the way one tries on occasion to display the kind of person one wants to seem to be. This may include managing the signs of such matters as social class, bodily potentials and so on. While his original study referred to displays of character in a rather broad sense, the later work *Stigma* (1963) looked at the management of all sorts of 'identities', such as ex-jailbird, race, social position, ethnicity and so on, which one might not wish to display or might wish to conceal by displaying a plausible discursive alternative.

Self 3 has aspects. There is the persona as the person intends to present it, in ways of speaking and acting, and then there is the ways such displays are interpreted by others, when they attribute personality or character to someone. These are putative attributes of the person, and so possibly aspects or components of Self 2. But in the actor's self-concept they will be registered only as the person he or she believes is being presented.

But even here the water is muddy. The notion of personality as a public display of the kind of person one is, or wishes to be seen to be, has been linked with a thoroughly unsatisfactory explanatory theory. This theory has been offered to account for the alleged fact that each person tends to display the same personality on different occasions.[4]

The logical mistakes in the revival of trait theory are instructive for the general project of building a scientifically respectable psychology. The fundamental error shown in most of the recent writings on the topic, for example McCrae and Costa (1995), is to confuse dispositions (traits) with powers and liabilities. A disposition is an observable property of a thing, be it a lump of dynamite or a person. It is ascribed in a conditional proposition of the form, 'If certain conditions obtain then the thing/person in question will display a certain kind of behaviour (*ceteris paribus*).' *Both the conditions and the elicited behaviour are observables.* Dispositions could not be unobservable, explanatory properties of anything. Behind the dispositions of many complex material things are microstructural properties: for example, the chemical composition of nitroglycerine explains its explosive disposition and its destructive power. But behind the basic particulars of the physical sciences, such as electrons or field potentials, are nothing but powers. If persons are indeed the basic particulars of the psychosocial world, then the only explanatory concept that could be imported to explain personal dispositions would be that of personal powers. But unfortunately for logic McCrae and Costa offer that impossible beast, the unobserved disposition, one or more of the Big Five traits, as explanatory devices to account for personality traits. The revival of trait theory in personality psychology with the re-emergence of the Big Five is a textbook case of a classificatory hierarchy being deployed as an explanatory hierarchy. Higher order traits are offered as hidden mechanisms to account for the dispositions that are displayed in those performances in which we discern the dynamic structures of public self-presentations.

Turning quite properly to philosophy of science McCrae and Costa pick up the wrong form of theorizing for the job in hand. Realists in the physical sciences assert that making models of hidden mechanisms is the appropriate methodology for theory construction in physics and chemistry. But in so doing they are careful to point out that the entities, properties, processes and so on of which the explanatory model is built up must be ontologically plausible, that is they must be possible existents (Aronson et al., 1995). The 'trait' ontology of the McCrae and Costa explanatory model does not pass the test of existential plausibility.

Identifying two main uses of dispositional concepts in personality studies, 'one corresponding to patterns of behaviour and experience, the other to the underlying causes of behavior' (McCrae and Costa, 1995: 236), they opt for the latter: 'we use the term *trait* in the second sense . . . we regard *trait* as a theoretical term.' Yes, but in what kind of theory? Explanatory or classificatory? Clearly they think it must be explanatory. They go on to say: 'traits as underlying tendencies cause and thus explain (in general and in part) the consistent patterns of thoughts, feelings, and actions that one sees.' But despite the flattering citation of my own work, I have to say that Harré and Madden (1975) did not say that. They said that dispositions are explained by causal powers, not by more higher order dispositions. McCrae and Costa say, quite rightly, that 'Basic tendencies are hypothetical constructs that cannot be directly observed.' But why? Is it because they are the substance of hidden mechanisms or because they are higher order classificatory concepts? They cannot be the former because they are of the wrong logical type.

A disposition is created by linking two observables by a conditional, and so is itself always an observable. Higher order dispositions are classificatory. One cannot 'see' the primateness of chimps, orangutans and so on, though every chimp is a primate, and so is every orangutan. Primateness is a classificatory category achieved by abstracting common elements from the descriptions of the species under which it falls. We do not explain the characteristics of species by adverting to their genus. No more do we explain the display of Self 3 dispositions by adverting to higher order dispositional categories. Basic tendencies are logically related to observable traits as primateness is related to being a chimpanzee.

Of course we need higher order dispositional concepts in talking about people, but their only function is classificatory. The Big Five, the generic traits, are taxonomic concepts, related to observable dispositions as 'primate' and 'cetacean' are related to 'chimpanzee' and 'dolphin'. One can see this even more clearly by reflecting on how hypotheses about the alleged source-traits are arrived at. They are the result of analyses of the answers people give to questionnaires in which they are asked to describe themselves or others. Extracted from the answers to such questions they can be no more than classificatory concepts, since they pick up which first order descriptive concepts cluster together. To say that a chimpanzee is a primate does not explain anything about its characteristics. It does the important but quite different job of reminding us that chimps are more like gorillas than they are like tigers, at least in the Linnaean system of classification.

Knowing myself as a unique individual

What do we each know of ourselves, in particular of that singularity I have called Self 1? It is not visible to a behaviourist poking about on the surface of cognition. At best a behaviourist might have discerned consistencies in the conduct of a uniquely specified body. It is not visible to a phenomenological scrutinizing of one's own subjectivity. At the very best Husserl discerned an I-pole, a centred structure of experience, of which the central 'origin' was not itself given in experience, the *eigenheit* or unique centre of being, is known only indirectly.[5] It is not available to private introspection, which yields only a structured field of experiences, the origin of which in anything other than bodily location is elusive. The self, in this sense, is not available to public inspection. Only persons are publicly visible, tangible, audible and smellable beings.

The very idea of a private 'search for the self' opens up a familiar problem, even a paradox, made much of by philosophers, famously by Hume (1746). The self I seek is the self that seeks, so it seems that it is impossible to make introspective contact with myself. The force of this paradox comes in part from the attempt by Descartes to give substance to the personal singularity of point of view as an entity to which mental attributes and processes are ascribed, much as physical attributes and processes of the human organism are ascribed to protoplasm. The Cartesian 'ego' is certainly not the Self 2 of the above analysis. It is not the totality of personal attributes, but is proposed as that which possesses them. But it is not the person either. The public person, the embodied active human being, would strike one as the obvious candidate for the individual 'substance' which possesses personal properties. The materiality of the embodied person precluded that solution for Descartes. It is the reification of the unique personal point of view which we have called Self 1. The Cartesian ego is a singular substance or entity invoked to explain not only my mental life, but also my experience of singularity of selfhood. As Descartes remarks, while our bodies are all made of the same stuff, each personal mind is a unique mental substance, individual and singular. The famous argument *cogito, ergo sum* may look as if it runs from a premise 'I think' to a conclusion 'I am', but as every philosophy undergraduate knows the conclusion is presupposed in the first person form of the premise. Perhaps saddling Descartes with the circular reasoning of the *cogito* argument does not do justice to his thought. Perhaps the assertion of 'I am' ought to be taken as the expression of a grammatical frame from which to draw the ways of interpreting thinking as something I personally do.

However hard Hume 'looked' within himself he could find only thoughts and feelings, never an independent revelation of that of which they are supposedly attributes. The Cartesian ego is not the totality of the mental attributes of a person but the alleged substance that has them. As such it could have none itself. Therefore it could never be apprehended introspectively as such. Hume's argument does not show that the Car-tesian ego does not exist. No failure to find something which could have no observable properties could prove anything. The point is stronger. A property-less 'something' has no role to play in psychology. In Wittgenstein's terms Self 1 is part of the frame and so not in the picture. But, as we now see it, the frame for my thoughts about myself is grammatical, not substantial. In asking whether the sword in the cupboard is rusty I first pick out the sword by identifying some of its attributes and then run over the rest to see if it is indeed rusty. In 'This sword is rusty' the expression 'This sword' refers to something having properties other than the one in question. But if the Cartesian ego possesses *all* the attributes of self, taken in itself as the bearer of all those attributes, it can have none of them. But what could it be that is a substance, but has no properties in itself? Our post-Wittgensteinian solution is unexciting, but deep. The Cartesian ego is a grammatical concept. Its alleged properties are nothing more than the grammatical rules for the use of the word 'I'.

Of course the Cartesian project is hopeless as Descartes conceived it. The postulation of the Cartesian ego appears to me to be the result of a familiar facet of scientific methodology, the hypothetico-deductive procedure on which physics and chemistry depend. Just as electrons are invoked to explain the behaviour of electrically charged bodies, and much else, so Descartes invoked the singular, personal dollop of mind-stuff to explain the cognitive aspects of human life. One way of accounting for the persistence of the 'ego' concept is because of an implicit adherence to this hypothetico-deductive mode of thought, appropriate to the natural sciences. In this way of thinking explanations are created by supposing that there exist unobservable entities and processes, the effects of which can be observed, and so used to support or undermine confidence in the existential implications of the explanatory hypothesis. The illusion of a substantive 'inner' being as the perceiver and actor, in addition to the person who looks and sees, listens and hears, thinks and chops wood, cannot easily be dispelled. In the end the case against Descartes and his account of the nature of persons must depend on the exhaustion of useful work for the substantial ego to do, work that is not already done by the concept of a person. Then a single slash with Ockham's razor ought to dispose of it.

We need to turn our attention from the flawed metaphysics that powers a hopeless 'pseudo-scientific' project with respect to the self, to a consideration of the grammar of those language games in which the sense of self as a singularity, Self 1, is expressed, and in which the self as the shifting totality of a person's attributes, Self 2, is manifested in the talk that displays the self-concept.

A summary of the grammar of 'self' talk

The study of selfhood involves the investigation of three conceptual patterns within which our understanding of what it is to be just this person are framed. There is that around the idea of a unique point of view and of action, a singularity, having a different spatio-temporal trajectory from every other. There is the idea that each person who persists as the same person through different times and situations has different attributes from every other, though the totality of such attributes is forever in flux. Then there is the idea that each person, however diverse and dynamic their personal attributes, is nevertheless a unity of sorts. A person is singular, unified and unique.

Two questions apropos of the experience we each have of our own identity and individuality, and of the identity and individuality of others, seem to be legitimate:

1 'How do I know you are the very person I met before and in different circumstances?'
2 'How do I know I am the very person I was before and in different circumstances?'

Much philosophical trouble and psychological confusion comes from thinking that both questions should be treated in the same way, namely answered by setting out criteria by means of which questions of identity in each case would be settled.

Anticipating something of the Wittgensteinian conception of the 'grammatical framing of discourses' Joseph Butler (1736) remarked on the necessary role that the concept of 'myself' plays in the very notion of memory. That something is for me a memory already incorporates the notion that it is a recollection of an event that happened to me. Memories could not constitute the self, since the very concept of 'memory' presupposes that the person remembering has at their disposal a robust sense of self. But that cannot be the apprehension of a substance of which my memories are attributes, dispositional or occurrent.

While I can rightly be said to know or not to know that you are the same person, to be more or less sure, to look for and assess evidence for or against the judgement, it makes no sense to say 'I know I am the same person I was yesterday.' Why? Because to use the word 'know' is to make conceptual room for all the other concepts that are part of the cluster invoked in considering the first question, such as making sure, having or lacking evidence, inferring rightly or wrongly from it and so on. But the sense of self is not a knowing of this kind at all. There is no place for such a judgement as 'I thought I was the same person as I was yesterday, but I turned out not to be.' Does the question 'Which person am I? Perhaps you?' make any sense? Plainly not. I do not grope my way to the bathroom mirror each morning to check whether I am the same person today as I was yesterday. What would it be like to discover I was not? To suggest this is already to presuppose a surviving 'I'. At most I might realize I was not the same kind of person I thought I was yesterday. This indeed is all too common an experience. Though of great psychological interest it has no bearing at all on the question of the continuity of personal singularity, since it presupposes it. It is just this way of looking at selfhood that we find scattered throughout Wittgenstein's *On certainty* (1969). The framework within which our interpersonal discourse and my reflections are put together is constituted by a shared background of grammatical commonplaces, including the unquestioned continuity of the ordinary person. But like every other aspect of the frame of the human form of life, my self-identity can, in certain circumstances, be subject to doubt. But then we are entering into a new pattern of language games, and the grammars of the old no longer guide us. By the same token the fact there are possibilities of pathologies of the self does not cast into doubt the framework with which we ordinarily live our lives. The statement 'I know I am the same person as I was yesterday' has no place in our lives, since it has no real work to do.

In *On certainty* Wittgenstein draws attention to a feature of selfhood that has not been considered very much in this context except by anthropologists, namely the relation between a person and their name. Am I making any more sense with 'I know my own name' than I am with 'I know I am the same person'? Part of what it is to be the same person is to be the person named 'Ludwig'. What stands in contrast to 'knowing my own name'? Do I have to collect evidence for my belief in what I am called, to check it up every day, for example sneak a look at my passport? Could I be a bit uncertain as to what it was? Not, it seems, with respect to the name I go by, the name I think of myself as bearing. Doubts about one's name might arise if it is one's baptismal name that is question. It is said that a certain Spanish family discovered that their 'official' name was not 'Estrella' only after four generations had lived under that name. It was great-grandfather's nickname! The amnesiac's worries about the name he or she has forgotten are not the worries the name sceptic entertains. But the name sceptic's doubts are empty since none of the cluster of concepts around 'knowing', 'checking', 'making sure' and so on has application here. Our names belong in all that frames our actions.

The public person and the private self

The unique public personhood of each human being has to encompass unique embodiment, not least because it is as embodied beings that people have a point of view and a point of action in the world. Bodies are, in the jargon of the law, 'non-fungibles'. A fungible is a commodity for which, in certain relevant contexts, any member of the same class will be an acceptable substitute. Thus the monetary unit 'one pound' is a fun-gible, since to repay a borrowed pound any coin of equal value will do. If I take away your child and return to you a similar infant, you will not be satisfied with the exchange since persons are not fungibles. To get the same one back one requires the return of the numerically identical being that was borrowed or abducted in the first place. Looked at this way non-fungible identity is given in human affairs, as a necessary part of the concept of what it is to be a person. But appearances of non-fungibility may have to be worked at. Where everyone looks alike and dresses alike and talks and behaves alike, as did the survivors of the Chinese 'cultural revolution', public non-fungibility was achieved by introducing minute but idiosyncratic characteristics into dress, particularly, that are unique to a particular individual. To break the fungibility of models of mass produced cars people customize them, that is add unique marks to their vehicle, marks that no other vehicle of the same model possesses. People, threatened by incipient fungibility, customize themselves.

The role of the body in personhood

Whatever may be the ultimate fate of the soul, in this world at least persons are necessarily embodied. We have already seen how far the sense each person has of their own being is deeply tied to the spatio-temporal singularity of their point of view on the material world, including their own body. What it is to be just this person is, in great part, to have just this location in the world of things and, among those things, of other people. And that location is the location of one's own body. Self 1, the substantialist metaphor for one aspect of personal being, just is bodily location.

But it is equally fundamental to our sense of our personal being that we realize that our skills and abilities, tendencies and dispositions, are grounded in states of our bodies, in particular in states of our brains and nervous systems. Common discourse is full of this principle. When being admonished for our inability to solve a problem we are told to 'use our brains'. When troubled by a minor pain we unthinkingly swallow an aspirin or two. We are not at all surprised that, when granny has a stroke, not only her ability to pick up a cup of tea but also her powers of speech and reason may be impaired. Thus embodiment is an essential feature of what we have called Self 2.

But quite apart from its deep role in the underpinning of the concepts of Self 1 and Self 2, that is in the grammar of our personal talk, the body plays another vital role in our lives. It is worth reiterating that it is a richly equipped tool kit for the accomplishment of all sorts of public and private tasks. Hands, arms and legs are needed for tennis, fingers for playing clarinets, and relatively permanent structures in the nervous system and brain for implementing the tasks in question. While the body is the material grounding for skills and dispositions it is also a tool kit for the exercising of them. Human beings have extended the kit beyond the confines of the limbs, the vocal cords, the cerebellum and so on, to include swords, pipe organs, electronic organizers and so on. But the basic kit is still the one we build up on the basis of our embodiment. Extensions of this sort are, in a way, extensions of our bodies. In *Personal being* (1983) I discussed the extension of embodiment into files and records far removed from our bodily centre and for that and other reasons not as easily accessed as our own memories and beliefs. This idea was not taken up, but its exploration would be a matter of even greater interest now, since the intervening years have brought a huge amplification in these protheses.

Narrative and personal unity

What holds together the three selves into a single person? This question sounds at first hearing as if it were the same sort of question as what holds the sides, base and top of bookshelves into one piece of furniture – as if we were on the look-out for some kind of psychic glue. In the light of the analysis deployed in this study we must reject the question as wholly misdirected. It goes out with the idea of substantial mind-stuff and other bad ideas. There are persons and their conversations, with others and with themselves. The latter are of course made possible only by the appropriation of the means for the former. What then is the unifying principle of a personal conversation? The generic answer that has gradually come to the fore in the development of discursive psychology is the idea of the organizing narrative. A great deal of our time is taken up telling ourselves and others bits and pieces of autobiography, but not just as a single chronicle. Narratives follow story-lines and autobiographical narratives are no exception. According to Sarbin (1993) narratives give form to the development and maintenance of one's identity. Bruner (1991), too, has pursued this idea, and indeed so have many others. The most systematic and empirically detailed demonstration of the principle that personal unity is a product of the narrative conventions of personal story-telling comes from McAdams (1997a). McAdams uses the expression 'personal myth' to describe the unfolding story of my life that I tell myself and with which I manage many of the choices of my life. The burgeoning field of autobiographical psychology is devoted to systematic studies of the forms, varieties and diversities of the ways we 'tell our lives' (van Langenhove and Harré, 1996). How is the psychological unity of person maintained? The answer is not to be found in the Self 2, the ever-shifting set of attributes that characterizes a person at any time, or in the Self 3, the local and variable presentations of personae, drawn from a culturally available repertoire. It is in the continuity of embodied point of view, one person for each body. The exceptions to this principle will not be overlooked, but it is for the most part a grammatical rather than a pervasive empirical fact about the human world. But unity also lies in the stories I tell myself and others, my personal myths. As McAdams says, strange as it may seem, we are the stories we tell.

Anthropologists on persons and selves

Anthropologists can usually be relied upon to offer clearer and more convincing images of human life than other students of the human domain. In preparing for cross-cultural, that is comparative, studies of how people think about themselves and other people in different societies and at different epochs, anthropologists (more than historians) have undertaken surveys of the multiple uses of the word 'self'.[6] This has proven necessary since even so sophisticated a commentator on the diversity of human life as Clifford Geertz (1977), can slip and slide between Self 1 and Self 2 in glossing the concept of personal identity common in the Western world. For instance he says it is:

> a bounded, unique, more or less integrated motivational and cognitive universe [Self 2], a dynamic center of awareness [Self 1], emotion, judgment, and action organized into a distinctive whole and set contrastively both against other such wholes and against a social and natural background. (1977: 9)

But the 'dynamic center of awareness' is not itself 'organized into a distinctive whole'. It *is* the centre point of that organization. Clearly there are two senses of 'self' in this passage.

However many anthropologists tend to use the word 'self' in the sense of Self 2 alone. For example Erchak (1992: 2) writes of 'individual selves shaped by culture' meaning 'sets of attributes of individual people'. The question of their possible uniqueness is not addressed, nor is their sense of self as centres of perception and action, Self 1. But one cannot rely on a stable pattern of usage even within the writings of a single author. For example Fajans (1985) tends to use 'person' and 'self' as synonyms, though not always. She writes 'The person is not a fixed entity but one whose attributes and positions evolve as much through particular contexts as through enduring "human qualities"' (1985: 325). This passage seems to be about what I have called Self 2. But later she writes 'person as a bounded entity invested with specific patterns of social behaviour, normative powers and restraints' (1985: 369) which is pretty much 'person' in the sense I have been trying to maintain in this essay. Catherine Lutz, who can be guaranteed to keep a tidy conceptual tool kit, writes of the psychology of the Ifaluk. 'The point at which the self stops and the other begins is neither fixed nor conceptualized as an impermeable wall' (1985: 47). Here she surely means Self 2, the attributes of an individual person. There are some valuable surveys of the conceptual foundations of person talk especially that by Johnson (1985). With some exceptions anthropologists seem to have settled on a conceptual system that is more or less the one I have been setting out as the 'standard model', in which there is just one substantive entity, the person, and a trio of grammatical fictions, Self 1, Self 2 and Self 3.

Despite some minor terminological differences anthropologists offer the student of persons and their selves an array of examples of the diversity of how Self 2 is realized among diverse peoples. According to Gaines, adopting the terminology proposed by Crapanzano (1980), the self (Self 2) of Protestant Europe is 'presented as a coherent whole independent of the particular context of interaction. As a distinct, autonomous entity, facts about that entity become meaningful and relevant to clinical and other encounters' (1996: 183). This he calls the 'referential self'. In contrast the Latin version of Self 2 'is not defined as an abstract entity independent of the social relations and contexts in which the self is presented in interaction . . . the self is perceived as constituted or "indexed" by the contextual features of social interaction in diverse situations' (1996: 182). Yet these contrasts only make sense against a background of a common sense of personal uniqueness both north and south of the Alps, namely Self 1.

Equally instructive is the work of Liberman (1989). He took the trouble to learn an Australian Aboriginal language sufficiently well to begin to live within their form of life. Later he followed up this *tour de force* by a long stay in the Tibetan community in exile in the Indian subcontinent, becoming sufficiently proficient in their language to learn the practices of formal debate and even to take part. In investigating selfhood in any human context Liberman remarks:

> It is more productive to address ourselves to that system of naturally organized social practices that constitutes the ordinary life of a community . . . We must relocate self and personal identity within a system of interaction that provides the places and orientations for self-presentation and self-assertion. (1989: 131)

This is the presented self, Self 3. When he says 'An Aboriginal person does not wish to be a unique human being; on the contrary he or she wants only to be the same as everyone else', it is not personal singularity that could be in question, rather the beliefs I have about myself and how I should conduct myself in public. 'Participants [in a discussion] do not voice "personal" views so much as produce summaries of their image of the consensus at any given moment' (1989: 133). And yet though Aboriginal people are not 'autonomous centers' they do have names and they do undertake individual projects, such as the quest that they call 'going walkabout'.

To return finally to Geertz's elegant paragraph, we see there the duality between the self as the totality of the attributes of a person and the self as the active centre of experience. There are all sorts of problems of detail about the self as the sum of personal attributes. For example does this include an unconscious domain? Does my sense of Self 2 necessarily omit a great chunk of what I am as a person, my unconscious? Most of what I know about myself are my dispositions, powers and skills. What about the occurrent neural states of the embodied person that ground these and make their display possible? Should we count these into the Self 2? These will be amongst the topics of later chapters, where I will pick up the current debates over just exactly what cultural diversity in selfhood amounts to and with what conceptual tools it is best discussed.[7]

Olfactory identity

We are inclined to assume, in these days of daily showers and deodorants, that the relevant physical characteristics involved in identifying some person again as the same person would be visual appearances, and sometimes tactile. But there are cultures that make use of other sensory modes. There is olfactory identity.

This is a stronger concept than merely the idea that for certain peoples at certain times smelling the same was criterial for being the same person, a criterion put to daily use by dogs, both for others of their species and for people.

> The Ongee hold that a person's odour emanates from his or her bones, which themselves consist of condensed smell, just as the odour of a plant or tree originates in its stem or trunk. It is through catching a whiff of oneself, and being able to distinguish that scent from all the other odours that surround one, that one arrives at a sense of one's own identity in Ongee society. (Classen et al., 1994: 113)

Other cultures believe that each person has a characteristic smell, but this is just another among the criteria that are in public use for answering the unproblematic question 'Is this the same person I met yesterday?', when the person in question is not myself.

Summary: concepts of personal identity

We have something like the following semantic field of conceptual tools for expressing the idea of a person as a *unitas multiplex*, a diversity in unity (Stern, 1938: 73). We must distinguish between how the identity of a person appears to others and how that person experiences and expresses his or her own identity.

The identity of each person for others is expressed in criteria for judging whether this is one and the same person as the one who has been identified at some other time and place. These criteria are based, for most purposes, on material attributes of the embodied person, especially those bearing on the question of whether the person has enjoyed an intact spatio-temporal trajectory. The multiplicity of public appearances of one and the same human being can be described by drawing on a local and historically variable catalogue of human personality and character types. Any individual person can exemplify more than one type in different settings and in the company of different people. However, each person adapts the social types available to his or her own particular and momentary needs (Taylor, 1991).

The identity of each person for him or herself is expressed in the grammar of first person discourse by which each individual's sense of self as a singularity is expressed. The diversity of beliefs and opinions each person has about their personal characteristics and their personal history appears in the autobiographical tellings of everyday life. Any individual person can tell more than one story and each story may display a variation on the person's self-concept.

There is nothing simple about this network of concepts. Its complexity is a consequence of the diversity of the concepts with which we try to deal with the many ways people can be the same and different. The study of the empirical realization of this complex network of concepts in everyday practices will require an investigation into how these very different aspects of personhood find expression in personal discourses.

Taking all this together requires a settled vocabulary for the many aspects of personhood that analysis has revealed and that the literature touches upon (Mühlhäusler and Harré, 1993).

At the apex is the principle that, all else being equal, each human being is a person, a unique, embodied centre of consciousness with a history. Some authors use the word 'self' as a synonym for 'person'. But this usage is surely not advisable, in that it adds to the possibilities of confusion that are rampant in this branch of psychology.

What is singular in me is my point of view. My field of awareness, though centred in a singularity, is a complex structure of relations to my environment, past present and future, involving the cognitive skills of perception, action and memory. To be one and the same person my point of view must be continuous or potentially continuous relative to an encompassing material framework, including the world of other embodied beings. The use of 'self' to refer to the indexing of point of view, I have called Self 1.

But each one of us as an individual has a unique set of attributes that differ at least in some respects from those of any other. Some

differences are insignificant, others important.[8] Among these attributes are our beliefs about the attributes we have. The attributes that
a person possesses at any one time we can call the restricted Self 2.
A more encompassing concept of self would include not only the
current attributes a person possesses, but all the attributes that
person has, has had and will have over a life-span. We can call this
the unrestricted Self 2. This distinction will prove to be of importance when we look closely at the predicament of Alzheimer's sufferers and others on the margins of personhood. The pattern of
stability and change, of persistence and evanescence, that characterizes the Self 2 will be a thematic thread throughout these studies.

My beliefs about myself are unique probably only in their totality. Any belief I may have about myself could be similar to the belief
that another person has about some aspect of his or her Self 2,
except of course those aspects of the belief that pertain to spatial
and temporal locations. These beliefs at any moment are the content
of my self-concept. My beliefs about my Self 2 are also part of my
Self 2. Any belief I have about my attributes including my beliefs is
one of my beliefs and thus one of my momentary and ephemeral
attributes. As annexed to 'I believe . . .' it is indexed as a belief of
the speaker, who thus takes responsibility for it, and with whose
bodily position it is marked.

However displays of personality and character, centred on a
unique body, are usually readily assigned to local types. According
to the dramaturgical account of personality these must be drawn
from a local repertoire to be 'legible' to other people. Unreadable
personality displays are evidence of madness or eccentricity. My
presented self or persona I have called Self 3. It is how I display my
Self 1 and Self 2, as I conceive or want them to be taken by those
with whom I am then in a dialogue, or sometimes even amongst
strangers and people with whom I may have no direct dialogical
contact at all. But Self 3 is more complex than this simple Goffman-
like account would suggest. There is the persona as the person
intends to present it, and as it appears in the speech and action of
the person as that is interpreted by others. They attribute a personality and character to the actor. In so far as there are different groups
of people with different relations to the actor and different circumstances of interaction, both the personality and the character of
someone, taken at large, may, in the eyes of others, were all those
people to get together to compare their stories, be quite diverse.[9] A
person's beliefs about the attributes that he or she believes they are
presenting are themselves attributes of that person, and so part of
the Self 2. But in the actor's self-concept they will be registered, for

the most part, only as the persona he or she believes they are presenting. This belief may not be fully conscious or well articulated.

Conclusion

Where must I be singular to pass as a normal person and where can I be multiple without threatening my standing as a proper human being? To ask 'Is the self as person singular or multiple?' is to press for a tidy answer to an untidy question. My Self 1 cannot but be singular within the normative constraints of all cultures that we know of. Amnesia and multiple personality disorder are taken as pathologies of personhood. But all the evidence points to the actual multiplicity of the Selves 2 of any one person and the self-concepts that partly describe them. Multiple too are each person's Selves 3, though they are meant to express people as singularities and to display a unique collection of personal attributes. My beliefs about myself shift and change with context and companions as do my self-presentations. And so does the totality of my personal attributes. How far can multiplicity range without censure? This is a vital question for anyone in real life, but it can be answered only *ad hoc*. The fuzzy boundary between multiplicities and pathologies of self is never stable, drawing different distinctions at different times.

Nothing less than this vocabulary will do justice to the person as *unitas multiplex*, and allow us to manage research into the many aspects of personhood where identity and diversity, singularity and multiplicity are in question.

Notes

1 I adopt, on occasion and where it seems natural, the obsolete 'they' as non-gendered third person singular, from ordinary usage, and in the light of the historical justification for this use (Mühlhäusler and Harré, 1993).

2 I owe most of my meagre knowledge of the personalist psychology of William Stern to James T. Lamiell, whose 'Stern' seminar has been an invaluable introduction.

3 New translations by Michael Bamberg.

4 The fact that empirical studies have shown the personality as displayed to be modulated as a person moves into different social environments seems to have been overlooked by those who have revived the once-discredited 'trait' theory.

5 I shall return to a more detailed account of Husserl's struggle with the problem of the phenomenology of personal experience.

6 Cultural psychology has moved, rightly, from comparing other cultures, usually with our own as a benchmark, to giving free-standing accounts of other

forms of life. This requires the taking seriously of the embedded cultural commonplaces in the language of the anthropologist author.

7 I am greatly indebted to my colleague, David Crystal, who has kindly kept me up to date on the relevant literature.

8 J. Lamiell has pointed out two important points about uniqueness of personhood in the context of a psychology of identity. Uniqueness can be expressed in the concepts of the recently revived trait theory, in that any individual could have a unique position in the 'space' defined by the Big Five dimensions of the current version of the theory. He has also reminded us that in practice we work with a weaker notion of personal identity than uniqueness. We need only that degree of distinctiveness that differentiates each of us from every other person playing a role relevant to our personal life courses.

9 This rarely happens. The diversity of Selves 3 presented by one and the same person was forcibly brought home to me as a member of four different committees each of which interviewed the same four candidates and then came together to discuss the applicants. Each candidate appeared to have presented a radically different Self 3 to each committee.

CHAPTER FIVE

The Self in Perception and Action

The idea of every way in which the human body is affected by external bodies must involve the nature of the human body, and at the same time the nature of the external body.

Benedict Spinoza, *Ethics*

Apter (1989: 76) rightly remarks that consciousness is implicated, as a necessary condition, in both the recognition of my distinctness from all other beings, both material and social, and in my sense of my own continuity. My sense of myself as a singularity in space and time is bound up with the structure of my perceptual fields, particularly the visual, auditory and tactile fields. The argument of this chapter will be developed around the general principle that the psychological study of Self 1 as perceptual point of view requires the study of consciousness, and is more or less exhausted by the psychology of perception. In this way we shall reach an outline of an understanding of Self 1, the centred structure of a person's perceptual fields. It is this centredness on the body's location that is indexed by the use of the first person in reports of what the speaker can see, hear, touch, smell and so on. 'I' is used not only to qualify reports of how the world and the speaker's body are, but also as the mark of the responsible authorial voice in assertions about matters with which we are acquainted by other than perceptual means. Though in many cases expressions like 'I am aware of . . .' can be transformed immediately into 'I am aware that . . .', by which perceptual knowledge is transformed into propositional form, the reverse is by no means always the case. I can be said to know my opinions, thoughts and so on, but not through perceiving them with the help of an 'inner eye'. I was recently reminded by Richard Bernstein of the widespread use of perceptual metaphors for commenting on the possession and acquisition of knowledge the origin of which is not in the use of the senses. For example, 'Are you aware that you still owe me $10?'

draws your attention to something you might have been presumed to know but have forgotten. This is not the attending that is called for in my asking whether you have noticed that you have a spider on your sleeve.

In this usage the pronoun 'I' and functionally equivalent constructions index what is said with the personal responsibility of the speaker, as well as his or her spatio-temporal location. In the first part of this chapter I am concerned only with the indexing of the content of a report of the state of the world and of the speaker's body, with the location of the speaker as a thing amongst things. But in every use of 'I' there is a second indexical force, since it indexes the utterances it qualifies with the authority of the speaker. As the author of my words I must stand by them, particularly in relation to what you take me to have said. Not only my words but all my actions are, in a sense, mine. My sense of myself as an agent or mere patient finds expression discursively. In the second part of this chapter I examine the discursive presentation of Self 1 as a responsible and active being – person as agent.

Consciousness talk: 'I' as reporter

Some uses of the word 'consciousness'

What is it to be conscious of something? Surely to be aware of it, whatever it is. And what is it to be aware of something? Surely to perceive it, by whatever perceptual system is appropriate. Taken this way the study of consciousness should follow two paths. There is the investigation of how the structure of experience is expressed, from which we can infer a good deal about the phenomenology of awareness. Then there is the investigation of the material means by which perceptual tasks are carried out. But if we begin with a general question like 'What is consciousness?', the hope of progress is very slim. This seems an intractable question when posed in this blunt way. Instead of trying to answer this question perhaps by some Procrustean definition, it is a good rule in psychology to begin an investigation by a careful analysis of the pattern of use of the expressions which are used in everyday life to describe, comment on and generally talk about the field of phenomena in question. Instead of asking 'What is it to be conscious?', we would ask 'What range of uses do we find for the vocabulary based on the word "conscious" and cognates?' Having settled the latter we might find ourselves already in possession of an answer to the former.

One pattern of use of this vocabulary can be illustrated with phrases like 'gained (lost) consciousness', 'was knocked unconscious' and the like. In these examples we are referring to some general state of the organism that makes possible certain specific experiences. We could call this state an enabling condition. Transitions into and out of this state are commonplace in such phenomena as falling asleep and waking up.

Another pattern of use of the 'conscious' lexicon is illustrated in statements like 'I was conscious of a strong smell' or 'The thought of a large slice of Tin Roof Fudge Pie popped into my consciousness' and so on. These statements express or describe a relation between a person and a phenomenological entity, the content of an experience. A more mundane vocabulary could be used without any loss of sense for these cases. Phrases like '. . . aware of . . .', '. . . noticed . . .', '. . . attended to . . .', '. . . was struck by . . .' and so on would cover the same ground, and express various subtleties and refinements in the content and structure of the local environment, including the speaker's place in it. Moreover 'Noticing something' can become 'Noticing a capybara' only if we have a more or less secure grasp of the criteria for picking out that species of rodent. I shall say that these uses express the 'reporter' sense of 'conscious of'. However a good many of these cases are 'epistemic', knowledge engendering, in that there is an unproblematic translation from the phenomenological mode to the knowledge mode. By that I mean that 'aware of' and 'notice' can be replaced by 'aware that' and 'noticed that' without invoking any mediating principle at all, given that the appropriate vocabulary of the task-relevant categories is in place. I shall say that these uses express the epistemic sense of 'conscious that'.

Generally then 'consciousness' may refer to an enabling condition for certain relations to obtain between a person and an entity, or to report or express some relation of a person as embodied to things and other material occupants of the material world. These relations are picked out from all possible such relations as those which exist for any one person at any moment. From the point of view of the establishment of research programmes, the study of enabling conditions is part of neurophysiology, and has prompted such speculations as Penrose's hypothetical brain structures and activities, and many other less exotic proposals. These researches can tell us nothing whatever about the relational patterns of awareness – the study of the perceptual systems by means of which a person performs all sorts of perceptual acts is the study of tools, not tasks. This is the second main programme for the student of consciousness. The investigation of these mechanisms is a highly technical matter and mainly the work of neurophysiologists.[1]

To set about research into how the world looks, sounds, feels and so on to a human being a quite different technique is required, the study of the public expression of personal experience of a centred and ordered world. It is to that project that this chapter is dedicated. It is in that study that clues to the nature of the polarized structure of perceptual fields can be found, expressed by the indexical force of the 'I' of experiential reports. This leads us to try for the best description of being aware of different kinds of objects, and of how that awareness takes different forms in different circumstances and with respect to different ways of perceiving. The work of describing perceptual experience requires the cooperation of philosophers to wrestle with the task of forging the most apt conceptual system for the task in hand, and of phenomenologists to use such concepts to express experience. Since perceptual verbs are used of others, as of oneself, the study of awareness and of the structure of perceptual fields is as much a matter of how other people are related to their environments as I am to mine (Strawson, 1959: 108).

Explaining consciousness

The conceptual difficulties with the idea of 'explaining consciousness' begin with a familiar ambiguity in the very expression 'explain'. On the one hand it often means 'account for', which in many cases is done by citing a cause or reason: 'How do you account for the smoke coming out of the exhaust pipe?', 'How do you account for your losing your temper?' and so on. Often it means 'analyse' or 'paraphrase', in such expressions as 'Would you explain the rules for electing a chairman?' and so forth. Since in the case of consciousness we have two fields of enquiry – 'What is it to be conscious?' and 'What are the enabling conditions that someone or some animal should be so?' – we have just the right conditions for slipping and sliding between the two senses of 'explain'. 'What is the phenomenon?' calls for an explanation in the latter of the two senses, while 'What must the neurophysiological machinery be like to sustain activities and experiences of that sort?' seems as if it might call for an explanation in the former sense. But the skill to grounding relation is not that between an effect and a cause, since neither the skill nor its grounding are of the right categories to be causes and effects, for instance neither are events. An exhaustive account of the grounding of a skill is not an explanation of the exercise of it, in the 'account for' sense. Thus Dennett's title *Consciousness explained* (1991) sounds thrilling but the study it covers turns out to be just another, if nicely done, account of the grounding of a skill or capacity and not thrilling at all. It includes neither an analysis nor a causal account of the phenomena of conscious experience.

In a passage of dazzling clarity Mary Midgley gets it absolutely right:

> The approach which looks always for the cause is of course very often the right one. It is suitable when we are trying to 'explain' some phenomenon such as global warming, when we are already confident that we grasp an effect adequately and the cause is then the next thing we want to find. But the project of *explaining money*, or *elections*, or *time*, or *marriage*, or *football*, or *grammar*, or *art*, or *laughter*, or *gambling*, or *the Mafia*, or *post-structuralism*, or *the differential calculus* is not like this at all. Here, what we need is to know more about the thing itself. (1996: 501)

What if we find a mechanism that will do what people do when they are conscious? We need to keep in mind the distinction between grounding a capacity and analysing it. Just as manual skills are grounded in permanent states of the brain and nervous system, and in their exercise we employ neural mechanisms to accomplish our projects, so too for that cluster of capacities loosely (and perilously) lumped together as consciousness.

The three major 'theories' of consciousness – organic (Searle), non-computational (Penrose) and computational (Dennett) – when looked at closely, turn out to be rival accounts of how these capacities are *grounded*. They are not analyses of consciousness as a phenomenon or as a capacity. Perceiving offers each of us a world to which access is dependent on the existence of the perceptual tools, and how it is presented to us is not independent of the processes of these systems. But we must be careful not to slip into the mistake of trying to explain the ditch the road mender has dug from the properties of the spade that was used to dig it.

It seems to me that much of the thrill of recent publications on the topic of 'consciousness', for example the book by Francis Crick (1994), comes about through slipping and sliding between these distinctive parts of the work of making sense of how human life goes on. Let us look closely at how Crick approaches and then slides by the problem without actually touching on it at all. Early in the book he sets out his basic assumptions:

> [1] People are not conscious of all the processes going on in their heads . . .

[2] It seems probable, however, that at any one moment some active
    neuronal processes in your head correlate with consciousness, while
    others do not. *What is the difference between them?* (1994: 19, Crick's
    emphasis)

It ought to be obvious that far from these two observations standing
together as one assumption, they are in tension. If I were conscious
of a process, 'in my head', it would have to be of the neuronal sort.
Those are the sorts of processes that happen in people's heads. But
how would I become conscious of such a process, that is perceive it?
Only by arranging a mirror or some other device to observe what has
been revealed by a suitable trepanning, or with the latest equipment
in an on-line PET scan. Otherwise I am still in the condition of the
ordinary person who is aware of the usual paraphernalia of the local
environment. Thus if the processes in the second clause above are to
be compared they must be seen in the mirror, as neuronal processes,
and we are still in the realm of correlations. But now the correlations
are phenomenal: how *my brain looks* with how *I feel*. Note the different grammatical subjects required to express the correlation. We are
not correlating attributes of the very same thing, as we might correlate the green colour and acidic flavour of a Granny Smith apple.

It should be clear that Crick does not even begin to realize the
nature of the problem with which he is grappling. We need only
look at his remark 'we do not yet know, even in outline, how our
brains produce the vivid visual awareness that we take so much for
granted' (1994: 24) to see this. What would such knowledge be like?
Let us look to chemistry for a model answer to what looks like just
such a question. A hundred years ago a chemist might have
remarked that we do not yet know, even in outline, how muriatic
acid produces the corrosive etchings on zinc. The answer is
achieved by imagining and later confirming the existence of a
causal mechanism that is responsible for the correlation. *But both
cause and effect are of the same category, material entities.*

Long ago Locke got this right. While it makes perfectly good
sense to look for the causal mechanism that relates one material
state to another we must be content with correlations between
phenomena of awareness and states of the neuronal mechanism,
since neither a neuronal nor a phenomenal explanation could be
forthcoming. It would be like saying that in a tennis match the racquets have scored 40/30! Of course there is no problem of that sort
for Francis Crick and his coworkers to solve, other than the
humdrum one of finding out which states of the system, which
architectures of the brain and so on are correlated with being
awake, catching sight of a snowdrop and so on.

And the 'astonishing hypothesis' that there might be 'awareness neurons' is no better off than the macrohypothesis that there are people who are awake when their brains are in a certain state of excitation. The situation is rather worse since being awake, noticing a daisy or smelling the drains is something people do. Their brains are the tools or instruments by which they do it. It is nice to know the mechanics of the strung racquet, but the score, the victory and so on are attributes of whole games.

Chalmers (1996) has recently proposed a novel argument in an endeavour to stop materialism in its tracks, by defending the view that human organisms have both material and mental properties, and that these are logically independent of one another. We can use a brief discussion of his argument to sum up the view of the brain/mind relation that I am basing the whole of this study upon. The former are the familiar properties assigned to matter by physicists, chemists and ordinary folks, while the latter are qualia, elementary, simple sensory 'atoms', such as coloured patches in the visual field, timbres and pitched sounds in the auditory field and so on. According to Chalmers the latter are not logically tied to the former because a creature could have the full complement of physical properties that were observed in some similar being which was perceiving something while lacking the usual mental attributes, such as qualia. His argument runs as follows. Suppose we manufactured a duplicate (a zombie) of a human being, molecule by molecule. It is logically possible that while the original should have a mental life rich in qualia, the duplicate should not. Leaving aside the implausibility of building a 'big' argument on logical possibility where natural possibility and necessity seem to be called for, consider the following zombies. We manufacture a duplicate of a corrosive acid, atom by atom. Is it possible that the zombie acid will lack the power to corrode? Now suppose we manufacture a zombie tennis player, drawing on the blueprint of a real tennis player skilled in the game. Is it possible that the zombie tennis player will lack the ability to serve, to volley, to play a drop shot and so on? It hardly seems possible since the perceptual system and brain, muscles and nervous system of the player and the zombie will be identical, including the networks of connections inculcated by training. Why should a zombie perceiver be different in any case? Perceiving is a capacity that people exercise using their perceptual systems as tools, in much the same manner as people play tennis using their arms and racquets as tools. Heroic though Chalmers's attempt is, it quite misses the point in dropping into subjectivity. The question is not how a person's sensations are related to the state of that person's brain, but what he or she can find out about the material environment and the state of their material body.

If we now turn to Crick's third assumption we can see its inner incoherence. He says:

> you are aware of many of the results of perceptual and memory processes but you have only a limited access to the processes that produce this awareness. (1994: 19)

This sounds as if I could become aware of the processes of perception in much the same way as I become aware of a noise at the window. But the processes of perception are Gibsonian activities of my brain, which I would need my mirror and my trepanning assistant or my PET scanner to gain access to, that is if I am going to perceive these processes.

Even the otherwise excellent Nick Humphrey falls into this pit. Within two pages (Humphrey, 1983: 47–8) he says:

> Yet, in so far as I am conscious, I can see as if with an inner eye into my own [internal nervous mechanism].

That this is the intended object of the verb 'to see into' is clear from the previous sentences. Yet he then says:

> I [qua lay person] have long ago come to regard my conscious mind as the very same thing as the internal mechanisms which control my bodily behaviour.

The proposed link destroys the whole structure. Humphrey then goes on to suggest that:

> the workings of my conscious mind do in reality correspond in some formal (if limited) way to the workings of my brain.

The conscious mind cannot at the same time correspond to the workings of the brain and be the very same as the internal mechanisms and be seen into by the inner eye. I have to confess I simply do not understand what the author of these remarks is driving at.

The brain and its states and processes are related to perception and proprioception, I shall argue, as tool is to task. Framed within that broad distinction I hope to make a few things a little clearer, and take away as much of the thrill as I can. Of course there are all sorts of ways in which the nature of the tool limits the possibilities of the tasks that can be carried out with it. It seems that our perceptual systems have evolved to pick out certain invariances in the energy flux in which we live, and not others, thus shaping the general forms of the material world we see, hear, touch and play around with (Gibson, 1979). Studies of the perceptual capacities of bees suggest that our confinement to a certain part of the electro-magnetic spectrum for vision is a limitation in our perceptual system compared with the capacities of the bee, for whom the ultra-violet offers useful views. Soldiers with their enhanced infrared capacities can perceive things in the material world in conditions the unaided lay person cannot. Dog whistles demonstrate the contingency of our auditory capacities and so on. Brain lesions restrict the effectiveness of our perceptual systems. The degree to which the perceptual systems of human beings are preformed to pick out certain sorts of material things is even greater than those identified by Gibson. Movement is even more potent than he supposed. Kellerman's (1997) studies of the development of perceptual capacities have demonstrated the role of movement, both by the perceiver and by the perceived, in the automatic search of the ambient energy flux in which a perceiver is embedded.

A broad distinction can be drawn between a person-based ontology and a molecular-based one. In the former people are the basic particulars of the science of psychology while in the latter molecules are the basic particulars of neurosciences. The point is, to what logical (grammatical) subject should such skilled activities as seeing, hearing, touching and tasting be ascribed: human beings as people, or human beings as structured molecular aggregates? Since human beings have a central place in both ontologies there is no simple answer to the question. The phenomenology of consciousness must be framed in the former (*people* see, taste and feel things) while the neurophysiology of perceptual systems must be framed in the latter (molecular structures are the tools of experience). Why should we treat qualia, the sounds we hear (as opposed to the things we listen to), the hues we see (rather than the things we look at) and so on, as properties of the material 'apparatus' that is our brain and nervous system? There is no more reason to offer that interpretation than to interpret backhand passing shots as properties of tennis racquets. People perceive and their perceptual systems are the tools they use to do it. There is a persistent and malign tendency in philosophy of psychology, no less than in psychology itself, to assimilate the task to the tool.

If these remarks seem so obvious and banal as to be not worth the making, one has only to turn to some of the recent publications on the subject of 'consciousness' to be forcibly reminded of the need to keep one's feet on the ground in this heady field. My interest is focused on how the complex network of 'self' and 'person' concepts is realized in reports of what we can see, hear, touch and so on and what we can feel within the envelope of our own bodies. The crossing of incommensurable ontologies is overt in the title of Siever and Frucht (1997): *The new view of self: how genes and neuro transmitters shape your mind, your personality and your mental health.*

In the world of persons, perception is prior to sensation

How does sensation become perception? This sounds like a well thought out question, the sort of question that sets research programmes into motion. It sounds like the question 'How does flour become bread?', as if there were a process involved in which ingredients were transformed into finished products. Just as we would find that yeast and sugar must be added, so it might seem as if we are getting somewhere with our problem when we realize that concepts are somehow added, so that we come to perceive patterns of light, sound, texture and so on as instances of this or that type of entity. But a field of perception is centred on the embodied person, that is it is organized around a point of view. Sensations are a flat and undifferentiated field. A field of perception is structured. Objects are perceived as standing in spatial relations to the embodied perceiver. Is 'point of view' yet another ingredient? Our problem seems to be: how does the centred pattern of perceptual fields come into being? It cannot come from sensation since in a field of qualia there is no such centring, nor can it derive from the acquisition of a system of categories, since without some preliminary differentiation into different kinds of objects as things other than myself, categories could get no grip.

But suppose that the question we began with was infected with a deep but defective presumption. It seems that the early work of Bruner and Sherwood (1977) and Vygotsky (1962) relates the origins of a sense of personhood to the manipulative practices with which, when verbally enriched, an infant begins to appreciate its world as ordered, with respect to its own position as an embodied being among other things and beings of that or similar sorts. This appreciation appears first in the growing capacity to seek and to manipulate things, and finally to manage indexical expressions of all sorts, particularly pronouns and demonstratives. To be able to distinguish 'this' from 'that', 'here' from 'there' one must have a sense of a field of things centred on one's own embodied self with which one is in a material relation. This is the point of view at the origin of all perception. There never is a Jamesian 'blooming, buzzing confusion'! To reorder the world as perceived into an array of elementary sensations is a very sophisticated and late developed skill, which has to be learned painstakingly. I suppose many people, for example those without some formal training in the arts, never acquire it.

Against representations

The proper question is this: how does the world of material things, of bodily feelings and so on, come to be categorized and structured in the way it is for developed human beings? Two major classes of answers to this question have been proposed:

1 Consciousness is awareness of representations of something other than itself. Various images have been offered in the history of psychology to enlarge on this suggestion, for example the imprint on wax of some hard object, or a picture of a landscape, and so on. In each of these images there is a sharp line drawn between the conscious state of the organism and that of which it is conscious. A striking example of this point of view is Locke's theory of ideas and qualities. According to Locke a person is aware only of their ideas, some of which resemble the qualities of the material things that cause these ideas. Let us call this the 'representationalist account'. It did not perish with Locke and the theory of ideas. It has its advocates to this day (Fodor, 1981) and others persist in theorizing with the concept of 'mental represen-tation'.

2 Consciousness is awareness of a material environment of spati-ally distributed things and temporally distinct events and evolv-ing processes ordered as a centred array of which the perceiver's embodied position serves as the origin, in the geometrical sense. Everyone is also aware of certain states, events and processes within the envelope of their own skin. In this formulation there is no need for a concept of representation.[2] It is entirely consist-ent with a Gibsonian account of perception as grounded in 'direct' pick-up of invariants in the flux of energy in which per-ceiver and perceived are embedded.[3] The state of the body of the perceptually active person is as much a material environment as the world outside the envelope of the body. Let us call this the 'objectivist' account. We are aware of a world of things and our-selves as things having a place within it.

In considering the structure of the 'worlds' within which percep-tion and action occur, there is a strong temptation to work only with what can be seen. For many philosophers and psychologists perception is almost synonymous with seeing. Locke raised the question of how the tactile/auditory world of the blind is related to the visual world of the sighted. Our sense of self as a location in an array of things some of which are people, with which and amongst whom we perceive and act, may have features that would be absent from a sense of self of one who has a sense of location in an auditory and/or a tactile/kinaesthetic world. To express the sense of self as of a thing amongst things is to presuppose the primacy of the visual or perhaps the tactile/kinaesthetic world in the formation of personhood.

The reason for this is deep. It is that the body has a necessary role in the very idea of persons as individual beings actively engaged in the material world. The necessary character of the framing of the human form of life in material thing-like embodiment has been examined by Strawson (1959). He looked in detail at one seemingly viable alternative, the possibility of developing a sense of self as an embodied point of view in a world without material things, as a sound amongst sounds. In order to do this he constructed ana-logues of spatial displacement and of the reidentification of audi-tory particulars in relation to master sounds, locations in a pitch world, with which each person was endowed with a point of view. This study showed that while some features of indexicality could be reconstructed, the essential condition of reidentification of sound particulars in the course of the coming and going of the sound with respect to the master sound becomes extremely tenuous.

The tactile/kinaesthetic world has a somewhat different charac-ter. The idea of identifying and reidentifying something as the same thing can be well grounded in the sense of touch, since it will permit judgements of both qualitative and numerical identity, provided that kinaesthetic experiences are included in the sensory repertoire. Furthermore, as Merleau-Ponty (1962) has pointed out one's own body as a tactile/kinaesthetic entity is bounded in that sensory modality by a striking phenomenon. In touching a part of myself I am aware both of being touched and of touching. Rubbing two fingers together illustrates that. But for tactile/kinaesthetic entities other than myself there is only the experience of touching. Persons stand out from trees in the tactile array in that there are character-istic expressions of bodily experiences, such as being touched, whether it be by another person or by a thing. According to Wittgenstein's private language argument it is just these expres-sions, as part of the natural endowment of human beings, that permit the establishment of a way of conversing about one's feel-ings with others of one's own kind. So in the tactile/kinaesthetic world there is the wherewithal for developing a sense of self as a location, as a thing amongst things and as a person amongst persons. The sense of self of the blind and of the sighted is for that reason, I contend, essentially the same, in so far as it is a matter of location.[4]

Which of the above ways of formulating our approach to consciousness and to the involvement of the singularity of self as an embodied point of view in it should we adopt? I believe that it is not too difficult to recruit an array of arguments against the representational account and for the objectivist account. Consciousness, being aware of something, is a relation between a person and an intentional object. The objects of a perceptual field are structured in various ways, but in all cases are centred on the perceiver.

Resisting representationalism

This popular account of the human psyche is tied in with the compu-tational account of cognition, which is itself an intimate part of the point of view in psychology which draws on the analogy between human cognition and the running of programs on computers. What follows is a mere sketch of how the argument would run, leaving open the issue of the value of the computer/brain analogy.

Let us begin with a surview of the way the word 'representation' is used, reminding ourselves of its etymology as derived from 'standing for'. To avoid the repetition of the somewhat clumsy 'representation' and 'that which is represented' I shall use the dog-Latin 'representans' and 'representandum'. I go to Geverny to visit Monet's garden. I wander down to look at the water lilies, and then in the visitor centre I look at a representation of the water lilies. The painting is a representans and the pond a representandum. I see both and I have no difficulty telling which is which. Later, I close my eyes and imagine the water lilies. Here again I might say that my mental image is a representans and the lilies themselves the representandum. I may even conjure up an image of one of Monet's paintings, so that now I am playing with a representation of a representation. My image is representans to Monet's painting as representandum. The grammar of 'see the water lilies' is quite different from the grammar of 'see a representation of the water lilies'. For example while it makes good sense to discuss the merits of the painting as a representation, the merits of the water lilies are quite another matter. Any number of representations could be destroyed without materially affecting the water lilies in the slightest. But if the water lilies are destroyed the status of that which represents them is immediately transformed. The representationalist as cognitive 'scientist' would have us treat seeing the water lilies, seeing a picture of the water lilies, and conjuring up a mental image of the water lilies as all mental representations caused by the water lilies. But now the old solipsistic bogey reappears. What is the status of the final 'water lilies' in this sequence? A theoretical entity needed to explain what I see? If all I see is a representans, what could the representandum be?

Certainly there is a causal relation between the water lilies and something, without which no one could see them. They must affect the state of the brain and nervous system of a being possessed of the necessary perceptual apparatus and the skill to use it. But these are not mental representations. They are material, of just the same ontological category as the water lilies. Given the equipment and a heroic interest in neuropsychology I could see both the water lilies and the material representation of them in my brain and nervous system, just as I could take a photograph of the lily pond down to the pond and look at it in juxtaposition to the lilies. Of course the PET scan would not look like the lily pond, though the photo should. There are at least two different senses of 'represent' at work here, and no doubt plenty of opportunities to transfer the grammar of the one to the other, creating yet more pseudo-problems.

What is the perceiving relation between? Surely a person and an entity, be it within or without the envelope of the skin. The confusion in the representationalist psychology of some cognitive 'scientists' is between a psychological phenomenon and its material grounding. Or more generally it is an exemplar of the widespread failure to distinguish attributes of the tool from attributes of the task. The task is to pick out water lilies. The tool is my brain and the relevant perceptual subsystem.

How does it come about that these mistakes are so commonly made? The slippage seems to be in dismantling the perceptual relation, as if it could be reduced to nothing but a property of the individual person who is doing the perceiving, that is to one of its terms. Perception is a *relation* between a person and an entity, not a property of a person alone. The terms of the perceptual relation cannot be detached and still be what they are. The relation is internal. But causes and effects can be detached. The state of the brain and nervous system that is caused by a lily pond can be described in neurophysiological terms that need make no mention of anything outside the neuronal system. The mistake of detaching the personal 'end' of the perceptual relation from the object perceived goes back at least to John Locke's psychology of 'ideas'. It is a grammatical error. It is to treat the grammar of 'I spent the morning looking at Monet's lily pond' as if it were a special case of the grammar of 'The material set-up, L-pond, caused the material set-up, R-brain, to be in a certain state for so many hours.'

There are mental representations, notably images of something that is not a mental representation, something that has been seen, heard or touched or that might be seen, heard or touched. There are material representations by means of which a person sees, hears or feels something. But what is seen, heard or felt is not a representation, mental or otherwise, unless it is meant as a picture of something else that is not a picture.

How could anyone come to hold the representationalist theory? Perhaps it comes from a false generalization of the realization that there seem to be two such fields superimposed upon one another. There is the field of material things and events, ordered in space and time, including those that exist both outside and inside the body. As we learn from Wittgenstein, treating the objects of proprioception as if they were a certain special class of things is a serious mistake. He showed too how they formed one system of spatially ordered beings, through the role of natural expressions of private feelings in the public world.

But there is another field also to be discerned with, it seems, no more than a shift of attention, the field of qualia, the sensory qualities of that of which we are aware. These too have a structure. It is as if the fields of awareness inside and outside the body were doubled. It is as if we experience qualia out of which objects seen, heard and felt must be constructed, as if qualia were the primitive building blocks. Even more telling the metaphor of 'the inner', which is literal for proprioception, is used to try to locate qualia so that privacy and inwardness become entangled. Qualia, like the hues of regions of a visual field, share their privacy with bodily feelings, though they are not much like them. Does this mean that they shared their innerness too? Soon we generalize all this into the idea of a sphere of sensation, centred around each human being, out of which they must somehow break into a common world. We slip into thinking we know representations but not things.

In summary then we can say that we are aware of the same world in two different ways. In one way 'it' is a world of material things and events centred on our embodied selves, the point of view indexed by uses of 'I' and other first person devices; in another way it is a pattern of qualia with a different organization, since in this way of paying attention there is no privileged point of origin, no Self 1. To the content of the first way must be added the states of our bodies, the domain of proprioception, which is structured around the same point of view. Perhaps we could say that for things and events outside the body, for the most part the body serves as a somewhat lumpish centre, while for the states and events within the envelope of the body the centre condenses to a spot a few centimetres behind the eyes, at least for the normally sighted. The difference between the domain of what is perceived and what is proprioceived is a distinction between what is outside the bodily envelope and what is inside it (the strange case of a sip of hot tea finding its way down to the stomach!). By a slippage of metaphor we tend to treat the world perceived as qualia as if it were just like the proprioceptive domain, but now in a special sense of 'inner', the domain of private experience. Of course the domain of proprioception is just as easily transformed into a domain of qualia. The mental representations theory is yet another category mistake lubricated by a slippage from 'the inner' as a genuine spatial domain, inside the skin, to 'the inner' as a metaphor for 'the private'.

In short the study of consciousness is nothing but the study of perception and proprioception, particularly the structure of the world we encounter with the help of our perceptual systems, and, for the neurophysiologist, the study of the tools, the perceptual system that people employ in looking, listening, touching, feeling, and so on. This is or should be another almost perfect exemplar of the essential duality of psychology as a discipline. While the personal experience of the world can be studied only in the analysis of the personal *reporting* how the world looks, feels and so on to the speaker, the latter requires the methods and the theories of the natural sciences. The former involves not only the expression of point of view of an embodied being in a material world, but also questions of the reliability, skilfulness and indeed honesty and competence of the speaker, and the willingness to listen and the linguistic competence to follow what is said by those to whom a report is addressed. There is no speaker without, at least potentially, a listener.

Singularities in experience

How is the ordered structure of what I perceive and proprioceive given to me in what I am aware of? If awareness is a relation between a person and an array of intentional objects, and the objects are perceived, ought not the person at the centre of the array also to be an object of perception? This seemingly innocuous question becomes intractable when the person as reported is transformed into an inner self, by turning the centre of a field of experience into a kind of thing. Two famous treatments of this apparent conundrum are worth pausing for. Each, in its own way, shows that there are only persons and the geometrical centres, their points of view, just as there are only planets and the geometrical centres, their poles.

Hume and the elusive self

In one of the most trenchant passages in Hume's robust discussions of human understanding the thesis that there is a perceiving and acting being, within a person, at the centre or origin of the arrays of things and events perceived, when they are treated as subjective states of the perceiver, is dismissed out of hand. We have already looked at the argument in the context of the Cartesian ego. But it can also be used against the homunculus perceiver. If the self as one pole of a perceiving relation between the person and what is seen, felt, tasted etc. is supposed to be an 'inner' correlate of perceptual relations, it should be as discernible as the subjective ideas and impressions perceived. But looking inwards, Hume says, he never finds anything but more sensations. He never arrives at the inner pole of the bipolar relation. But this would indeed be just the result one would expect if the perceptual relation is between *persons* and things! There is no entity as inner pole. Hume is entirely right to emphasize the fruitlessness of this search. As we have seen it takes hard work and some training to shift one's attention from things perceived, whether by sight, touch, hearing, taste and so on, to become aware only of qualia, of hues and sounds, rather than flowers and the buzzing of bees. Of course Hume did not see his argument quite this way. He worked with a psychological ontology of impressions and ideas. The perceiving self was neither an impression nor an idea. But then neither were what a person perceived! Point of view cannot be perceived, but the body with which it is spatio-temporally and necessarily collocated certainly can be. Just as the North Pole is a place, but not a geological feature, so the Self 1, as point of view, is not a psychological entity either. The eye is not part of one's visual field, but its location is given in the structure of the whole field of person–material environment.[5]

Husserl and the ego

Shorn of the special terminology of Husserl's phenomenalism we find in the *Logical investigations* (1900) a view that seems rather like the one I am advocating in these studies.[6] Husserl says:

the [empirical] ego in the sense of common discourse is an empirical object . . . If we cut out the ego-body from the empirical ego, and limit the purely mental ego to its phenomenological content, the latter reduces to a unity of consciousness . . . The phenomenologically reduced ego is therefore nothing peculiar, floating above many experiences; it is simply identical with their own interconnected unity. ([1970]1900: V, Chapter 1, Section 4)

Put another way Husserl seems to be saying that if I delete that aspect of my sense of my own singularity that comes from my unique embodiment which has one and only one spatio-temporal 'world-line', the remainder is just the unity of my experiences as those of one being, that which I have called Self 1. Put the two back together again and I have a sense of myself as one being, uniquely embodied, and thus as one and only one Self 1. The singularity of self is none other than the uniqueness of personhood, since each person has his/her own unique point of view in the world of things and events, with which, for the most part, a person's point of action is closely associated.

However in *Ideas* ([1967]1913, Section 57; 1967: 172) and later in the *Cartesian meditations* (1960), Husserl seems to be offering another treatment of the conundrum. The 'pure Ego' does seem to be needed to account for the structure of experience: 'it belongs to every experience that comes and streams past, its "glance" goes through every actual *cogito*, and towards the object.' Though every act of thinking may be different from every other, 'the Ego remains self-identical . . . [and] appears to be *necessary* in principle.' Husserl seems to be offering the very thing he dismissed in 1900, namely an ego as an explanation of the unity of consciousness, since each person's experience is unified because the experiences belong to that ego. It is not given in experience, but is required by the structure of what we do experience. It is *a transcendence in immanence*. In *Cartesian meditations* this 'glance' becomes a kind of vector, characteristic of every experience, anchored to a centre which does not itself appear as itself: only an I-pole is intimated as the polar origin of the 'glance'. Thus we get the transport of the 'public person is aware of object' relation into the private realm as 'ego is aware of phenomenal presentation of object.' This is just the fallacious transportation we have already identified in the illegitimate extension of the phenomenon of proprioceptive awareness into a general analysis of perception. It is just the same transportation that the terminology of 'representations' tempts us to make.

Double consciousness

The idea of 'double consciousness' has appeared in several different areas of psychology. As with most uses of the word 'consciousness' there is an essential equivocation in its use, which can lead to
problems in interpreting the claims of those who describe this or
that phenomenon as a case of 'double consciousness'. If each 'consciousness' is centred on a distinct ego, the double consciousness
seems to suggest a duality of personhood. But if we distinguish the
indexing of bodily location from the taking of responsibility, both
functions of Self 1, then we could have the latter without necessarily disrupting the former. As we have seen the contemporary
'consciousness' lexicon includes two broad patterns of use. There is
that which derives from the origins of the expression in the Latin
sciere, by which some mode of knowing or some corpus of knowledge or belief is referred to. There is also a phenomenological
flavour in that which has accreted to the use of these expressions,
which appears in the various uses in which 'conscious' could be
replaced by 'aware' or 'notice' and other phenomenological expressions.

According to the former pattern of use 'double consciousness'
refers to two sets of beliefs about oneself that are distinct but held
together, clusters of beliefs that may in extreme cases be logically
incompatible. In most cases of 'double consciousness' of this sort
the incompatibility is pragmatic, in that in implementing the one,
implementation of the other is blocked. For example feminists have
used the expression to point to the fact that a person may be at the
same moment a professor and a mother, and these roles involve
different and incompatible beliefs about what one should be doing
and attending to at any one moment of the working day. In this
context 'self', if used to gloss the phenomenon, would be a cluster
of beliefs about oneself, the person. The singularity of the centredness of perceptual awareness would be intact in such cases, indeed
the phenomenon could not exist unless it was. There is nothing
more exciting here than an emphasis on the complexity of Self 2.

The other sense of double consciousness is used to refer to
phenomena which suggest that there are two centres of awareness
existing contemporaneously and distinctly in the one human being.
In so far as the criteria for 'selfhood' are founded upon the principle
of singularity there would be two selves in the one human being.
The phenomenon of 'blind sight' is often cited as an instance of such
'divided consciousness'. Less plausibly, multiple personality disorder and self-deception are also occasionally interpreted in this

manner. I shall try to show that interpreting them as grammatical features of personal discourses makes better sense. The deep point about these suggestions is that if they were taken seriously they would appear to be exceptions to the strong principle that there is only one person per body, since that bodily location is now the centre of awareness of two perceptual fields. In the case of 'blind sight' these centres are supposed to exist contemporaneously in the one body while in the case of MPD they are supposed to exist successively.

Altered states

There are some experiences the expression of which suggests that the relation between body and person, preserved even in multiple personality disorder, can be disrupted, with a consequential difference in the sense of self. Of the many cases recorded two seem to me specially instructive.

Carlos Castaneda (1968), in describing his time with a Mexican magician, Don Juan, refers several times to flying about the desert with his mentor while their bodies remained behind at the cabin. Here the sense of self as having a perceptual point of view that is fixed in the body of the perceiver is disrupted or changed. The perceptual point of view is disembodied, as it might be in a dream. This is the general character of out-of-body experiences, that the perceptual point of view no longer coincides with the spatial location of the perceiver's body. This is not a new claim. The word 'ecstasy' originally meant 'placed or standing outside', by implication the body. Clearly ecstatic discourse must be using the reporting 'I' in a way that relieves it of its normal indexical force identifying its perceptual point of view with the location of the body. What are we to make of the moral indexicality, the act of standing behind the verisimilitude of the perceptual claim that is also an important feature of the indexical uses of 'I'? This too must be changed. The tie between spatial and moral indexicality is tight in normal discourse since perceptual claims can be checked by occupying the position from which the speaker issued the original claim. But it is not at all clear that Carlos Castaneda's claims can be checked in the same manner. What would it be to occupy the point of view of one flying with Don Juan? It is the same sort of question that might arise by querying the verisimilitude of a dream. How could anyone other than the dreamer say anything relevant to the reporting of a dream? The film *A Nightmare on Elm Street* plays with the indexicality of dream discourse as the beings in the dream worlds of more than one dreamer begin to take physical shape in the waking world.

The practice of meditation is also said to transform the sense of self. A common form of meditation involves the selection, from the general field of objects of which one is aware, of just one on which to concentrate attention. The object chosen might be visual or auditory. It is rarely tactile, olfactory or gustatory, and that fact needs explanation. A mantra is a short verbal formula which is chanted over and over again, until it occupies the whole of the meditator's attention. Or the focus might be a material object like a flower or a stone, again attracting the whole of someone's attention. The steps with which a mantra becomes a meditative focus might go as follows: first one hears the chant among a number of other sounds; then one hears only the mantra. It is not heard as here or there, which would require some sort of auditory reference system. It is the only sound heard. In reporting this experience 'I' is no longer needed as a spatial indexical since there is nothing but the sound, which it makes no sense to index with a spatial location as a sound among sounds or as the production of a thing amongst things, one of which is the body of the listener as the centre of an ordered auditory field. In meditation on a flower, in the end there is nothing but the flower, and again no role for the spatial indexicality of 'I'. In this sense then the self has melted away, been transcended and so on. Any number of metaphors may find a place in the expression of what is essentially a grammatical feature of the reporting of decentred experience.

In a way meditation is the very opposite of ecstasy. Though in both cases the routine indexical force of 'I' as centering experience in the body is suspended, point of view is robustly maintained in ecstasy and dissolved in meditation.

Action talk: 'I' as responsible agent

Conceptual foundations for the psychology of agency

I turn now to the second mode in which singularity of self is manifested in our daily doings, displays and exercises of agency. Taylor (1985: 263) remarks that 'a person is an agent who has an understanding of self as agent'. According to the discursive point of view, 'understanding' refers to a complex pattern of abilities and dispositions, including the ability to create stories in which a speaker can adopt a variety of roles. One can present oneself as agent, exercising one's personal powers and be fully responsible for what one has done. For other purposes one can present oneself as a mere plaything of fate and of forces beyond one's control. But before this suggestion can be worked out in any detail it will be necessary to set aside a way of tackling the phenomenon of human agency that has a very long and frustratingly unsatisfactory history. In taking responsibility for my actions, presenting myself as an agent, I do so as a person, as a basic entity of the psychological realm.

A proliferation of redundant entities

I have already pointed out that there are several ways in which explanations are constructed in both lay and scientific styles. The simplest is to look for antecedent conditions that seem to vary with the phenomenon to be explained. Then there is the hypothetico-deductive technique in its logicist and realist forms, in which a hypothesis that links conditions and outcome is proposed interpretable as referring to a hidden mechanism. Finally there are rock-bottom explanations in which the ultimate active powers of the basic particulars of a domain are cited in an explanatory role. In psychology the first is typical of behaviourist psychology, in which the concept of human agency has no role. The second is typical of 'mental muscle' accounts in which faculties like connation ('the will') or structures like 'belief/desire pairs' are introduced as explanatory hypotheses. In both versions of hypothetico-deductive theorizing a part of a person is cited as endowed with agentive power, that is power to initiate action. In the one it is the will, in the other desire. Kenny (1975), in an early work in which he followed the hypothetico-deductive pattern rather closely, proposed the concept of 'volit' for the activating states that brought resolution to execution. None of these accounts are satisfactory. The supposed 'internal' subpersonal agencies are hard to find, and equally hard to credit with authorial powers if offered as hypothetical entities.[7] The best answer to the conundrum of human action is right in front of our eyes, so to say. It is the agentive powers of persons as the basic particulars of the psychological realm. People have powers of action, that we can see quite easily. Only if we hanker after a hypothetico-deductive style of explanation, looking for a mental mechanism to account for the agentive powers of people, would we feel dissatisfied with the thought that in psychology the agentive powers of people can be no further grounded. Something now needs to be said about those powers, picking up the themes of earlier chapters.

Dispositions and powers

I turn now to develop the brief sketch of a physics/psychology parallel offered in Chapter Two. Dispositions are observable properties of individuals or samples of substances. Each component of the conditional form 'If C then B' refers to an observable phenomenon. C is filled out with a description of the eliciting conditions and B with one of the behaviour elicited. Amongst the varieties of dispositional concepts relevant to human life are skills and temperaments. Dispositional descriptions can be in either the indicative or the subjunctive mood, thus expressing the relative likelihood of satisfying the conditions described in the first clause. Thus 'Were C to obtain B would be displayed' expresses a more remote possibility than 'If (when) C obtains B is displayed.' Clearly the notion of an unobservable disposition makes no sense.

The corresponding theoretical concepts by which reference is made to unobservable states or entities responsible for the possession by individuals and substances of dispositions fall into two groups: there are passive liabilities and there are active powers. The former are ascribed when it is assumed that the agentive influence is extrinsic to the individual to which the disposition is ascribed, the latter when it is assumed that the agentive influence is intrinsic to that individual.

The application of this conceptual system in a research programme which has lasted over four centuries is very clear and unequivocal in physics. Agentive power is ascribed to elementary poles and charges, which are structurally simple, having no internal constitutions as such. Dispositions through which such powers are manifested are properties of spatio-temporally distributed fields. How would this ontology apply to people? To get this right we must have a second look at the physical sciences. In chemistry, metallurgy and the science of materials generally it is assumed that the samples of substances that are studied in the laboratory are complex structures of more fundamental or elementary substances. The powers and liabilities of the complex materials are explained in terms of the powers and liabilities of their component parts. Elasticity is explained in terms of the electrical fields (distributed dispositions) of the elementary charged particles of a typical microstructural explanation. This pattern of explanation is continued until a fundamental level of unanalysable basic particulars, elementary particles with their charges and associated fields, is reached. In psychology people are the powerful particulars. There are no deeper levels to look for, and so there is no place for a realist application of the hypothetico-deductive method. To use it shifts us from psychology to physiology.

There are two qualifications needed to tie this conceptual scheme to ordinary language and lay explanatory formats. In lay use the concept of a causal power has more than one common application. It is used both for a property, having a power, and for an entity, being a power. This duality of meaning can lead to equivocations and confusion. For this reason the expression 'powerful particular' as a generic term for such beings as elementary particles and magnetic poles is the expression of choice. The second qualification has to do with the way that hierarchical structures have been disclosed in nature. For example the dispositions of chemical elements are explained by the valencies or 'combining powers' of chemical atoms, the relevant powerful particulars. But chemical atoms are not elementary. Their powers are redefined as dispositions and explained by the invocation of the powers of sub-atomic particles, like electrons which for a long while played the role of powerful particulars. Physicists have no trouble with either of these qualifications, since the entitative and qualitative uses of the notion of 'power' are fused in the concept of a powerful particular and the analytical schemes of power/disposition hierarchies are firmly established. Physics does not need to deal with infinite regresses since hierarchies of this sort are terminable in a class of powerful particulars which are deemed elementary until there should be evidence of their constitutional complexity, for example as revealed in the products of a high energy collision between particles previously taken to be elementary.

Numerous attempts have been made to transfer this scheme to the understanding of human behaviour. In the field of personality psychology the 'trait' theory has appeared, disappeared and reappeared from time to time (Cattell, 1965; Eysenck and Eysenck, 1969). In philosophical psychology the scheme has been famously exploited by Ryle (1947), and developed and refined by many others, for instance Armstrong (1968). Neither the advocates of Cattellian traits nor the critics of Rylean dispositions have paid close attention to the uses of the scheme in physics. They have missed the opportunity to learn from the experience of generations of experimentalists and theoreticians from Gilbert (1600), who reintroduced causal powers into the physics in his studies of magnetism, to the charges and fields of the present day. Sooner or later one reaches the level of elementary *active* beings, which serve as the ultimate groundwork of agentive explanations.

Applications in psychology

There seem to me to have been two major omissions in the application of dispositional concepts in human studies.[8] The explanatory
pattern is structured as a powers/dispositions hierarchy with intermediate steps only if it is the case that the entities to which powers
are assigned in the first step of the hierarchy are, as a matter of fact,
internally complex, such as chemical molecules and atoms and, of
late, subatomic particles. Powerful particulars may or may not have
internal structure. If they do the power concepts must be reassigned
to the entities constitutive of that structure. In the human world
people, as psychological beings, do not have parts, though they
produce complex patterns of action that give the illusion of psychological parts. Of course people's bodies, their most fundamental
tool kit, are intricate systems of interacting organs. There can only
be a one-step hierarchy in which psychological dispositions and
skills are used to describe people, since these are observable properties. The relevant powers and liabilities, which, when exercised,
appear as dispositions and skills, are ascribed to people to explain
those manifested dispositions and skills.

The second omission is evident in the mistaken idea that traits or
dispositions can be arranged hierarchically, as if generic traits
explained specific traits or dispositions. This is a familiar error in
the thinking of psychologists and should therefore be guarded
against vigilantly. The only hierarchy that could obtain among
traits ascribed to the same level of powerful particular, in this case
'person', is taxonomic. 'Feline' is a generic term that comprehends
hierarchically 'tiger', 'lion' and 'pussy cat' but the fact that this is a
pussy cat is not explained by citing the fact that it is feline.

The attempt to use dispositions as the basis of hidden mechanisms in contrast to a causal powers account in which people are the
powerful particulars is a symptom of something deeper to which I
have drawn attention from time to time. It is a symptom of the persistent tendency to try to substitute causal accounts for normative
explanations – and so to extrude the category of person as such
from psychology.

This observation draws our attention to the fact that there is yet
another aspect to agency that needs to be taken into account. It is
that of control. This aspect has been explored by Dennett (1984).
There are a variety of targets for control: parts of one's own body,
one's acts of speaking, one's thoughts and feelings, other people,
dogs and so on. These taken-for-granted powers come into promi-
nence only when they are in question. Thus the paraplegic, the

sufferer from coprolalia (perhaps as a species of Tourette's syndrome), the schizophrenic, the unassertive, and so on, are or should
be well exploited sources of knowledge of that which we take for
granted. Like pilots of complex aircraft we use our neural mechanisms to carry out our projects. Sometimes one of these mechanisms
gets out of hand. We cannot help but cough at a crucial moment at
the concert. More embarrassing is the predicament of the sufferer
from Tourette's syndrome whose 'shouting mechanism' sometimes
runs free, especially if the result is coprolalia (the polite expression
for obscenity). Our discourses make a perfectly clear distinction
between bodily equipment that is under the control of the person
and that which is running free. Case by case problems of great complexity occur when the basic distinction does not have an unambiguous or uncontestable application. But they need not concern us
further here. They are defects of the tools only in relation to socially
acceptable and legitimated tasks.

The discursive view

In everyday life actions are embedded in intentional discourse,
stories in which a person gives an account of what they are proposing to do, or what they have done. What work do we find such
accounts are used to do? For the most part they turn around two
issues: the taking or repudiating of responsibility. These forms of
talk were first distinguished into 'excuses' and 'justifications' by
Austin (1961) and later identified in everyday talk by Backman
(1977). The distinction between excuses and justifications is itself
dependent on a prior distinction, between those constraints from
which a person cannot escape and those he or she is free from. This
distinction cannot be drawn in general, but must be made *ad hoc*
and case by case, situation by situation. Only if a person is hindered
by a constraint from which they cannot escape can they successfully
repudiate responsibility for the relevant action or failure to act.

Large scale studies of 'agentive' story-telling have been made in
recent years, particularly by Westcott (1988). However I would like
to fill out my account of the expression of personhood in agentive
story-telling by a brief sketch of the treatment proposed by Aristotle.
In some ways I think it is still the most convincing psychological
treatment of agency. Aristotle (Ackrill, 1987) makes a broad distinction between voluntary and involuntary actions, but not in terms of
the empirically woolly concept of 'could have done otherwise'.
Voluntary actions are those for which the actor has a goal to the ful-
filment of which the action is directed. Wittgenstein (1953: 437–44),

in discussing thoughts about the future, points out that an expectation can only be for an outcome of the same *type* as the one envisaged, thus cutting through a tangled mass of philosophical theorizing about the role of the future event in goal-directed processes and teleological explanations. This fits very nicely with Aristotle's account. One acts to realize a goal without being able or willing to offer reasons for it. However there is another type of voluntary action where the actor not only has a goal but can give reasons why just that goal was picked from among others that seemed possible. So the category of 'voluntary action' is a discursive category, namely those actions for which a goal can be avowed, and in some cases a story replete with reasons can be told. Involuntary actions are those which are driven by impulse. Is this distinction ontological? Are there two kinds of processes that are the material foundations of action in the human organism, the voluntary and the involuntary? Would it make sense to go from the cognitive models of hierarchical organizations of means and ends, visible in the grammars of accounts, to a search for something similar in the state of the brain and nervous system, while the actor was doing something voluntarily? I suggest that no such mechanisms could be found. The category distinction 'voluntary/involuntary' is a distinction in types of stories, of ways of making sense in one's local context, especially if the propriety of what one is doing comes into question.

Voluntary actions are explained by reference to the future, though only by reference to a special kind of causality, final causality, to which we might give the Wittgensteinian twist, while involuntary actions are explained by reference to the present, the impulse that caused them, caused in the sense of efficient causality. The futurity and pastness are also discursive categories, since there is no suggestion that something in the future brought about the action directed towards *it*. There is no 'it'. The tricky question of akrasia, or incontinence in the sense of lack of self-control, doing what you know to be wrong or foolish or self-indulgent, is explained by Aristotle in terms of inattention. For some reason one's focus on the reasons for doing something is distracted. Perhaps one forgets, in the heat of the moment, what would have been best. Only the young are distracted by bodily impulses. The elderly suffer other kinds of distraction.

Aristotle's treatment of the psychology of action is exemplary for the analyses proposed in this book. In it he reserves agentive power to the whole person. He finds the distinctions between kinds of actions, those in which personal powers are displayed and those in which they are not, in the stories in which the actions find a place.

The treatment is very systematic. As the analysis unfolds it becomes clear that voluntary action, things done by the person, is, as we now say, the default case. Aristotle's attention is mostly on the involuntary. Voluntary actions are those for which the 'moving principle' is in the agent himself, he being aware of the particular circumstances of the action.

Involuntary actions are those for which the person whose actions they are contributes nothing to their genesis. This could be either because of compulsion or by reason of ignorance. But there is a large class of actions which are 'mixed'. In a particular situation and on a particular occasion an action which would not be chosen in more common circumstances is the right thing to do. A person may do something unsavoury for 'fear of greater evils or for some noble object'. These are more like voluntary than involuntary actions because in the situation they are worthy of choice and the person exercises his or her personal powers to execute them. Considered independently of the actual situation such actions would usually be involuntary, that is either forced on someone or done out of ignorance. The important point is that actions can only be classified as voluntary or involuntary as particulars, that is in concrete circumstances, and not according to the type of action they exemplify. With this as the groundwork, Aristotle turns to discuss actions done out of ignorance.

Things done out of ignorance that the actor neither suffers for nor regrets Aristotle calls 'non-voluntary'. 'Only what produces pain and regret is involuntary' (Aristotle, *Nichomachean ethics*: [1110^b] see Ackrill, 1987: 389), since no one in their right mind would do such a thing. This distinction is also very much in the line of recent discursive accounts, since what distinguishes such an action is the slices of life that unfold in which the action has a place. It is a thoroughly relational conception. No action, considered only as an instance of a type, could be classified into any of the three categories, voluntary, involuntary or non-voluntary. Since the psychological explanations of actions draw on just these distinctions, such explanations are always concretely situated. In what would an explanation consist? It must be in what would justify the action, show it as a matter of choice.

Running over some candidates for the underlying psychological account of choice, Aristotle rejects much the same candidates as Wittgenstein might have: particularly mental states such as 'appetite', that is thoughts of what would be pleasant or painful, or emotions such as 'anger'. It cannot be based on wishes, since 'choice seems to relate to things that are in our power' (Aristotle,

Nichomachean ethics:[1111^b] see Ackrill, 1987: 391); nor on matters of fact, since choice is about what is good or bad.

Now the analysis turns towards the psychology of choosing. And once again we find Aristotle firmly in the discursive school. It involves previous deliberation, the construction of a discourse, framed by principles of reason. It is interesting to run over Aristotle's characterization of discourses of deliberation. We deliberate only about what we think we can bring about, and only about those matters where things could turn out in different ways, or where the event to be achieved is obscure or indeterminate. Deliberation becomes dialogical, as we now say. Aristotle (Aristotle, *Nichomachean ethics*: [1112^b] see Ackrill, 1987: 393), more homely in his vocabulary, simply remarks that 'we call in others to aid us in deliberation on important questions, distrusting ourselves as not being equal to deciding.' Furthermore deliberation leads to thinking of hierarchies of procedures or means until 'we come to the first cause' relative to the case in point. Unlike contemporary activity psychologists, Aristotle does not think that it makes sense to deliberate about ends. We could hardly deliberate as to whether to try to cure someone if we were a medical expert, he seems to think. (Could he have imagined Dr Crippen? Is it too slippery to declare him to be not a real doctor?)

Be that as it may, the outlines of Aristotle's treatment are clear and much to be admired: 'man [in the species sense] is the moving principle of actions ... deliberation is about the things to be done by the agent himself, and actions are for the sake of things other than themselves' (Aristotle, *Nichomachean ethics*: [1112^b] see Ackrill, 1987: 393).

To round off the discursive account of agency as a social construction created in the course of telling the story of an action, as the captain in Aristotle's example tells the story of throwing the cargo overboard to save the ship, we turn once again to grammar. We have already noticed that the first person is used not only to index a statement with the location of the embodied speaker in space but also as the means by which responsibility is taken. The default position is that he or she who uses 'I' is responsible for what is said and for the consequences of the saying of it, unless that responsibility is specifically repudiated.

However, a glance at other cultures shows that all is not so simple. Students of Japanese, for instance, have pointed out that the first person expressions in that language are used to diffuse rather than to take responsibility. The first person indexes a commitment with the relevant group to which the speaker belongs for the purpose in hand (Bachnik, 1982). The internal relation that obtains in individualistic cultures between the user of 'I' and the presumed agent is quite different. Who or what then is the *agent*? Does group responsibility entail 'group agency'? No such question is called for. Groups and individuals play their roles in the story of the activity. Who was consulted? Who said what? Who had been elected captain? And so on. These are the relevant questions. In agentive stories they are answered.

When I declare that I did it myself, the relevant entity is the person. None of the 'selves' of the standard model are invoked.

Conclusion

Indexing reports of experience and accounts of actions with the first person invokes the self as the centre of an array of material things as I perceive them. But the responsible actor using his or her bodily tools to accomplish material projects is the person. I can also act upon my actions, and upon my thoughts and feelings. We have looked briefly at the agentive discourses that address and express our powers of self-control. Again it is the person, as powerful particular, that is invoked in the discourses of self-monitoring and self-control. In these discourses 'self' is used as a synonym for 'person'. The standard model, Person {Self 1, Self 2, Self 3}, still works well in the two contexts discussed in this chapter. While we need the Self 1 to express the structure of the world as each embodied person perceives it, we have seen that agentive discourses work by ascribing to persons the basic powers and capacities that are utilized in action. That is nicely in accordance with the general account offered in this book, namely that persons are the fundamental entities of the psychological domain, the powerful particulars with whom the *psychological* analysis always terminates.

Notes

1 The most interesting question in this arena, at least for me, is how far the whole of humankind employs the same perceptual tools. There are differences in what people from different environments can routinely perceive, but how is that to be accounted for? For a superb summary of past and present research on this matter see Cole (1996).

2 One wonders why the 'representation' theory persists to this day. Of course in tracking the neurological processes by which perceiving is accomplished it is necessary to look for the representations of states of the world, and of the body of

the perceiver in the perceptual system. But that this representation should resemble that which is represented has had a long run from Locke's primary qualities to Gestalt properties to Wittgenstein's common logical forms. The metaphor of 'symbol' has been used to try to bridge the gap between what is experienced and the necessary neural representations. Neural network models of the brain tend to sideline this ancient problem, by rejecting the very idea of representations. The Lockean thesis, in whatever guise, involves two mistakes. It treats perception as secondary to sensation, and encourages the interpretation of perceptual activities in terms derived from studies of the tools we use for perceptual tasks.

3 Some misunderstandings of 'direct' as Gibson uses it have led to doubts about the Gibsonian approach. By 'direct' he meant 'not *mediated* by sensation'.

4 It turns out that people blind from birth do not centre their world as perceived in just the same point as do the sighted. But that is hardly surprising. I shall return to this point in more detail in the next chapter.

5 Taking the phenomenological stance to the search for the singularity of self, G.H. Mead (1934) offered an ingenious solution to Hume's conundrum. There were two singularities in our experience of ourselves: the current 'I' which perceives and acts, and the retrospective 'me', a current representation of the 'I' of the past. The former is imperceptible for the reasons Hume gave, while the latter is readily identified in the remembrance of things past.

6 I am particularly grateful to Tom O'Hagan who kindly put me right about the way Husserl's views changed.

7 Of course a person may make use of body parts and organs, including the brain, to accomplish various projects.

8 Ironically while freedom loving Americans developed a psychology which cast them as automatons with the framework of a psychology built around causal concepts, the Russians, supposedly the dragooned citizens of an authoritarian regime, developed an action-based psychology built around the agentive notions of means–end pairs and the goal setting for projects of their realization. So entrenched has the cause–effect metaphysics become that none of William Stern's personalist psychology rooted in a personal teleology, Leontief's activity psychology or the 'competence' point of view of Rommetweit have been taken seriously outside Europe.

CHAPTER SIX

The Self in Reflection and Recollection

Hence, for all its vulgar embodiment, a person's relation to and cognition of himself does seem to have certain unique features.

Irving Thalberg, *Encyclopedic dictionary of psychology*

When the subjective self-authorization of knowledge is allowed, the pretence of truth is replaced by inter-subjective negotiation. The responsibility of each knower for his knowledge and to the other party is necessarily an item in the discussion.

D. Bleich, *Subjective criticism*

In the last chapter we saw how a person's sense of self as a perceiver and actor is expressed discursively. Self 1 is conjured up in the expression of what one is conscious of but it is to Person that the actions one performs are assigned. The word 'self' is also used for the totality of attributes that each person possesses. The Self 2 includes both one's dispositions and powers, one's current private and public thoughts and feelings, and one's personal history. However psychologists have long been aware of and taken into account the common-sense observation that what each person believes about their personal attributes differs along many dimensions from what, from a God-like stance, those attributes could, in principle, be known to be. Thus we need the notion of the self-concept, as a person's beliefs about their nature, as well as the Self 2, what that nature is, to do justice to psychological reality.

In this book I am concerned only with how people appear to themselves and others as singular, individual and even unique beings. How do we come to have an opinion about our personal attributes, and how are our reflexive beliefs expressed? In short how is Self 2 manifested discursively? For this purpose I need only sample the huge field of the possible content of reflexive beliefs. In the first part of this chapter I examine a model case of self-knowledge, that is particularly instructive as an illustration of the general thesis of this book, that personal psychological attributes are generated in the flow of talk and other forms of action. In the latter part I turn to the creation and expression of autobiography, the beliefs that a person has about their past. There, again, the same general point obtains; we create autobiographical versions for ourselves and for others, in the working out of this or that project. Taken together we have two aspects of Self 2, what one currently is, and what one has been.

Self-consciousness, self-awareness and self-knowledge

Awareness of my own attributes, my ever-changing 'take' on my ever-changing and largely relational Self 2, when reported to myself or to others, makes use of the first person, but now takes on more of the second aspect of its indexical force, namely my responsibility as a reporter. At the same time as the self-reports are those of the speaker, their reliability is tied to the standing of the speaker in the community of speakers, and the speaker as him or herself as interlocutor. In this chapter I shall be facing sunny-side up, in that discussion of the innocent, and not so innocent, pathologies of self-reporting, such as self-deception and 'denial' will be postponed until Chapter Seven.

Native cognitive powers and their maturation

What do we believe about ourselves? Prominent amongst the more lasting contents of the self-concept are beliefs about our capacities and powers. Since our powers and capacities mature, change and decay, this fact about our Self 2 induces a progressive character into the continuously transforming self-concept. As the work of Kellerman (1997) and others have shown there are native cognitive and perceptual powers that become the powers of an ordered human mind by the acquisition of first person skills of all sorts, prominent amongst which are linguistic and practical competencies. Infant perception of arrays of things in motion becomes adult perception of person centred external and internal environments, action becomes agency, dependency becomes respect and memory becomes autobiography. The key to understanding the transformation of natural into acquired powers, I believe, is in studying what is involved in talking as a person. We could have focussed on what is involved in sawing and hammering, walking and jumping as a person. Organisms walk, human beings walk somewhere for some reason and take what they believe is the right path, and are usually ready to account for their perambulation before, during and after it.

Starting from the discursive foundations of thought and action we can also see which aspects of the sense of self are likely to vary culturally and historically and which are very unlikely to do so. We can also see where pathologies of the self could take root, and even conjecture what might be their expressive forms (such as the oft-reported favouring of 'me' over 'I' in the talk of schizophrenics). Anthropological studies show that the sense of unique embodiment and so of spatial location of the embodied person is a transcultural and robust feature of all discourses, readily identifiable in the grammar of first person expressions (Wierzbicka, 1992). Even if multiple personality disorder were to be a real disordering of mind in some cases, each of the set of multiple I's that express this strange form of life is embodied in just one body. Serial re-embodiment, belief in which is widespread outside the boundaries of the Christian/Judaic/Muslim world, is an interesting claim and the grammatical devices used to express it would be well worth studying. As one might expect, anthropology and history show that the grammatical embedding of social 'standing' is the most variable and unstable. Many people change their social standing and many have more than one, depending on the immediate social context. Titles, which mark proper names with *indelible* social positions, have all but disappeared in most cultures. Even when social standing is expressed linguistically it is most likely to be qualitative rather than numerical identity that is marked. There are some exceptions. There is only one King or Queen of England at any time just as there has been, mostly, only one Pope. When there have seemed to be more than one King or more than one Pope, the alternative has been retrospectively redefined as 'a pretender'.

Though the use of grammatical analysis as a psychological method depends on the Wittgensteinian distinction between descriptive and expressive uses of language, not all contexts of application of the technique are alike. While there is an ethology of feeling there is no *ethology* of the expression of selfhood. In accord with the Vygotskian view of the development of the higher cognitive faculties, the self-organization that is expressed in the grammars of indexical pronouns and other functionally equivalent grammatical devices comes about in the very learning of the grammar and other intentional, normatively constrained skills with which it is expressed. However, as Shotter (1971) and others have argued, there are natural powers, some of which are listed in this discussion too, which, so to say, play the part of an ethology of self.

Why has this constructivist account of personhood sometimes been called '*social* constructionism'? The use of this expression has led to all sorts of misunderstanding and misalliances. The variety of societies does not justify the claim by certain persons (some calling themselves 'postmodernists') that selfhood is therefore relative. All that is properly to be concluded is that:

1 The arrays in which one's location is the source of one's sense of self are all external to the embodied person, and include other persons and things.
2 Amongst the arrays of beings within which a person has a unique place there are opportunities for variations in the sense of self of a person over time and between persons in different cultures, in which these arrays are differently arranged. We have seen that the English 'I' is uniquely indexical only of the spatial location and temporal trajectory of the embodied person. The question of whether more than one person can occupy the same position in a relevant local moral order and whether positions are disputable has recently been the topic of a new research programme in social psychology (positioning theory). Some of these variations have been charted in van Langenhove and Harré (1991).[1] Japanese permits the indexing of social position in the first person and Kawi of indexing the relation between the events referred to and the act of uttering their description, in any person. We shall delve further into the details of the variability and multiplicity of the indexical features of the first person in the next chapter.

What could be the content of a person's self-concept?

Ideally my self-concept should be an accurate resumé of certain truths, palatable or unpalatable, about myself, that is about the person in question. This is an exercise in self-awareness, as perceiving or knowing my own personal attributes or at least having beliefs about some of them. This ideal is rarely met. Candour about oneself is rare in public discourse and though it may be more common when I think about myself, it is by no means guaranteed even in my most honest self-reflections. So we must say that the self-concept of any person is the cluster of beliefs that that person holds about him or herself rather than the attributes that person actually, at that moment, possesses, his or her Self 2. Both Self 2 and self-concept are labile, but it seems can change only within certain limits, more or less well defined, which depend on situation or epoch or both. In this cluster there are at least the following:

1 what I am currently thinking, feeling, saying and doing;
2 what I currently remember about what I thought, felt, said and did;
3 what I could remember about what I thought, felt, said and did;
4 what I know or believe about my history, my capacities, liabilities and powers, and my bodily characteristics;[2]
5 what I know or believe about my position in the social and moral worlds in which I live.

Many of these have been researched in some detail.

'Self-esteem' as a model case of the grammar of self-assessments

Beliefs about oneself include beliefs about the quality or standard of one's attributes and skills as well as beliefs about my past and likely future. Any beliefs I have about my attributes including my beliefs are amongst my beliefs. As annexed to 'I believe . . .' a belief is indexed as a belief of the person who is writing or speaking, that is of the person who is responsible for it and from whose point of view it is arrived at. The study of the ways in which the authorship of utterances is managed in everyday life in matters other than reportings about one's self is outside the scope of this study, but it has been investigated with his usual flair by Goffman (1981). That much we have abstracted from an examination of the self-concept, the beliefs I have about my Self 2. But there are also beliefs I have about the worth or value of that Self 2 and of what I believe to be its components.

I shall illustrate the forms of self-criticism and self-assessment in just one case, that which has been called 'self-esteem'.[3] There is a substantial and instructively muddled literature on this topic, so that it is an ideal worked example. Since the 1970s, the measurement of self-esteem has become a major preoccupation for psychologists. High and low self-esteem are presented as if they were levels of a property of a person, like their weight, which has different magnitudes in different people. So an individual can have more or less self-esteem than another. Just as the weight of an individual can vary from time to time so a person's self-esteem may be higher or lower at one time rather than another. Some of the current discussions of self-esteem are concerned with whether there are several such attributes, personal, collective and global, ascribable to each person.

In the terminology of experimental psychology, questionnaires are described as 'instruments' for measuring this alleged property. An instrument is a device with a variable property that is causally affected by the property it measures, and the effect on the instrument covaries proportionally to the magnitude of that property. Self-esteem is supposedly a causally efficacious state of a person which would bring about the answers to questionnaires. The 'experimental procedure' only makes sense if it is believed that the beliefs expressed in the answers as a personal narrative are caused by this property and vary with its magnitude. But if we look at the procedures used by those studying self-esteem we find that an alternative explanation for the differences in the answers given is also plausible, one which makes no use of mysterious cognitive properties. According to the alternative view, in answering a questionnaire participants are required to construct a formal narrative in which they are asked to express some of their beliefs about their likes and dislikes. Hence they must draw on certain implicit conventions for talking or writing about oneself to others, such as when it is proper to give a catalogue of one's achievements, whether self-deprecation is in order and so on.

This alternative view brings into question the idea that there is some personal property, 'self-esteem', which is other than and explanatory of people's expressed beliefs about themselves. How do we know the property exists independently of the 'conversational situation' set up in the 'experiment'?

Greater clarity in this area can be reached by looking closely at the way people write about 'self-esteem' and by trying out various alternative formulations of their claims. In the terminology of traditional psychology we have the following (Crocker and Luhtanen, 1990): (a) 'Social identity theory posits that individuals are motivated to achieve or maintain a high level of self-esteem.' This statement could be rephrased something like this: (b) 'People like to think well of themselves.' There is no mention of a personal attribute, 'self-esteem', in (b). If (b) captures the psychological content of (a) then the alleged property 'self-esteem' comes into being simply in the rewriting of (b) in the currently approved form (a). There seem to be no grounds at all for the belief in the existence of self-esteem as a *property* of people. Of course people favour one style of personal discourse over another from time to time and depending on who they are talking to and how things are going and what the point of the conversation might be.

Let us now look at some of the ways that assessments of 'self-esteem' are actually expressed. We note that in commenting upon the characters and behaviour of other people with respect to their sense of their own value and virtue we more often use expressions like 'He's pretty pleased with himself', 'She's so stuck up!', 'Have you ever come across such a swollen ego!', 'She's a shrinking violet', 'He's a modest soul' and so on. Or expressing your own sense of self-worth you usually express yourself indirectly: 'Well, I'll make up a four but I'm not in your class at tennis', 'If you need some help with the language I have a smattering' and so on.

Among the supposed personal attributes that are cited to explain these judgements of self and others are various varieties of self-esteem. The pervasive use of the term 'self-esteem' in modern North American discourse perhaps reflects the growing influence of psychology, through popular literature and the media. Be that as it may we can identify at least the following.

PERSONAL SELF-ESTEEM   This is defined in relation to 'positive personal identity' as 'high personal self-esteem'. Both of these expressions seem to refer to some property that is responsible for a person's evaluations, in some context for some task in hand, of the characteristics that at that moment they believe themselves to have. But as we have seen unless there is a good reason for introducing a new and additional concept, we should use Ockham's razor to eliminate it from our explanations. It is rarely advisable to put a mysterious causal property behind a discursive style or genre, when citation of the conventions for expressing oneself in a certain way is explanatorily sufficient. Looked at this way 'self-esteem' does not refer to a hidden causal attribute of people but sums up my evaluations of the characteristics I believe myself to have. High self-esteem *is* the favourable way I present myself.

COLLECTIVE SELF-ESTEEM   This is derived from the concept of 'social identity',[4] defined by Tajfel as 'that aspect of an individual's self-concept which derives from their knowledge of their membership in a social group (or groups) together with the value and emotional significance attached to that membership' (1981: 255). When we substitute 'beliefs about oneself' for 'self-concept' we get the unsurprising remark that amongst one's beliefs about oneself are the beliefs about which group(s) one belongs to and beliefs about those groups, including some evaluations of them. Not surprisingly it is suggested that one may think something like this: 'I'm okay because I'm a Georgetowner', which only makes sense if one also thinks 'Georgetowners are tops'.

All we have to do to keep our heads in discussing these topics is

to stand fast against reifying aspects of discourse as causal properties of persons. It is a mistake to think that in addition to the things
I think about myself and the groups I belong to there is something
else 'in me', my self-concept. It is a double mistake to think that
included within the self-concept is yet another attribute, my social
identity, which causes me to think and say these things. My social
identity just *is* the things I am inclined to say and do. Again
Ockham's razor can help us avoid inventing imaginary attributes,
such as 'high collective self-esteem', offered by Crocker and
Luhtanen (1990).

GLOBAL SELF-ESTEEM   A third distinction in the alleged generic personal
attribute, 'self-esteem', has been proposed by Tafarodi and Swann
(1995). Starting with the assumption that global self-esteem is 'influ-
enced' (as if it were an independent property of a person) by more
specific self-judgements, they propose to analyse it into a conjunction of two attributes, 'self-liking' and 'self-competence'. The latter
is responsible for the degree to which one expresses a belief in one's
personal abilities and powers. Working through the 'method' section
of Tafarodi and Swann's paper discloses that the authors came close
to realizing that their studies relating questions to answers were
actually revelatory of discursive conventions. They separated the
questions into two groups, those to do with competence and those
to do with what we might call approval. Instead of interpreting their
results as the discovery of a discursive convention they added 'two
new variables' to their analysis. In this way they created two distinct
aspects of 'global self-esteem'. The time consuming running of statistical tests on the answers to their questionnaires was redundant.
Questionnaires are not instruments in the sense that thermometers
are. They do not measure a property. They are invitations to a conversation. The way the conversation goes is governed by discursive
conventions, not by underlying causal processes. Tafarodi and
Swann have found out a little bit more about how people currently
think it proper to talk about themselves, and which aspects of their
lives and characters they feel they ought to emphasize.
      The diagnosis that seems to me most illuminating for explaining
these conceptual misplacements is an unexamined *metaphysical*
assumption of a great deal of contemporary psychology. It is widely
assumed that to be scientific an investigator must offer causal
explanations rather than normative ones. So instead of looking for
rules and conventions for genres of discourse, causally potent but
unobservable properties are invoked. They are supposed to cause
the person who has such a property in some degree to talk and act

in a certain way, say boastfully. Of course questionnaire-based studies will make it look as if there is such a property, since the hidden attribute cannot fail to be correlated with the relevant discursive phenomena it is supposed to explain. It was invented by reifying some aspect of the content of just those phenomena. The step from discursive convention to causal property is very clear in a paper by Crocker et al. (1994), in which they say 'self-esteem is a better predictor of satisfaction with one's life than any objective characteristic of individuals, such as income or age', and they claim that individuals who are high in self-esteem also tend to be less at risk for depression. But the correlate in each case is discursive. So these seeming 'discoveries' are semantic tautologies. There is no point in doing elaborate statistical analyses of answers to questionnaires, since the results are already there in the discursive conventions of this genre of discourse. At best these analyses will bring to light hitherto unnoticed discourse conventions. They cannot bring to light causal relations between unobservable causal properties (self-esteem) and overt discursive effects because there are no such properties.

The target of self-assessments

What can be praised, blamed, traduced, defended and so on? A person. But some of a person's attributes can be singled out for praise and criticism. A person can judge themselves to be worthless or worthy, successful or unsuccessful, but so can other people make that sort of assessment of someone. Is self-assessment a special case of 'other' assessment? How we answer this question depends on the complexity of the Self 3 aspect of personhood. Clearly the criteria must come Vygotsky-wise from the community, but it does not follow that a person's assessment of themselves or of their attributes is simply a reflection or summary of how they understand the assessments that others make of them.

When does an unworthy attribute depreciate the value of a person? In the eyes of others? In their own eyes? The answers will surely be local and hugely various. In some cultures epilepsy is a stigma, in others a mark of divine favour (Taylor and Harrison, 1977). In our culture sufferers from Alzheimer's condition have to fight for public recognition of their surviving capacities against the tendency of their interlocuters to generalize word-finding difficulties into marks of senile decline (Sabat and Harré, 1995). Each case must be investigated within its own milieu and its unique grammar unravelled. But the role of the first person will be characterized by this essential duality, as an index of location in a material world, and an index of moral position in a world of discursive values.

Being aware of oneself is as much a relational phenomenon as being aware of a cow or of an itch. But in this case it is a relation between a person and Self 2. The body centredness of Self 1, indexed by 'I', is of lesser importance than the role of 'I' in taking responsibility for what has been said, for instance in answer to a questionnaire.

Autobiography and the expression of Self 2

The idea of the self picked out as Self 2, in what I have called the 'standard model', is complex in that at any moment in a person's life there are several strands to it. There are the powers and skills, liabilities and other basic psychologically ungrounded dispositions that are sufficiently stable and long lasting to characterize a person. Then there are ephemeral flows of activity, both private and public, in which that person engages, producing thoughts and actions, sometimes but not always displaying repeated structures and forms. The third strand consists of the beliefs a person holds as to their own nature. Autobiography should be the story of one's Self 2, a set of beliefs, offered to oneself and/or others, at some moment in one's life. As such it is itself part of one's Self 2. However the public display of Self 2, or some aspects of it, occurs in the production of what I have called Self 3, a self which can exist in its recognition by relevant others. By and large the expression of Self 2, what I am, occurs in the display of Self 3. There are all sorts of complications possible within this general pattern. My self-concept, that is my beliefs about my Self 2, which are part of that Self 2, may not accurately reflect it. There is also the possibility, made much of by ethologists, that I inadvertently display aspects of my Self 2 which I would prefer to keep private. Then there is deliberate management of public identities to conceal a discredited or discrediting identity of Self 2 that Goffman (1963) describes in *Stigma*.

What then is an autobiography? One might say 'the story of a life as told by the person whose life it is'. A little reflection shows that this common-sense definition is simplistic. For a start one has to acknowledge that there are many stories that one could tell about one's life. Which one reveals the 'real me'? Postmodernists would answer 'None – there is no real me.' I would answer 'All – each reveals an aspect of what I am.' But how are the various stories I might tell about myself tied into a personal bundle, since there is no one story-line that expresses the singularity that is my one and only life? Here is the problem: each person does lead one and only one life. Yet each can tell a multitude of stories. What is the link that makes them *my* stories? To answer that question we must return to the basic layout of concepts in which the singularities of self are expressed. I turn again to what I have called the 'standard model' – one real entity, the embodied person, accompanied by three or more grammatical fictions, created in ways of talking with others, and soliloquizing with oneself, and larded over with all sorts of discursive activities, such as those in which a Self 3 is manifest.

The basic particular or elementary being in the realm of discourse, the subject of all psychological attributions, is the person. But that is an illusion created by the grammar of the first person. Psychological phenomena are attributes of the flow of action, not of the person who created or produced that flow. Persons have no inner *psychological* complexity. The grounding of every psychological skill, capacity and power is some state of or process in or architectural feature of the brain and central nervous system. Persons, considered psychologically, are the point sources from which all else flows. Yet each person has a sense of self, of having singular locations in manifolds of things, persons and events. This, I have argued, is a property of the flow of action that the person engages in with others, privately or publicly. Somehow this multiplicity of 'stuff' I create in my thinking and doing is fused into a complex singularity, that of myself. Each person has beliefs about themselves, about their capacities and skills, and the happenings that constitute their life. This we have called the self-concept, fitting into the 'standard model' as portrayed above. It too is multiple. My beliefs about myself are expressed in soliloquies and stories, in action and refraining from action. There is no one pattern of self-presentation that recurs in all the contexts of my physical and social being. These three aspects of selfhood are related as follows. The self-concept consists of what P believes about P. The stories of my life are indexed with the first person, Self 1, the mathematical 'origin' or centre point of the structure of P's phenomenal experience. This is expressed in the grammar of the discursive presentations of self-concept, which P makes to him or herself and to others, using the word 'I' or its functional equivalent. In this way the Self 3 is constituted from moment to moment, from context to context. The autobiographical 'I' is not a name of the person talking, but indexes the content of autobiographical utterances with the spatio-temporal locations, the world-line, commitments of various sorts entered into, mostly implicitly, by the person who is telling this or that version of their life.

The matter is yet more complicated, in that a person's expression of the singularities of selfhood in the indexical aspects of the grammar of their reflexive discourses is not part of what someone knows about themselves, but is the frame within which people acquire knowledge and come to have beliefs about themselves. The grammatical devices for expressing one's sense of oneself, as one and only one person, define the frame in which the discourses of self are to make sense. We have made use of the whole gamut of 'self' concepts as already discussed, namely 'person', 'sense of self' as Self 1, and 'self-concept' as both beliefs about and a part of the dynamic entity we have called Self 2. But to understand the self in autobiography we need yet another concept, that of the 'presented self', Self 3. In telling one's life, consciously or unconsciously, one is presenting the author of it, oneself, not only as a being with a unique panoply of attributes and a unique history but also as a certain kind of person. Even if the presented attributes do not quite hang together in what is locally regarded as a proper kind of person, nevertheless there is a presentation of the subject of the story as having these or those qualities and capacities, on which the reader or hearer may form a judgement. We have called this pre-sented self 'Self 3', the Goffman self. It is now time to develop the concept further.

Wittgenstein's (1969) insight, that the frame of discourse, its grammar, is not something to which concepts like 'know' should be applied, lies behind this discussion. We cannot properly say we know ourselves as singularities, because that way of speaking is part of a discourse in which concepts like 'making sure', 'gathering evidence' and so on also have a place. But the grammar of selfhood, the sense of singular locations in multiple manifolds, is the frame within which self-reflective discourse is set. My life story is a story about me. And that requires a common subject of predication. The multiplicity of stories in self-concept and the threefold multiplicity of manifolds within which a person has a sense of singular locations are features of the discourse of one and only one person.

As human beings we are located in space and the use of 'I' indexes a point of view with the one and only one body of the speaker. As located in some complex structure of local moral orders the use of 'I' indexes the social force of what has been said with the moral standing of the speaker. But we have seen that as we look into the indexical force of first person expressions in languages other than the Indo-European we find that the simple unitary 'one-person' indexing of English 'I' gives way to complex and subtly contextually shaded indexings of responsibility to groups of which the speaker is, in one of several different senses, a representative or spokesperson. As human beings are located in time, that is their lives are sequences of events embedded in other sequences of events, the use of 'I' as narrator of a life indexes events as belonging in that *continuous* life course. My sense of myself is not as the locus of an event among events, but as the locus of a trajectory in a larger history.

Since the subtle and profound criticisms of Locke's self-as-memory thesis launched during the eighteenth century, above all by Thomas Reid (1788) and Joseph Butler (1736), we must concede that the sense of self as a being in time is not compounded of memories. The gaps that are everwhen present in my recollections, for instance during sleep or by virtue of infant amnesia, do not count, for me, against my sense of being in time. The continuity of my memories, in so far as they do form a coherent life story, cannot be my temporal self, but presuppose it. A thought is a *memory* only if it is a thought of something *I* did or that happened to *me*. In short the English (Indo-European) 'I' expresses continuity of personhood in the very narration that creates it (McAdams, 1997b). It does not express the sequential layout of events. That is presented in the tenses of the relevant verbs. But the psychological history of a person as it is presented by that very person includes not only what did happen, but what might, could, should and would have happened, as well as what will, might or should happen in the future. In using 'I' I am indexing all this material as *this person's*, presupposing 'being in time'.

'Time' in these locutions is not the absolute time of Newtonian physics, but the relevant totality of sequences of events in the environment of the person narrating a life to him or herself or to others. What then is the source of the sense of a continuous being in time? It cannot be the continuity of embodiment since I do not need to reidentify my body every time I wake. Indeed I do not need to reidentify myself. The thesis of this chapter is that my sense of continuity is at root the sense of continuity of a narrative. My life is not a sequence of historical events but a story which I tell myself and which is forever being updated and revised. It is the story of *this person*. As Jansz remarks, 'self-narrative is indeed a *linguistic tool* for providing a person with a sense of stability across time and situations' (1991: 120).

At the same time for every story I tell myself about this person that is myself and that I tell to others, many alternative and complementary stories are possible. This is partly because what I remember is enormously variable, and what I consider consequential or important equally so. Furthermore each story has an actual or poten-tial auditor, and my story for you will be very likely to be somewhat different from my story for someone else. Each of these stories has a measure of veracity and plausibility, though each is likely to cast me, as the story-teller, in a different light.

In presenting the temporal aspect of the sense of self I have emphasized that the singularity of a continuous trajectory in time is not a simple function of the ability to present just one auto-biography, since most people not only can but do have different stories to tell about themselves. Studies of how people tell their lives show that each of us, having a sense of our singularity in the three dimensions of our relations to other embodied persons, experiences our lives retrospectively and prospectively in relation to more than one autobiography. Like positions, autobiographies are functions of the situation and persons to whom they are told, including autobiographical soliloquies which are more often than not directed to some imagined other. Furthermore, as I have pointed out, autobiography has both a backward and a forward direction. There is not only what one is telling oneself about one's past, but also what one is telling oneself about one's future. The future dimension of autobiographical telling is no more unitary than is the past. At each moment one locates one's present self at a moment, this moment, on some suitable world-line, and so estab-lishes one's temporal singularity as a self. But that trajectory may be abandoned for another at some subsequent moment. Whereas in space one has and can only have one self, since one exists in one and only one body, in time one can and does have many selves. How is this possible? Provided we keep the two major senses of 'self' distinct there is no paradox. Self as singularity is different from self as a moment by moment totality of personal attributes, including the current state of the shifting pattern of beliefs (both dispositional and actually then and there being expressed) one has about the person one is. While in relation to the body the former must be singular in non-pathological life stories, the latter is under no such constraint. Whereas the criteria of identity of human bodies are such that at one place in the material world there can exist only one body at one time, say at the moment of an act of speaking, the criteria of identity for events, as they form elements in the temporal trajectory of a life, are potentially multiple. There is always the interpretation that lies between sentences and the statements they are used to make, between actions and the acts they are used to perform. Indeed, the study of real symbolic interaction shows that most linguistic and other symbolic acts are to some degree indeterminate (Pierce and Cronen, 1980). Sometimes the situation requires that we must make them more precise, but we rarely need to bother. There are huge numbers of events in our lives, so the possibility of making different selections for different purposes also makes multiplicity possible.

There are then four ways in which the pronominal systems of languages index one's speech acts with one's sense of being located at some point in some ordered array of persons. Each array is created by the use of a way of ordering a group of people with respect to one of three possible relations, spatial, moral and social. Of course the same people may be arrayed differently according to whether they are seen as arranged in space, as standing in relations of mutual duty and responsibility, or as occupying social positions. Only the first of these arrays is immune to transformation in the shifting patterns of inter- and intrapersonal discourse. Our sense of individuality is also expressed in the telling of stories to ourselves and to others in which the events in which we have a part are related to larger, but potentially multiple orderings of the events of the social and natural world.

Following through Wittgenstein's insight that a grammar of expressive devices could be established only on the basis of a root ethology, we can discern, in the fourfold indexicality of a theoretically complete pronoun system combining grammatical features from many languages, four 'native' capacities: to perceive material things and the states of own bodies, to initiate action, to find a place in a status hierarchy, and to recollect the past and anticipate the future. Non-linguistic forms of expression of an animal's sense of location with respect to the conditions for the exercise of these capacities are well known from primate studies. Just as in the case of pain and other private sensations the substitution of verbal for more primitive expressive devices opens up the possibility for great elaboration and refinement in the very phenomena themselves, by the acquisition of finer grained discriminations that are borne by the richer vocabularies of expression that their discursive transformation allows. But above all it provides us with the power to express ourselves as persons. So too the indexical labelling of discursive acts allows for a similar enrichment. The opening up of research possibilities in this matter by the introduction of concepts like 'positioning', the momentary distribution of rights and duties to speak and act in certain ways with respect to others reciprocally positioned among the persons present in the encounter, has shown particularly the many layered multiplicity of relational systems that can be found immanent in the practices of a cultural group.

What of how people actually tell their personal stories? In a recent collection of studies of autobiographies produced by people from many different social groups of different ages across Europe (Hammerle, 1995) there were many ways in which story-telling differed, not only in style but in content. Above all there was a broad distinction in authorial voice, between '"us" as the narrating subject' and 'I'. Tied in with this is the expression of isolation in contrast not so much to solidarity, but to finding a place in relation to the larger historical events within which one's life is lived. Contrastingly, the personal stories of young people tend to be set almost wholly in the grammatical present. In these studies the complex patterns of the indexical grammar of the first person in expressing a life seem to be clearly displayed.

Narrative

Narratological studies of many discourse genres, including the reporting of scientific experiments (Nash, 1994), the presentation of environmentalist arguments and so on, have revealed the somewhat surprising fact that the overall structure of most tellings and writings exemplifies story-telling conventions rather than patterns of logically ordered premises and conclusions or straightforward chronicles of a 'this happened then that happened' sort. The power to persuade for example seems to reside more in the plausibility of a traditional story-line than it does in the fulfilling of the strict criteria of logic. One of the most powerful analytical devices for revealing the step by step pattern of a discourse is the scheme of Vladimir Propp (1924), originally abstracted from a study of the plots of folk tales. Propp identified more than thirty steps that appear in the plots of traditional stories. Every folk tale draws on some, and always in the order they lie in the ideal totalized plot. Thus the hero suffers a loss, is sent on a quest, receives the help of a powerful being, and eventually triumphs. The same patterns are evident in Greek myths and the Homeric tales. The stories we tell about our own lives and the lives of others, the fictions we elaborate to instruct or amuse, follow a limited number of patterns, patterns the narratologists call 'story-lines'. Not surprisingly one cluster of such patterns can be seen to fit into the Proppian repertoire. As Harriet Hawkins (1990) has argued, classics and trash obey the same dramatic conventions. *Othello* and 'Dallas' share patterns of character relations and of plot. This must surely be a matter of interest to psychologists intent on explaining the unfolding of episodes of human interaction, and in the longer run the development of a life among the developing lives of others.

The strongest narratological thesis that would link the study of the patterns of story-telling to the problem of explaining human action is this:

> Lives are lived according to the same conventions in accordance with which lives are told. (Bruner, 1991)

This thesis has profound consequences for the concept of autobiography. It is the fact that an autobiography has both retrospective and prospective dimensions that makes autobiographical telling a prime subject for psychological research. Not only do we tell ourselves and others versions of the lives we have led, but we tell ourselves and others anticipatory stories that express the pattern of those parts of our lives that are yet to be lived. Shakespeare was very good at presenting this aspect of human psychology. His grasp of this phenomenon appears in such famous soliloquies as that of Richard III over the corpse of his predecessor and that of Hamlet attempting to resolve the existential dilemma at the heart of his struggles to find a way to deal with the murder of his father. Should his autobiography end in suicide or in revenge?

Anticipations of this line of thought can be found in Bruner's (1993) discussion of autobiography, as well as explicitly in more recent works. The most systematic attempt to develop a narration-based psychology of persons has been made by McAdams (1996). Redrawing the Meadian distinction between the 'I' and the 'me' McAdams refers to the process of 'selfing', of narrating experience to create a self, 'whereas the Me may be viewed as the self that the I constructs' (1996: 295). This fits snugly onto my terminology in which the agentic person is McAdams's 'I', and the 'Me' is the complex pattern of interweaving productions of psychological phenomena I have called Self 2 and Self 3.

At first glance the concept of autobiography could hardly seem more innocent of complications. It is just the story of my life as told by me, from my point of view. Autobiographies may differ in degree of candour, and self-absorption, but who is the best authority on what I did and why I did it other than myself? But reflection on the matter, and empirical studies of autobiographical telling, quickly disclose all sorts of complexities.

An autobiography is above all a narrative, and in each age narrative genres have their own conventions. Caesar's *Gallic wars* and St Augustine's *Confessions* share some narrative conventions but not others. Both are self-exculpatory. But Caesar wrote *The Gallic wars* as the plain tale of a bluff soldier (however disingenuous that style may appear to us). He begins his 'simple tale' thus: *Gallia est omnis divisa in partes tres*, as boring a geographical observation as one is likely ever to encounter. However the great 'one-liner' *veni, vidi, vici* is more appropriate to the implicit drama of the narrative. St Augustine's psychological epic is as much a story of the 'inward-ness' of a soul at odds with itself as it is of public action. It could hardly be more different from the style of Caesar's fragment of autobiography.

But an autobiography is a narrative in the first person. As I have pointed out, grammatical studies show the first person is a complex indexical device expressing at least four aspects of the user's sense of self, as a singularity in arrays of other people, ordered by various and shifting sets of relations, spatial, temporal, moral and social.

An autobiography is not just one story, my story, told to some generic and anonymous listener or reader. The written tale is just one of the autobiographies that a person did tell or that they could have constructed. Research into autobiographical telling in every-day life discloses how the quality, value, detail and arrangement of the episodes recounted depends on the person to whom the tale is told, the context of the telling and the aim of the story-teller at that moment in the telling of it. Everyone has a multiplicity of potential autobiographies, though few may see the light of day. That multi-plicity is evident in the practice of retrospective telling. But, as I pointed out above, at least as important in the everyday practice of autobiography is the prospective telling, how my life is going to evolve, in the next hour, the next day, in the next decade, and in eternity. Autobiography not only reports and interprets action, it shapes action.

Learning to remember

Remembering is a cognitive/discursive skill, not a native endow-ment. In learning to sort out the verisimilitudinous from the fan-tastic, memory from imagination, there are no intrinsic clues in the thoughts themselves (Neisser and Fuvish, 1994). Most psycho-logical studies of remembering make use of 'subjects' for whom this distinction is already in place. Even in studies of 'infant amnesia' the adult capacity of the psychologist seems to be presumed in the methodology, since what happened, what was remembered and what was forgotten by the neonate or the infant, are defined within adult categories. At some point in development 'remembering' as a cognitive skill must have been in the 'zone of proximal develop-ment'. What were the discursive interactions among adults and infant that established memory?

To find a clue to what might be looked for in the conversations that establish this skill one might draw on studies of collective remembering as we find it among groups of adults. Pioneering work in adapting the concepts of adult collective remembering to the memorial interactions between mothers and children has been done by Middleton and Edwards (1990: Chapter 2, from which the following quotations are taken). The standpoint of discursive psychology is clearly defined as follows:

> Rather than looking at how conversational competence is represented cognitively, we are interested in how cognition is represented in ordinary conversation. As far as memory is concerned, the aim is not to specify how putative mental models might represent knowledge and experience, but rather how people represent their past, how they construct versions of events when talking about them.

It is when engaging in such practices that children come to acquire the skill of establishing each his or her own past, as a discursive competence. In these interactions the idea of 'my memories' and 'my past' are developed. Here is a transcript of a brief segment of a memorial conversation, constructed around a photograph:

Mother:	oh look/there's where we went to the riding stables wasn't it?
Paul:	yeh/er er
Mother:	you were trying to reach up and stroke that horse
Paul:	where? [*laughs*]
Mother:	you don't look very happy though
Paul:	because I thought I was going to fall off

Such conversations 'are used by parents as opportunities for marking past events as significant, recalling children's reactions and relationships, cueing the children to remember them, providing descriptions in terms of which those rememberings could be couched and providing all sorts of *contextual* reminiscences' (1990: 39). As the authors say, these studies and others like them suggest 'the plausibility of a dialogical basis for thought . . . for an origin of self-consciousness, metacognitive and rationalized remembering, from within communicative pragmatics – from within children's conversations and arguments'.

Narration in Kawi

Middleton and Edwards's studies suggest that the forms of remembering are identical to the grammars of discourses of remembering, realized in conversations about the past. We can see a little of the possibilities of variety in memorial conversations in the pronominal grammar of Kawi, the classical language of Java.

I have described the Kawi grammar of the first person in the discussion of the grammar of self-presentational discourse in Chapter Three. We must return to it at this point to see how the possibility of inflecting the first person for tense bears upon the patterns of narration of a life or part of a life. There is no need to tell a story in the order in which the events narrated happened. Temporally inflected pronouns always reveal the temporal relations of autobiographical events to the moments of the utterance of their descriptions. Stories can follow more dramatic narrative conventions, organized according to such principles as significance for the narration as a whole. Kawi stories do not need to be presented in the 'X *then* Y *then* Z' format.

Of course autobiographies told in an Indo-European language do not need to adopt that layout either. For example the autobiography of Assata Shakur (1987) (a.k.a. Joanne Chesimard) begins with a dramatic event, the killing of a policeman, around which the tale unfolds, in such a way that events that occurred before that key moment are able to be seen as its precursors and those that occurred later as its consequents. Tense and calendrical marking permit this style very well. However, in the informal narrations of everyday life, a combination of these patterns occurs very frequently. The story I tell opens with a dramatic event, and then continues in a time ordered pattern around it, moving back and forth from past to present, enlarging each as it unfolds.

Conclusion

I am well aware of the narrow range of examples and the restricted references to the extensive and diverse literature on both self-description and assessment and autobiographical story-telling. For instance I have not discussed the important phenomenon of the emotion displays of judgements of self-assessment (Harré and Parrott, 1997). The point of this chapter is not to survey the literature nor to summarize the extensive empirical and theoretical studies in this domain, but to demonstrate the thesis of the discursive construction of personal psychological attributes and the role of the first person in their expression. I have tried to show that self-esteem is not a standing property of a person, causing certain kinds of answers to questions and certain kinds of behavioural manifestations, related to the degree or strength of the alleged attribute. Rather, like all such attributes, it is a property of the flow of personal action, context dependent and jointly produced. In the framework of the standard model, Person {Self 1, Self 2, Self 3} these attributes are assigned to the person regarded as the prime mover in the production of the flow of talk and action, and give the appearance of standing or permanent properties, aspects of Self 2. But, as we have seen, they are produced in the course of the *ad hoc* genesis of one of the repertoire of Selves 3 that socially competent people have mastered.

In a similar way autobiographical stories, presented as the work of memory, are also demonstrations of aspects of Self 3, indexed with first person authority, as amongst the permanent features of Self 2, the total, temporally extended, attributes of a living person. Autobiography is not simply reporting one's well remembered past. Life stories are narratives, and as such depend for their structure as much on the conventions for narrating lives as the historical verisimilitude of their accounts of the events they describe. From a psychological point of view one's effective past is not what happened to one, but which fragment of autobiography is salient at some particular juncture in one's life. Since one's life is lived and told with others, autobiographical story-telling, like all forms of memory work, is essentially social, produced dialogically (Taylor, 1991). We have also seen how the ways lives are told depend in part on grammatical resources of tenses and pronoun systems, through which the events described as indexed as happenings in the life of the speaker. In the next chapter I shall take up the question of autobiographical norms and the possibility of pathological autobiographies.

Notes

1 For a comprehensive survey of 'positioning' see van Langenhove and Harré (1991).

2 It should hardly need saying that what I know or believe about my past is not identical with what I remember about it.

3 I am grateful to Heather Fath for finding examples of the current literature on self-esteem.

4 We note here the recent use of the word 'identity' in the sense of the logician's 'qualitative identity', the respects in which something is similar to something else. As I noted in Chapter One this sense has become well established, for example in such expressions as 'identity politics'.

CHAPTER SEVEN

Diversities and Multiplicities of Self

'Identity', for my Polish friends, is not a category of daily thought, not an entity etched in their minds in high relief. My American friends watch the vicissitudes of their identity carefully: now it's firm, now it's dissolving, now it's going through flux and change . . . They see themselves as pilgrims of internal progress, heroes and heroines in a psychic drama. . . . For my Polish friends, an identity, or a character, is something one simply has . . . introspection is a process of dwelling on what one has experienced, rather than a means of systematic analysis or self reform.

E. Hoffman, *Lost in translation*

In what does the unity of a single life consist? The answer is that its unity is the unity of a narrative embodied in a single life.

Alistair MacIntyre, *After virtue*

What is it like to be someone else? The human resource of language joins the public realm of interpersonal and material interaction with the private realm of thought. These personal realms are open to one another not only by virtue of the power of language to report on how things are but more importantly by its power to express publicly how it is with someone privately, from a person's own point of view. Looking at the grammars as well as the semantics of expressive uses of language reveals the role of pronouns and functionally equivalent inflexions in expressing the structure of experience, as just this person's. From the discursive point of view singularities of self are not to be explained as the consequence of the existence of a Cartesian ego, a unique person substance. Rather they are patterns of discourse, the spatio-temporal uniqueness of personal embodiment anchoring expression to person through the indexicality of the personal pronouns. Pathologies of self are both aspects of and expressed in the form of pathologies of discourse. In certain cases at least it seems reasonable to claim that correction of such pathologies might be achieved by the relearning of locally valid grammars. This seems to have been Morton Prince's (1905) technique when faced with the pathological grammar of Miss Beauchamp's presentation of herself as three different people.

In my tidied-up 'grammar' of discourses of the self, the 'standard model', there are four main concepts in play: 'person' (the unique being I am to myself and others); 'Self 1', the centre or 'origin' of relational properties that make up my field of perception and action; 'Self 2', the totality of attributes both ephemeral and enduring of the person I am, including my self-concept, the beliefs I have about the characteristics I believe I have as a person including my life history, and 'Self 3', the personal characteristics I display to others. The 'self' of self-presentation is a doublet, including 'personality' and 'character'. The analysis I have presented shows I believe that while 'person' is a genuine substantive, picking out a category of real entities, for which questions of numerical and qualitative identity call for criteria of much the same sort as we use for simple material entities, the three 'selves' are ontologically quite different. Though phrases like 'the saturated self' and 'the dialogical self' are to be found throughout the literature, both academic and popular, selves are not entities, not substances of any kind. These expressions refer to attributes of the flow of personal action, and to the skills, powers and dispositions a person must have so to act. As entities, Self 1, Self 2 and Self 3 are fictions, though indispensable fictions. As I have argued in other places (Harré, 1983) they have something of the character of theoretical concepts in the physical sciences, such as the gravitational field. The public concept of 'person' seems to serve as a source for local versions of the triad of 'self' concepts. Indeed this would be just what one would expect, if the acquisition of a mind as an ordered pattern of thought were accomplished dialogically in the manner described by Vygotsky (1962).

A human being, in normal circumstances, can be only one person, and perceive and act from just one point of view in space and time, summed into a life trajectory as a thing amongst things. But what about people's skills and dispositions that are a large part of Self 2? And what about those patterns in the flow of action that we pick out as aspects of ourselves? What room is there for differences in the way these characteristics of human beings are manifested? There might be differences within the life of a person, but there might also be differences across generations, across cultures, across ages and across genders. I shall call these differences 'diversities'. It might be that individual diversity ties in with cultural diversity, in that some categories of persons are accorded more licence in displays of difference. It might be that some categories of persons find themselves with greater diversity in their lives in some of these characteristics than they would wish.

However there is another possibility. It may that a human being incorporates, that is embodies, more than one person, either contemporaneously as in multiple personality disorder (hereafter MPD), or serially as in certain kinds of amnesia.[1] While it is logically impossible for someone to be at the same time human and have more than one Self 1, it may be that at least some of their personal attributes and powers, particularly as these are expressed in momentary sets of reflexive beliefs and autobiographical stories, are sufficiently different for it to make sense to say that this person has more than one Self 2 (Hacking, 1995). Indeed it may be that in different degrees everyone has more than one Self 2. As to the self of self-presentation, it has long been established, if anything more than common sense were needed, that each person has a repertoire of Selves 3, called forth on different occasions and in dialogue with different people.[2] I shall refer to the fact that people display more than one personality, and that people have more than one story of their lives, as 'multi-plicity'.

I shall be working with the general principle that diversity becomes pathology when certain normative boundaries are violated, and in most societies these boundaries are quite strict. The case of multiplicity is more difficult in that while there are normative boundaries they are more open than the boundaries of diversity. Some degree of multiplicity is necessary to living well, so that excessive rigidity as well as too labile a self are both on the boundaries of acceptability.

Assessment of individual lives as displaying pathologies of self is common enough. But there has also been a place for assessment of pathology in the comparison of cultures, though the difficulty of defending norms for all of humankind is notorious. Often the notions of 'primitive', 'backward', 'undeveloped', and so on play the role of pathological characteristics, to be remedied or put right. The weaknesses of such judgements have been brought out by Wittgenstein in his *Remarks on Frazer's golden bough* (1979), from which we will draw some of the leading arguments.

The dimensions of possible diversity in selfhood stand out in this catalogue. It would be very surprising indeed if there were not great differences in how people in different cultures think of themselves, in the sense of their self-concepts, what was important, fateful and so on. It would also be very surprising if there were not great differences in the kinds of personality and character that were valued and so encouraged, from tribe to tribe. But it would be very surprising if the concept of person diverged much from that known amongst ourselves, and even more surprising if the Selves 1 of other cultures shed our body-centred point of view in perception. Within the indexicalities of the first person, spatio-temporal location must surely be universal. But we have good reason to believe that there are great differences in the degree to which a person's actions are taken by that person and others to be their sole responsibility. If the pathological is a difference between what the local norms prescribe and what someone does, there will be pathologies that stem from individual variations from standard discursive presentations, and there will be those which stem from interpersonal variations from standard discursive conventions.

Multiplicity

The double singularity principle

Using the simple terminology of Self 1 for singularity of point of view and Self 3 for the publicly presented self, and assuming there is an interplay between them, it is possible to spell out a pair of locally powerful normative constraints on how a person should be. Only those human beings who display a singular, continuous Self 1 as an aspect of whatever Self 3 they may from moment to moment be presenting are to be counted as psychologically normal, perhaps even as persons properly so called. Disruptions of the Self 1 singularity, such as fugue and amnesia,[3] and so on, are to be counted as disorders. Only those human beings who display or present a singular, harmonious, and coherent Self 3 are to be counted as morally acceptable. Thus dissimulation, machiavellianism, vacillation, insincerity, and hypocrisy are to be counted as vices. The fusion of psychological and moral standards for proper personhood I shall call the 'double singularity principle' (DSP). The principle is not an inductive generalization of the observable behaviour of human beings. It is a normative principle serving to delineate the boundaries of what it is to count as a proper person. Deviations from either singularity are to be taken as failings, to be remedied in the one case by reform and in the other by cure. Failings and moral deficits do not count as empirical refutations of the principle. Picking up the general distinction between 'frame' and 'picture', made famous by Wittgenstein, we could say that the double singularity principle makes explicit part of the frame within which many tribes of people live out their lives. This principle melds constraints on propriety drawn from two distinct but interpenetrating systems of norms: the social/medical and the moral.

Normative constraints can be challenged. It might be argued that life ought not to be ordered in accordance with the double singularity principle. The principle might be challenged in the particular form that it takes in a locally defined culture. Yet, we can hardly maintain our humanity unless we frame our lives within the DSP, even if the local criteria of health and/or morality are objectionable, according to some higher principles. The principle may be challenged in a more fundamental fashion, in that the very idea of personal singularity in either the social/medical mode or the moral mode is defective according to some broader or higher conception of how life should be lived. Challenges are the more effective when they are grounded in some real or presumed real forms of life, of other places and other times. The force of the principle can be explored through an analysis of an important set of challenges to its authority and hegemony. The challenges I have in mind come from feminist authors of a poststructuralist bent.

Challenges to the double singularity principle

One kind of challenge comes from Dorothy Smith (1987). Smith describes a woman's experience as typified by a 'bifurcated consciousness'. A woman's mind consists of 'two modes of consciousness that could not coexist with one another'. At a first reading, this observation seems to make no sense. Smith's state of mind could not literally be that of bifurcated consciousness, otherwise she would not be able to realize that she remembered, planned, or feared different things in different circumstances. Smith, however, does provide a gloss in which the two modes are explained as being 'different organizations of memory, attention, relevances and objectives, and even different presences'. If we take 'presence' to mean something like a Goffmanesque presentation of Self 3, it is clear that what I have called the Self 1, the embodied point of view, must have been conserved for Smith throughout her life. Her memory of the events of her one life is unimpaired. Her sense of continuous self-embodiment is not in question. But from time to time she entertains thoughts and undertakes patterns of action that either could not be performed together or that, though thought together, were mutually contradictory. It is easy to see that her identity as a person is robust and conserved as a singularity given that Smith's account of her 'contradictory' life depends on all the thoughts, episodes, and so on being indexed with the unique and singular spatio-temporal trajectory and moral standing of their author as an embodied being. There is no doubt that her sense of personal identity in the philosopher's sense is unimpaired and persists through sequences of the presentation of very different Selves 3 and the possession of a complex, many layered Self 2, about which she has had a variety of different beliefs from time to time.

It is clear from the tone of Smith's writings that she regards this kind of multiplicity as unsatisfactory, as if relative to some unspecified level of the tidy life, the ordinary lives of women (and many men too fit her description only too well) ought to be remedied. Smith's writings are a challenge to multiplicity.

Miss Beauchamp and Eve White: multiple personality disorder

If Smith seems to deplore an over-abundance of Selves 3 and a overly complex Self 2, by some standard of desirable normality, the contemporary attitude to the kind of multiplicities of self described by Morton Prince (1905) and Thigpen and Cleckley (1957) implies that the existence of more than one person in the one body is a condition to be remedied. If unique embodiment is a constitutive condition for personhood and the Self 1 is an ontological reflection of the spatio-temporal indexicality of the grammar of the first person, then multiplicity of the embodied *person* marks a sharp break with the human form of life.

The indexical properties of first person pronouns are centred round the unique spatial location of the embodied speaker. The structure of the perceptual field seems to carry considerable weight in the sense of self, much more weight than the temporal dimension of the sense of a life in time. This pattern of priorities could be summed up in the principle: one person per body and one body per person. Seeming to run counter to this principle are cases of multiple personality. These need to be looked at very closely to see how the seeming violation of the principle comes about. In this examination we shall come to a view about the nature of the phenomenon, that denies some of the more extravagant interpretations.

The phenomenon was first described in detail by Morton Prince (1905) and popularized by Thigpen and Cleckley (1957). Prince's patient was a young woman, Miss Beauchamp. Under hypnosis she began to address remarks to and about herself, as if from the point of view of someone else. Later, as her condition developed she would address comments from the point of view of yet another 'person'. Prince called these 'speakers' BI, BII and BIII. BII began to take on personhood as a characteristic pattern of pronoun usage marked a complementarity of address between her and BI, Miss Beauchamp proper. The 'I' – 'you' pair shifted indexical reference from Miss Beauchamp to her alter ego, who, it emerged, had a distinctive proper name, first 'Chris' (Miss Beauchamp's name was Christine) and later 'Sally'. The attitudes and characters of Miss Beauchamp's two 'selves' as 'persons' were very different. BI was polite and conventional, while BII was mischievous and provocative. A fourth 'person' eventually appeared in the form of yet another speaking standpoint. The third 'voice', referred to by BII as 'The Idiot', differed in attitudes and character from the other two. How did Morton Prince identify BI, BIII and BIV as distinct persons?

There seem to have been three main criteria at work in his analysis. There was first the pronominal usages which rested upon the indexical grammar of English, but called into question the force of the criterion of singular embodiment. This deviation was grounded, in Prince's analysis, in asymmetries in the knowledge displayed by each voice. The discourses marked by the second and third 'voice' displayed knowledge of the life and thoughts of BI while that of BI did not show any knowledge of what BIV had said and done. More important still was a memory criterion, used very much in the manner of Locke. Chris/Sally was treated as the manifestation of a person because her memory was 'continuous for the times of her own previous existence' (Prince, 1905: 33). And 'BIV remembers only that part of the episode in which she herself took part. She has no recollection of the scenes when BI and Sally were present' (1905: 211). The criterial force of memory is evident in Prince's description of the moment of cure: 'When Miss Beauchamp became possessed of the memories of IV, they awakened within her a consciousness not only of IV's doings, but of the thoughts, the feelings, and the emotions by which IV had been dominated' (1905: 407). The role pronouns play in all this becomes very clear in Prince's report of how the cure was effected. It came about by the incorporation of the memories of each voice within a common autobiography, that is as a temporally coherent and continuous story as indexed by the pronoun 'I'. Tying some recollections to 'you' and 'she' had ceased. From the point of view of the overall analysis of this book, Prince's description of the pathology and its cure highlights the internal or conceptual relation between autobiography and personhood, in that when Self 2, the facts about a person, are distributed through more than one life story, we are inclined to assign them to more than one person, despite the uniqueness and singularity of the embodiment of the various voices.

The importance of the multiplicity of autobiography in the diagnosis of dissociated personality as multiple personhood is confirmed in Thigpen and Cleckley's classic *The three faces of Eve* (1957). It is an account of the distinctive modes of self-presentation adopted by a young woman to whom they gave the pseudonym 'Eve White'. A quiet and seemingly moderately contented housewife and mother, she was being treated for severe headaches, when one day she suddenly began to talk in a wholly different manner, displaying a quite different personality. It appeared that a little earlier, on a visit to a relative, she had quarrelled violently with her husband, refusing to return home. But when she did come back she denied all memory of the affair. To simplify the story it emerged that when acting in this new style she did recollect these violent events. Just as Miss Beauchamp's alter ego had a different name, so the alternate called herself by her maiden name and sometimes denied ever having been married. And just as in the Prince case, a third voice came to be heard, calling itself 'Jane'. After Eve divorced White, her threefold discourse subsided quickly into a continuous and coherent pattern of autobiographical tellings. How are these multiple ways of talking to be interpreted? Are they, as we might surmise, at first acquaintance, expressions of independent persons, so that each of the speakers has its own sense of self, and so is genuinely multiple and each exists as a person? We should call this the 'radical interpretation'. Yet there are two features of this mode of speaking that militate against that interpretation.

The reported discourses are full of cross-references, particularly when the third voice enters the scene. Miss Beauchamp, Sally and the third voice 'know', though not fully, what the others think and do. In a sense then, while memory is divided among the fragments of autobiography, it is not like fugue, strictly separated into three non-overlapping compartments. In a sense there is just one autobiography, though it is fragmented enough to encourage Prince and others to give the pronominal aspects of personhood, as manifested in the diversities of Self 2, priority over singular embodiment as manifested in the stability of Self 1, the embodied point of view. The second feature that counts against the radical interpretation is the role that this manner of speaking plays in the lives of those who manifest it. It seems above all to be used as a defence, particularly against attributions of responsibility and blame. An alternative, more 'conservative' interpretation would treat the adoption of this manner of speaking as a discursive strategy, found useful in early childhood, and confirmed in adulthood as a way of avoiding all sorts of discomforts.

A very curious feature of MPD that also tends to confirm the conservative interpretation is that it is diagnosed only in the United States. It may be that the discursive strategy, and its diagnosis as a 'condition' rather than a device, go hand in hand. There seems to be something *ad hoc* about a device (a mere device) where there is something necessary about a syndrome that requires 'diagnosis'. It has been said (Fahy, as reported by Wessley, 1993) that psychiatrists, quite inadvertently, have been partly responsible for bringing forth this strategy, particularly, it seems, by falling in with the use of different names for each autobiographical 'voice'. If the strategy is successful both in establishing an interest in the eyes of psychiatrists and in defending the speaker against various kinds of troubles it is not hard to explain why it develops and persists (Aldridge-Lewis, 1990). Thigpen and Cleckley have reported that after their book came out they received a flood of requests for consultations, with the evident intention of the applicants to avail themselves of the diagnosis of MPD. If MPD is publicly presented as a condition and not revealed as a useful discursive strategy then responsibility and blame are necessarily deflected. You cannot reprimand a paraplegic for not running across the street to save a dog from being hit by a car.

Our analysis shows that the spatial integrity of the embodied person as having one location in the manifold of things is preserved through the shifting pattern of responsibility managed by the diversified structure of the pronoun grammar such persons have recourse to. It is also clear that there are complicated patterns of cross-reference between the bodies of knowledge that each speaking voice presents as information that it has of the lives of the other voices. This suggests that a generic lifeline is preserved since we can only explain the cross-referencing as based on shared memory, whether the trio are willing to explicate it as such or not. But there are indeed three different story-lines, each with its appropriate voice, through which the remembered events of one person's life are realigned into three clusters, and dignified 'ontologically' by two or more of these narrative voices being assigned a proper name.

The question of shared memory has become central to discussions of MPD. In the revised third edition of the DSM (American Psychiatric Association, 1987) the 'official' definition of MPD runs as follows:

A The existence within the person of two or more distinct personalities or personality states (each with its own relatively enduring pattern of perceiving, relating to, and thinking about the environment and self).

B At least two of these personalities or personality states recurrently take full control of the person's behavior.

There are several striking features of these criteria. 'Personality' is assumed to lie 'within the person', rather than an aspect of a Self 3, an invariant in the pattern of a person's actions. 'Person' and 'personality' are used in unusual ways. In received English a person is the 'author' of his or her behaviour, and 'personality' is a facet of that behaviour. In the above criteria 'personality' is doing duty for 'person', while the word 'person' is used in quite an opaque way. Another striking feature of this way of distinguishing a genuinely pathological state from extremes of the normal spectrum of socially skilled flexibility in self-presentation is the absence of any reference to memory, and to Locke's contentious thesis of a deep tie between reach of memory and selfhood.

The emphasis, we can see from our 'grammatical' stance, is on the temporal indexicality of the first person. If we tie 'normality' to singularity of spatial indexicality, locating the point of view of perceiver and actor in the point of embodiment of the speaker in an array of embodied speakers, and allow a measure of multiplicity to Self 2 and Self 3, then the only remaining dimension on which there might be multiplicity is that of autobiography, the story a person tells about their lives, indexed to their personal temporal 'world-line'. We do allow and even expect some multiplicity of stories within a single life provided they are told by the same narrator. However, we do not allow, so it seems from the DSM-III-R, a multiplicity of story-tellers, each occupying its own segment of *lived* time. How do we know that there are several narrators embodied in the one spatially unique body? By the memory criterion! How do the objections to Lockean use of this criterion to determine selfhood fit into the 'official' account of MPD? They would seem seriously to challenge it.

Degrees of diversity within the 'standard model'

Commentary on the challenge at level 1

In Strawson's (1959) account of persons as basic particulars, the practices of identifying and individuating persons as singularities are rooted in the singular material bodies in which persons are usually one to one embodied. Only as a persisting material being can a person be identified and reidentified by others. The principle of non-contradiction applies strictly, that is, grammatically, to material beings and their material attributes, so the 'contradictory self' cannot be a Strawsonian person. It is noteworthy that, in Strawson's treatment, it is the spatio-temporal singularity of each person's unique perceptual point of view that fixes limits to the resolution of 'contradictory experience.' It cannot, it seems, undercut the material singularity of the embodied person.

If 'knowing' is, like most other important psychological concepts, used both for a complex pattern of discursive and practical skills and for the ephemeral products both private and public of exercising these skills, a solution to the first level of attack on the double singularity thesis might take the following form. Person is to be mapped on to one term of the traditional polar concept 'knower'–'known' and the actively produced attributes that contribute to Selves 2 and 3 on to the complementary polar concept 'known'. This is in keeping with the thesis argued for in earlier chapters that perception and other 'epistemic' phenomena are one and all relational, tying a person to something other than the person, be it perceptual or proprioceptual. The Self 1 is the structural 'origin' of the total set of such knowing relations.

The actual multiplicity of Selves 3 can be made tolerable *ad hoc*. They could be temporarily successive as in the lives of those to whom the concept of 'working mother' applies. They could form a hierarchy as in the lives of those to whom the concept 'successful candidate for sex-reassignment surgery' can be applied. Or to one whose personal multiplicity of Selves 3 included 'timid accountant' Monday to Friday and 'daring mountaineer' on Saturday and Sunday. Selves 3 make their appearance and perhaps exist only in the contextually and historically various discursive and material practices a skilled human being can produce. A good deal of multiplicity is tolerated by every healthy human being, and always has been. Think of the social and personal necessities of the immigrant communities that have emerged for millennia on the shores of every continent, and by internal migration within. The Huguenot migrant, for a generation or two, kept to French ways within the family circle and entered fully and successfully into the host societies typical of such people. Think of the strange double and triple lives of the Sicilian immigrants into the United States, with their secret selves and their public displays as all-American social beings.[4]

The grammatical conditions for Smith to present her case publicly include acceptance of the complex rules for the use of indexical expressions, particularly for the iterated first person. But this is the very grammar that poststructuralist, feminist linguists must declare off limits. Smith can only state her claim by subverting it, in that the

grammatical forms that she must choose are those from the reification of which the person/self dichotomy arises and in which the
necessary singularity of the narrator's voice is constituted. But this
is the very singularity her discourse is directed at denying. If she is
to declare her *self* contradictory as the *many* who are known, she
must adopt the voice of the non-contradictory narrator as the *one*
who knows. So she does not have a bifurcated consciousness.

What were the material conditions for the intelligibility of her
claim that she suffered from multiple, because mutually incompatible, Selves 2 and perhaps Selves 3 as well? They are not the least bit
like the material conditions under which Morton Prince surmised
that Miss Beauchamp was a multiplicity of persons. Dorothy Smith,
the singular person, remembers very well both taking her children
to the park and discussing sociology with her (male) colleagues. The
phenomenological conditions include that she be aware that she is
simultaneously or successively engaged in the presentation of
herself according to diverse criteria for a proper display of personhood. Smith exists and functions both as a singularity, that is as an
embodied person, the one who observes and remembers, and as a
multiplicity, the ones who are observed and whose diverse activities
are remembered. In short, Smith is and must be the one person,
whose point of view on the world is expressed in the multiple ways
she views herself. The whole person, the Strawsonian person, and
the material conditions for that concept to have application can be
summed up as 'singular embodiment.'

The reflexivity that appears in this analysis is neither paradoxical
nor particularly the preserve of persecuted woman. The selves that
Dorothy Smith conjures up are grammatical fictions. There is just
one Dorothy Smith and the many things she does. Dorothy Smith,
the 'knower,' is not another entity, an ego, or something of the sort;
nor are the 'knowns', as clusters of incompatible actions and sets of
incompatible beliefs, entities either. There are just people, including
female people, among whom is Dorothy Smith. There is what they
have done and their reports of what they have done, their beliefs
about themselves and the reports of those beliefs.

Multiplicity as diversity

The structure that I have expressed as Person–{Self 1, Self 2, Self 3}
permits all sorts of variations. Feminist writings have drawn attention to the extent that both Self 2 and Self 3 are relationally and sit-
uationally diverse. This makes for a multiplicity at the heart of
personhood, a multiplicity which, though it has the appearance of

a multitude of 'beings', is essentially a manifold of discourses, over-lapping and diverging. But they are tales told by one and the same person. It is when the indexical force of the first person seems to fray into several strands that diversity becomes pathology. To demonstrate the degree of non-pathological diversity of multiple Selves 2 and 3, as displays produced by one and the same person, we can find no better example than Japanese personhood.

The local character of standards of normality is as much to be seen in matters of selfhood as in matters of cuisine. The case of Japanese selfhood is invaluable both in helping us to free ourselves from the illusion that only the self-structure of Protestant indi-vidualism is normal, and in illustrating one of the ways that multi-plicity in selfhood is a cultural norm.

The Japanese sense of self has been a topic of great interest to psy-chologists since the Second World War. Ruth Benedict's (1946) famous book set the agenda for many decades. It was based on the use of Western categories to reveal a psychology of contradictions. The problem for psychologists was to understand how these con-tradictions were resolved and surmounted. More recent scholar-ship, much more closely tied to the realities of Japanese life,[5] has revealed a structure of personhood no more but no less complex than that of other human beings, but differing greatly in the degree to which personal attributes are continuously created and re-created in adult life. It is as if a Vygotskian 'psychological symbio-sis' of great complexity characterized the whole of life. There is a plethora of literature on this topic, well summarized in a recent col-lection (Rosenberger, 1992) on which I shall draw in this section.

I have assumed throughout this book that the fourfold conceptual structure, Person–{Self 1, Self 2, Self 3}, is a universal analytical tool with which to understand the thought ways and personhood of all members of our species (Spiro, 1993). Within this framework the question for me is 'How does one map cultural differences, such as those displayed in the Japanese form of life, onto the scheme?' Let us first survey Rosenberger's summing up of the most recent work in this field. She identifies four points of importance:

1 It [recent studies] suggests that [Japanese] thinking will emphasise indexing rather than referencing . . . indexing multiple places along a range of meanings is more important to Japanese than defining oneself consistently according to fixed meanings.

2 A multiple concept of self implies the idea that power is inherent in the creations of selfhood. If self is not essential, but depends for mean-ings on differences and likenesses with other selves . . . then power in interrelations is inevitable.

3 These multiple identities concern not only power but meaning as well
   ... as people relate in multiple ways to people of different ages,
   genders ... to various arrangements of nature ... to changing
   demands of the political economy, they create larger patterns that
   carry cultural meanings important to their ongoing understandings
   of society and the universe.
4 A conception of self as multiple aims toward purity as a goal to be
   reached through dissolving dualities ... the ultimate aim of multiplicity: entry into a space beyond difference, at the level of the cosmos
   rather than self or the social. (1992: 16)

Where do we find singularity and where multiplicity in the type
of person-hood sketched in this summary? Plainly in Japan as elsewhere each human organism is just one person. Furthermore there
is no suggestion that changing relations with others, with the shifting forms of nature in the seasons, and with the structures of the
world of work induce fugue or other dissociations of Self 1, the
point of view from which each embodied person perceives and
acts on the world. However each person in Japanese society,
according to the above, not only has a shifting and ephemeral self-
concept, beliefs about their personal attributes or Self 2, but
because of the relational character of those attributes, also has a
shifting, labile and ephemeral Self 2, attributes other than a
person's beliefs about his or her attributes. Consequentially we
would expect there to be even more situational variability in the
presented self, Self 3, in the lives of individual Japanese than we
find amongst ourselves.

   The question of how personhood differs from place to place and
time to time has been the subject of a vigorous recent debate,
sparked by the well known paper of Markus and Kitayama (1991).
In that paper the authors tie together a psychological typology of
Selves 2 with a sociological typology of societies and (if we can
allow ourselves the word) 'cultures'. The psychological typology
distinguishes 'independent' from 'interdependent' people. The
psychological typology is spelled out in the contrast between the
'autonomous, independent person' given to 'expressing one's
unique configuration of needs, rights and capacities' (1991: 8) and
the 'interdependent construal of self' in which other people
'become an integral part of the setting, situation or the context to
which the self is connected, fitted and assimilated' (1991: 10). All
this is crossed with a distinction between 'inner', meaning roughly
'private', and 'outer', meaning roughly 'public'. The authors seem
to assume that 'the public self [Self 3?] ... derives from one's
relations with other people.'

The cultural complexes are differentiated by the use of expressions like 'individualist' and 'collectivist'. But in this way of expressing forms of life the points to be made are expressed in terms of attributes ascribed to abstract entities, such as 'societies' and 'cultures'. The discursive psychologist would require these points to be spelled out in terms of the actual practices in which these attributes are immanent. And indeed that is just what Markus and Kitayama do. So the alleged parallel between pairs of properties is actually a parallel between, or perhaps even an inclusion in, one set of practices and another.

This complex typology has been criticized by Raeff (1997) on the grounds that the 'independent/interdependent' distinction is not between people but between the different discursive strategies that one person might adopt from time to time and with respect to different contexts of action. As we shall see this point is very well taken. Killen (in press) has gone a step further and offered fairly convincing evidence that the sociological typology is defective in a similar way to that in which the psychological typology is defective. It does not pick out societies or cultures, but selects discursive strategies made use of from time to time by the people of this or that culture as context requires. Killen (1997) remarks that 'diversity exists within cultures, that is, that individuals, within the same culture, approach problems from very different perspectives.' She alleges, quite rightly, that 'researchers have asserted that the attributes associated with broad social orientations are applied indiscriminately without taking contextual, interpretative, and cognitive factors into account.' While I would not put the matter quite that way, the point is well taken, and given chapter and verse in her paper.

Throughout the whole of this literature we have a slippage between the style or characteristics of practices, meaningful activities in which people engage, and ascriptions of standing psychological attributes to the people so engaged. If it turns out that one cultural group favours one discursive strategy over another, we are inclined to explain that preference in terms of alleged psychological profiles of the people who do this. But it may well be, as Kitwood (1980) showed, that everyone is able to adopt both discursive strategies, but they use one for one task and one for another. Cultures are differentiated by the profiles of their typical task demands.

The link to Self 2 is tenuous. Each person has, among their attributes, the skills and capacities for a great many possible social worlds and tribal forms of life. Both sorts of practices are expressions of Self 2, and of course the beliefs people have about themselves are also part of their Selves 2. If we look closely at the material offered by Markus and Kitayama in support of their typology we find that it consists almost entirely of reports of different *practices*. So the idea that there are 'other-focused *people*' is grounded in a description of certain practices, such as deferring to others in a conflict. Of course one social group may favour deferral to aggressive responses to disagreement, and so people will more often adopt that strategy. But there is a further implication in the Markus and Kitayama typology. It is that the Selves 2 of people from the two kinds of society they accept, from Triandis and others, are different in that the independent have attributes that are intrinsic to that very person, while the inter-dependent have relational attributes. This suggestion is no more convincing than the general correlation, mentioned above.

A further aspect of the Markus and Kitayama paper deserves comment. They seem to be offering a psychological mechanism by which action-styles are differentially adopted. It is something like 'attention to the self-concept' or, as they say 'construals of self'. A person thinks 'what sort of person [Self 2] am I?' and answers 'interdependent', and so adopts a particular Self 3 style. Since all that is going on is the performance of practices of various sorts, the foregoing describes a discursive style. If we adopt the 'private/public' distinction, as a mere division of location of essentially the same discursive practices, it is hardly surprising that 'construal of self', a private discursive practice, and say practising a nur-turant style, a public discursive practice, should, in a certain situation, be similar. If the location in the private/public dimension is merely accidental, then it is close to tautological that 'construals of self' and 'social behaviour' will be stylistically similar. Nothing about causes can be drawn from the correlation. The problem of heterogeneity of cognition disappears (if inter- and independence were supposed to be attributes of persons, that is comprised in Self 2) when we see the differences in form of life pointed out by Markus and Kitayama as varieties of discursive conventions.

Further light on the complexity of comparisons between people of different 'tribes' is thrown by the studies by Crystal et al. (in press) into how American, Chinese and Japanese youngsters describe the differences between people. The American and Japanese participants tended to mention cognitive abilities and material resources, whereas the Chinese tended to mention behavioural characteristics. Older participants divided along different lines, the Americans mentioning more kinds of differences than the Orientals.

In what sense is 'the self not essential'? Not in the embodied point of view. That is part of what it is to be a human being. Not in the socio-legal concept of person. The very possibility of language depends on a moral recognition of others' rights and their recognition of one's own. But there is both diversity and multiplicity in the attributes that each person displays from time to time. If this is so, and the extent to which it is remains a researchable question, there is an essential core in the beliefs that people have about themselves, that they are in space and time, and that they are, in principle, the possessors of communicative powers. But everything else people believe about themselves, as if it were natural or ineluctable, can, it seems to me, be shown to be a local variant on what are only generic similarities amongst the people of the tribes there have been, that currently exist and that are to come.

Social pathologies of self-presentation

Variations in the forms of autobiographical telling

It might seem obvious that an autobiography is a window into its author's soul. But pathological 'souls' can find expression either in the unusual content of their stories or in the use of a strange grammar. The study of the expression of self in stories is part of discursive psychology. This development is based on a Vygotskian thesis about the shaping of mind in the learning of linguistic and practical skills in symbiosis with another person, and on a Wittgensteinian insight that how we feel and how our thoughts are organized are expressed in characteristic language games. The selfhood of autobiographical telling, analysed in Chapter Six is expressed predominantly in the uses of first and second person (indexical) pronouns and in the choice of narrative conventions within which to tell the story. Pronouns are used to index what is said with the various locations of the speaker as a person amongst persons in several patterns of relations. The uses of 'I' with the tenses of verbs, together with local narrative conventions, express the shapes of the many stories we can tell about ourselves. It is quite usual for each person to have many auto-biographies. But when non-standard uses of pronouns appear we must be alert to a kind of linguistic pathology which, given the strength of the expressive account of language use, may express a pathological structuring of the mind of the speaker.

I have shown how the use of the first person has indexical force in four dimensions, though not all of these are grammatically realized in the Indo-European languages. The sense of self, the possession of which distinguishes a human being as a person, is expressed in these four indexical markings. The sense of oneself as a singularity is an expression of the complex interweavings of one's perceived and expressed locations in at least three arrays of persons, arrays which are ordered by shifting and unstable relations. The fourth element in the indexical expression of selfhood is one's sense of a life history which is, at any moment, a selection from a variety of possible personal pasts related to anticipations that project one of a variety of possible personal futures. A pathology of autobiography can come from two sources. What one does may seem strange in many possible ways, when juxtaposed to the conventional life courses considered proper in a certain time and place. For example it is now well established that there is a sudden increase in the detail introduced into a story at the point at which something the speaker wishes to conceal occurred. But for the discursive psychologist at least of equal interest and importance are the pathologies that derive from failures in the four indexical aspects of personal story-telling.

An inability or unwillingness to index one's perceptual reports with the location of one's body seems to be a possibility. Reporting in the third person does occur, and while it is at first sight merely a device for repudi-ating agency, it may reveal a deeper malaise. The use of the third person to index reports of what has been perceived, either in the external world or subjectively, does not index the report with any particular place in space. Additional information must be on hand, namely where the person whose perceptions are reported was at the time they occurred. The use of the first person suffers no such defect since the point of view is fixed by the very embodied location of he or she who speaks.

Studies of the speech of schizophrenics have shown a defect in the agentic indexing of speech acts, in that the passive 'me' is preferred to the active 'I' when reporting life events and so contributing fragments of autobiography. Similarly it has been reported that autistic children, lacking a sense of personal responsibility for actions, adopt a passive mode – indeed, if they are speakers of English, failing altogether to make use of pronouns. In the absence of pronouns the indexical force of an act of speaking is indeterminate. I have been told by an experienced carer of autistic children that the moment at which she perceives them to be ready to take responsibility is also the moment at which pronoun use becomes firmly established. From the point of view of discursive psychology the question of which change is responsible for which is misplaced. I have already cited Michael Lewis's demonstration that the appearance of the self-regarding emotions, like shame, comes at about the time that competence in the use of pronouns can be observed. Wittgenstein's analysis of expressive uses of language depends on our seeing a subjective state and the tendency to express it as indispensable components of a unitary psychological phenomenon.

O'Connor's (1997) studies of fragments of autobiography offered by convicted and indeed self-confessed murderers brought to light a discursive convention that routinely presented the speaker as a patient. One might make a case, from the frequency and taken-for-granted character of the use of this convention, that 'telling a personal story in the patient mode' is the unmarked version of autobiography. The phrase that carries implication of passivity is 'and then *I caught a charge*'. The model for this construction is something like 'I caught a cold.' Things you catch are personal states and conditions all right, but they are, as it were, out there, floating about, and by chance and through no fault of your own you run into them. A killing may be reported as something that happened, in a neutral style that neither takes nor repudiates responsibility; but that the police should hold me responsible for it, to the extent of charging and ultimately trying and even condemning me, is something that positions the speaker in their own moral order as 'the one who should be held responsible for doing it'. This is a strategy of the sophisticated user of the standard discursive tools for the taking and repudiating of responsibility. It is as far as it could possibly be from pathology.

In European languages other than English, a mildly 'off-key' style of some autobiographical telling could arise in the use (and misuse) of the second person, as indexing the relation of speaker to presumed addressee: 'Como he dicho al Principe de Gales, "Tú tienes demasiado interés en el polo".' The sprinkling of gossip columns of English national newspapers with certain uses of the first person is at least partly responsible for the unpleasant 'taste' of the fragments of autobiography they contain. 'Sharing a table with *my* good friend the Duke of Somewhere, . . . I . . .': this suggests an intimacy, where the choice of other grammatical forms for reporting the incident would perhaps seem forced or too overt a piece of social climbing. The disappearance of the English 'thee/you' distinction in favour of the ubiquitous 'you' reflects a deliberate choice of speech pattern to distance oneself as a speaker from the Quakers, considered among the upper classes to be tiresome zealots.

The fourth component of the indexical grammar of English story-telling is the indexing of what has been described or avowed as an event in the life history of the speaker. Lacking the tensed first person pronoun, English speakers must use tense to order their autobiographies, and at the same time the continuity of the story-line is ensured by the transtemporal sense of 'I' and 'me'. The same is not true of 'we', since the collective, membership of which it expresses, can and does change with time. Lying about one's past and fantasizing about one's future are obvious possibilities in the telling of autobiographical tales, but in these studies of the self I am concerned with pathologies which infect the indexicality of story-telling. It is not only pronouns that bear temporal indexicalities but also tenses. What if someone lacked a sense of the past and had no antici-pations of the future? The first person might survive in their speech, but there would be no verbs inflected for tense. The widely reported case of the English musician Waring, a man without a sense of past or future but with his powers of speech, including the use of the first person, unimpaired, shows that the expressing of spatial location is an act distinct from indexing one's talk with a moment in an autobiographical trajectory in time. Or perhaps some reportings would be indexed as past and others as future but with those categories no order would be expressed, because, according to the discursive point of view, no order in recollection would be experienced. In the case notes of psychiatrists (for instance in those of the redoubtable Oliver Sachs, in whose consulting room some remarkable cases seem to congregate) there must be material that would be of the greatest interest to those discursive psychologists who are interested in the indexical pathologies of autobiography. There is lots to do in charting these divergences and using their light to reveal what, in this culture or that, counts as the right and proper way to order a life.

Pathological autobiographies

In the small English city of Gloucester there once lived a couple, Fred and Rosemary West. For more than fifteen years they pursued a way of life so extraordinary that our capacity even to imagine what they did, let alone explain it, is nearly exhausted. For the psychologist the question must be: what was it like to be Fred West? Or to be Rosemary? After his conviction Fred produced a vast auto-biography, some of which has been published in newspapers. The English pronominal system and associated positioning devices

allowed him to take all the responsibility for the appalling treatment of the victims upon himself. The indexicality of place that
pronoun usage offers a speaker was used time and again to locate
Rosemary far from the times and places of the events in question.
The indexicality of responsibility was used time and again to locate
the whole agentic power in himself. At the same time as we pay
attention to the grammatical devices by which Fred West's relation
to the events was constructed we must also take account of the fact
that this was an extended narration, many acts of story-telling.
Stories have their own logic, the narrative conventions of the
culture. During the trial many other people told the stories of their
encounters with the Wests. And in the discursive acts of the trial
itself various other versions were produced. From the standpoint
of discursive psychology the key not only to what the Wests have
said, but also to what they did, lies in the patterns of story-telling
within which these horrific episodes were embedded.

Broadly speaking there could be at least two ways in which autobiographical narratives might display a pathological form of life.
Subscribing to common narrative conventions and, so far as one can
judge, employing the grammatical resources of English in the
accepted manner, in a certain sense Fred West's autobiography was
not pathological. The story he told was horrific but it was a story
the form of which we can all recognize. Perhaps the disturbing
effect of these revelations was due in part to the commonplace and
even stereotypical use of pronoun grammar and narrative conventions in their telling. The lives of the Wests were pathological in
content but not in form. For this reason alone we must hold them
responsible for and thus guilty of their monstrous acts.

However, a familiar issue surfaces once again. What are the
boundaries of autobiography? One limit, that follows from my
general claim that the form of public expression is holistically
linked with the form of private thought, must, in each culture, be
the local conceptions of coherence. Adshead (1997) remarks about
the incoherence of narratives 'where the sense of self appears to
have been "disorganised" by loss or trauma'. From my point of
view there are not two things here, a disorganized self and an incoherent narrative, but just one, the narrative, with which, to use
Miller Mair's phrase, one speaks oneself both to oneself and to
others. If we think of mentation as essentially symbolic, then in a
way all psychology is 'grammar', that is the structure of the mind
and the structures of private and public discourse are the same
thing. What can be attributed to an individual is a disposition to
create certain kinds of narratives, but how they are read, or even if

they can be read at all, is a function of the social environment in which they are brought forth.

One must resist the temptation to slip back into the simplistic 'liberal' notion of the psychological and morally autonomous individual. The question of 'how we would distinguish the psychopath of peacetime from the saboteur of wartime' takes us to the heart of the matter (Norrie, 1997). The singularity of the Self 1 means that certain unities of time and place must be preserved. More labile and therefore, in a certain sense, more negotiable are the moral positions and social standings that are also indexed by the use of the first person. There is a contrast between the non-pathology of Fred West's discourse in the first two indexical dimensions, of spatio-temporal singularity and the taking of moral responsibility. The latter was very much in evidence since in trying to deflect the law from Rosemary West he needed to exploit the full force of the English 'I'. A deeper study would need to call on 'positioning theory', in which the pattern of rights and obligations between the people of a close community are mapped, and which are expressed in narrative, not directly in the syntax (if it is an English story) but in the story-lines and the illocutionary force of how we take up what has been said. The positioning of others as mere instruments displays a pathology of language. A mere instrument cannot be addressed or listened to, since as such it has no linguistic powers at all. If then we examine the full gamut of the indexical force of the first person, in its marking of the time, place, position and standing of the speaker *in relation to those addressed*, the victims of the Wests' activities, we might come near the pathology of Fred West's auto-biography. But how do we halt the slide in the other direction, the slide that would leave us with a wholly contextual account of evil? I confess I have no easy solution to this conundrum, but I believe it lies somewhere in the conditions necessary for there to be language at all.

It follows from the main thesis of the narratological version of discursive psychology, as set out by Bruner, that behind pathological lives there must lie pathological story-tellings. So it is to auto-biography, as the most psychologically relevant form of narrative for the understanding of disturbed and distorted lives, that we must turn. Of course the very idea of 'disturbed' and 'distorted' presupposes the existence of patterns of lives that are 'correct' or 'normal' and that must surely be a topic for the anthropologist and historian to explore. At any moment in the history of human psychology there will be patterns that are the taken-for-granted background of uncontentious ordinariness. But what was ordinary for

the Toltec (see Pizarro's *The conquest of Mexico*) or a medieval
Carmelite (see the *Héloïse and Abelard*) might seem very strange and
even pathological to a shopkeeper in the 1990s.

Self-deception

What is it that is going on when someone, as we say, persistently
deceives themselves? What is the cash value of the metaphor in
terms of the conceptual system deployed in these studies? How can
a person deceive themselves if the one who is deceived is the very
one who is the deceiver? I shall try to show that the paradoxical
appearance of the concept is an illusion. Once one homes in closely
on what sort of discursive activity is involved in cases that we call
'self-deception' the paradoxical air vanishes.

Iterated pronouns

By extending our analysis of the role of personal pronouns and
other devices functioning in the same way we can gain a surview
of the practices of critical self-examination. I shall try to show that
self-deception is a pathological variant on everyday practices of
self-examination. Following once again the Vygotskian way of
looking at things, I shall work with the assumption that person
practices of self-examination are special cases of and derive their
social practices from the critical examination of others, especially
through their conversational contributions. If we are to understand
the logical grammar of statements like 'I am not sure I understand
you', 'I think I am going to be sick' or 'I believe I am falling in love
with you', we must compare them with statements like 'I think he
is falling in love with you', 'I am afraid he is going to be sick' and
'I am not sure he understands you.' While the latter group are
clearly descriptive and predictive, and make use of evidence, the
former are performative and expressive. A statement like 'I am not
sure I understand you' is a weaker form of the performative utterance 'I understand you', which is not a description of my state of
mind but a confirmatory act with respect to what you have said.
This is even clearer in the case of 'I think I am falling in love with
you', which is a weaker declaration of affection than 'I love you',
but again not primarily a report on my affective state. Of course
affective states, nauseous feelings and a sense of cognitive grasp are
not irrelevant to the propriety of the first person statements but
their description is not the social role of these utterances.

The use of the substantive 'self', detached from such pronominal settings as 'myself', tends to emerge in discursive practices that seem to confirm a Cartesian ontology. But if, as I have argued, the 'self' vocabulary is not used substantivally, this appearance is an illusion. Let us look at the details of a self-examining utterance in the following:

Alpha: I_1 am not sure that I_2 trust you.
Beta: Why, what have I done?
Alpha: Well, you let me down once before.

Let us refer to 'I trust you' as *a* and 'I am not sure that *a*' as *b*. Alpha's second statement offers some evidence for retracting *a*. But what is its relation to *b*? Since *b* is a performative utterance, a weaker version of *a*, *a* must be a part of what Austin called the 'felicity conditions' for *b*, that is the conditions that make *b* proper or correct in the circumstances. The weaker performative is created by the epistemic qualification of the stronger embedded performative. Do the two occurrences of 'I' in *a* serve the same function? 'I_1' plainly indexes the whole utterance as the speaker's responsibility, and so is related to the speaker as a singular person. But 'I_2' would seem to have subtly shifted its point of application to what I have called Self 2, since loss of trust is a dispositional attribute of the speaker. The way is now open for a non-paradoxical account of self-deception, in that in these complex utterances we might find a model for the expression of false reflexive beliefs that do not need a doubling up of the person to make sense.

Monodrama

The concept of monodrama was introduced by Evreinov (1923) to describe a genre of theatre in which the characters in a play represented different aspects of a human mind. The discursive interplay between the characters was presented as a kind of model of the cognitive processes of an individual person.

The same thought has been echoed by Jerome Bruner:

There is within each person a cast of characters – an aesthetic, a frightened child, a little man, even an onlooker, sometimes a Renaissance man. The great works of the theatre are decompositions of such a cast, the rendering into external drama. The life too can be described as a script, constantly rewritten, guiding an unfolding internal drama. (1986: 137)

Both Evreinov and Bruner can be interpreted as suggesting that the forms of life come about through the projection of the forms of mind onto social interaction. However, taking my cue from Vygotsky, I am inclined to think that, at least in the case of Bruner's use of the general idea of monodrama, the cast of characters that can be imagined as components of the human mind are borrowed from episodes of real life. The attempt we might make to understand the ways in which we carry out such reflexive activities as self-criticism and self-exhortation, and the kind of language in which the 'I' addresses, exhorts and criticizes the 'me', must be understood by reference to linguistic practices borrowed from those originally developed for social purposes of exhortation, criticism and so forth, in which the commentator or critic and the actor are different persons. Accordingly from the monodramatic point of view, as thus revised, the concept of self-deception can be made sense of only with a model drawn from typical social episodes from within the moral order of the community in which the self-deceiver lives and from the language he or she speaks.

From this point of view it follows that we may not take for granted that there is any such thing as a universal phenomenon of self-deception. There may be, but that would emerge only after a prolonged and detailed study of concrete examples considered within the framework of the deceptive discourses of this or that particular society.

The first step then will be to consider some ways in which we can deceive each other. Broadly speaking there are two classes of deceptive acts. Complexities in detail are very great depending in part on whether words or actions are the main vehicle of the deceit. One may lie, or one may fail to disclose. In English law it is an offence not only to tell falsehoods about the state of a house that one is offering for sale, but also to fail to reveal hidden defects to the prospective buyer. In both cases the victim of the deception is prevented from *knowing* what he or she has a *right* to know. Matters of fact intersect with the local moral order in creating the local standards of impropriety in discourse.

But having a right to know something does not entail that one would like to know it. For example one has a right to know the result of medical tests, but most people are apprehensive with good reason about what is to be disclosed, and a significant proportion of those who consult their physician do not want to be informed about their true condition. So there are three dimensions of variation in deceptive interpersonal discourses: truth and falsity, rights to knowledge which may or not be recognized, and the wish to know or not to know. Jos Jaspers once pointed out that if we take a point somewhere in north-western Europe as the prime location of a moral order in which speakers intend hearers to take their remarks literally, the further south and east one goes the less can one rely on that intention. One may be told a version of the facts that the speaker thinks the hearer would like to have, or a version of the facts that throws the speaker into the most favourable light, or some fatal combination of the two.

If self-deception is a cultural practice modelled on the local styles of deceptive discourse, then we would expect there to be a Jaspersian diversity in forms of self-deception and attitudes to it that reflects interpersonal patterns of diversity in the conventions for (mis)informing one another of how things stand. So there will be no single, universal consensus as to the limits beyond which the self-concept of some individual is so different from what one might reasonably expect it to be that it must be treated as pathologically self-deceptive. Did the cult leader really believe that he had the power to lead his disciples through 'Heaven's Gate' to join the space riders of the Hale–Bopp comet? Since he joined them in their mass suicide we must presume that he did. But did not a smidgeon of self-doubt ever cross his mind?

Self-discovery and admissions of default

One way of reading such commonplace remarks as 'It took me ages to admit to myself that I had little talent for chess' is to see them as marking the end of an episode of self-deception. On the face of it two psychological beings seem to be referred to: one who admits and one to whom an admission is made. Taking 'I have come to realize you have little talent for chess' as the model for 'I have come to realize I have little talent for chess' might tempt one to take both remarks as marking a transition in the knowledge that A has of B. In Fingarette's (1969) study two self-like components of a single human being are interacting much as two persons might. According to Fingarette, in the psyches of self-deceivers there are two psychological centres around which knowledge and beliefs cluster, especially those concerning that very human being. If we were to return to Aristotle's account of weakness of the will (akrasia) at this point we would say that the self-deceiver is a person who attends to only one of these clusters. Are we under any philosophical necessity to follow the path of mono-drama rigidly and project the duality of persons indexed in the model sentence form onto the iterated 'I'? I shall argue that any such temptation can be blocked by a close look at the function of statements by which people confess their falling into self-deception, yet remain within the general monodramatic framework.

What does a remark like 'I realize I have been fooling myself', apropos perhaps of some capacity or skill I thought I possessed, do in a conversation? I suggest that such statements are a rhetorical framing, in terms of an acceptable public-collective grammatical model, of a change of mind. The model is one of mild interpersonal reproach, or a reminder of harsher realities, but there is a balance between candour and tact. What of the state of the person before this admission? Here we are inclined to say that they were deceiving themselves. But in this and similar cases the psychological reality is *simply* being wrong. The iterated 'I' is a rhetorical device, not the mark of a subtle psychological hypothesis. Interpreted this way there is no temptation to suggest that the being who knows is ontologically distinct from the being who was mistaken. It is just the same being. Nor is there any temptation to introduce the idea that there are beliefs which are conscious and others which are not, as the basis of a psychological explanation of how a person can be wrong about their capacities and skills, or, in the other large class of cases, about what happened to them. I could ignore things I know or, while not ignoring them, simply fail to acknowledge them or take them into account. Or in the most complex case, the accuser thinks I should remember or acknowledge something that he or she thinks is important in my life, but I do not: 'R.H. is deceiving himself again!'

To get an adequate surview of these practices we must look at a close relative of self-deception, namely hypocrisy. The hypocrite's discursive activities have a similar formal structure to those of the self-deceiver. The hypocrite knows or believes one thing and says or does something incompatible with it. But whereas the accusation of hypocrisy is based on the assumption that the hypocrite is aware of his or her covert beliefs, the self-deceiver at the moment of self-deception is not. This brings us to a second main point about self-deception, in that in the treatment I am proposing the thesis that beliefs are dispositions, not states of mind, is an important ingredient. The self-deceiver is thought to be in possession of the self-discrediting belief, but is not paying attention to it. That is possible only if the belief is a disposition. The hypocrite can formulate beliefs privately that would have been contradicted by other public disclosures had they been allowed to filter through into the public arena. There is no temptation to create a double ontology of deceiver and deceived in the case of hypocrisy, other than the person and those others who are taken in. Self-deception is distinguished from deceit, prevarication and hypocrisy simply by the extent to which the speaker has paid attention to or delved into and assessed his or her dispositions and powers, such as beliefs, resources, talents and skills. While hypocrisy is taken to be a vice we are a little more forgiving of self-deception, though it too is reprehensible. Its moral deficit is laziness, inattention, and so on. The self-deceiver ought to have acknowledged those matters that are germane to what he or she is planning to do or is giving expression to.

Erving Goffman (1963) has drawn our attention to an intermediate case that lies between hypocrisy and the mildly reprehensible self-deceit that candour resolves. He has remarked on the extent to which people need to present themselves in public in such a way that they conceal certain events in their past and certain attributes they have that, if known, would discredit their current publicly presented self. Goffman called these facts 'stigmata'. In his subtle and entertaining book he explored the strategies by which discrediting facts are routinely withheld from public knowledge, particularly by the careful management of public display. Sometimes there is even a kind of collusion between people to protect one another's public faces by refraining from that kind of public interrogation which, mutually indulged, would reveal the stigmata that each has so carefully kept from public view. This is neither hypocrisy nor self-deception. It is not hypocrisy because it does not attract the same kind of moral condemnation. It is not self-deception because the stigmatized person is privately paying attention to the facts that must be kept concealed.

According to the account I have offered self-deception is no more puzzling a psychological phenomenon than any other form of inattention. Of course why one does not pay attention to failings and faults may be different from why one does not pay attention to something repeated so often that it has lost its power to fascinate. Thus instead of a double self we have a person whose attention wanders. However this still seems to require the concept of motivated inattention, and perhaps even motivated forgetting. How can I have a motive to forget something that is disagreeable to me? How can I have a motive to attend to something else than that which is too painful or humiliating to attend to? If beliefs are dispositions and iterated first person statements are simply qualified declarations indexed to the person who is speaking, then the temptation to double up centres of consciousness or to invent a realm of thoughts of which one is not conscious can be resisted.

The rhetorical treatment of these moral and psychological failings can be extended to other phenomena, as for instance in Warner's (1986) account of 'self-betrayal'. Instead of taking the heart of self-betrayal or self-deception to be the proposition that A does not know, believe or remember that which he or she wishes to forget, which requires that A does know, believe or remember the matter in question to have any wishes with regard to it, Warner argues that both sides of the seeming contradiction are mis-descriptions. Instead of a style of self-presentation that involves adopting an apologetic, self-accusing and self-denigrating rhetoric, A adopts a self-glorifying and self-justifying rhetoric. There are not two 'persons' embodied as A, one reflecting on the capacities and achievements of the other. There is just one person who has the option of all sorts of rhetorics of self-presentation. When adopting the self-glorifying style, lack of attention to matters that are discrepant is hardly surprising. The difference between honesty with oneself and self-deception is not that of psychological levels, one visible and the other invisible; or that of quasi-persons or 'psychological centres', of tricksters and dupes. Rather it is a difference in moral tone of ways of relating a part of one's life. The telling of a slice of life in the rhetoric of self-aggrandizement precludes the telling of it in a rhetoric of self-deprecation, self-accusation and the like. The ordinary business of displaying oneself in a good light becomes pathological when the display and the personal facts drift too far apart. These ways of managing reflexive discourses are made possible by the adoption for reflexive story-telling, for private thought, of the conventions of a monodrama as those of the drama of everyday life.

Conclusion

The very idea of 'singularity of self' brings to mind the possibility of multi-plicity and diversity of self. I have tried to show that there is indeed both multiplicity of selfhood in the (sometimes untapped) discursive resources of ordinary people on ordinary occasions. I have also tried to show that there is diversity among people and among cultures in several dimensions of self-display and self-disclosure. But the major point of all this has been that a certain picture, suggested by that very way of talking, is seriously defective. It suggests that within a person there are selves hidden away to be brought out, to be displayed, or to be disclosed. There are no such 'inner' states, structures, 'authentic selves' which might or might not appear in the public world of everyday action and conversation. There are, to be sure, a person's skills, capacities, dispositions, tendencies and so on, which may from time to time be realized in private and public action – action that the person, as active producer of meanings, brings into existence in symbiotic relationships with others. Those skills are not grounded in anything psychological or mental. They are the 'bottom line', the ultimate features of mentality that analysis reveals. How is it that my skills and dispositions, beliefs and memories, are 'there' to be recovered in future discursive acts? They exist in the only way they could in a world of our sort, in the material groundings of my personal powers, in the relatively robust and permanent properties of my brain and nervous system. This thought takes us back to the very beginning of this study, where I argued for psychology as an essentially dual science. It is dual in its ontology. The basic particulars of the world of thought and action are people, having all sorts of resources for interacting conversationally with one another, and in ways that have the same form as conversations, joint actions mediated by rules and conventions. The basic particulars of the world of bodies *per se* are molecular clusters. In the conversational world people are not hierarchically organized; only their action patterns display such structures. But in the organic world human bodies are hierarchically organized, organs and their parts, and ultimately the basic particulars are molecular clusters. Given this ontology it ought to be obvious that Wundt was right, in all essentials. Psychology is also dual in its methodologies. The conversational world can be made sense of by the use of techniques drawn from history, literary studies, linguistics, anthropology and philosophy, which are no less strict in their criteria of good work than are the biological sciences. Indeed in some respects they are demonstrably tighter. The groundings of discursive capacities in the bodies of those who have them can be made sense of by the use of techniques drawn from anatomy, physiology, molecular biology, and the like. Two new sciences link these seemingly diverse aspects of human life. Ethology, the study of naturally occurring signal systems, serves to bring out the natural endowment without which the cultural forms of life could never have arisen and without which they could never be passed on to new generations. Artificial intelligence, in trying to achieve machine simulations of at least some human thought patterns, can provide us not only with schematic formal grammars of the discursive skills we do possess, but also with schematic models of the groundings of those skills materially. The singularities of self are to be found, on the one hand, in the unique embodiment of each person in one and only one body. But they are also to be found in the discursive resources for personal expression, the pronoun systems and other indexical devices of diverse cultures. In this as in all other matters, human life is lived in two worlds, one material and the other symbolic.

The four main concepts of personal identity that were introduced in Chapter One as the standard model, to bring order to our intuitions about concepts of person and self have now been shown to be the ordering principles of the actual fields of usage of words by which the sense of personal identity and singularity is routinely expressed. The results of our grammatical studies can now be set out as an ontology of selfhood as follows:

Person: the embodied, publicly identifiable and individuatable and unanalysable being around which the human form of life revolves. Persons are subject to criteria of numerical and qualitative identity. The question of which person it is that one encounters is a factual matter. It makes sense to raise questions of doubt and certainty in this context. However there are no criteria which I myself might use to decide whether I am or am not the same person I was on other occasions at other times. In consequence expressions like 'I know I am the same person as before', if they are declarations with respect to the sense of self, are radically misleading, since they make place for such notions as 'having or lacking evidence', 'making sure', 'being doubtful about' and so on which have no application to this concept.

Self 1: the concept of self that is embedded in a person's sense of self, of occupying one and only one standpoint from which to perceive and act upon the environment both external and internal to the bodily envelope. It is manifested in and exists as the spatial indexicality of the use of the first person.

Self 2: the totality of attributes of a person including that person's beliefs about him or herself. Reflexive beliefs encompass ideas about what sort of person one is, what one's strengths and vulnerabilities are and what one's life history has been. The concept is manifested in the self-concept which is none other than the stories one tells about oneself and the actions one performs as oneself.

Self 3: the sort of person that we are taken to be by others. This concept is complicated by the fact that there is the self I intend to project in what I say and do, and the self that others read in my speech and action. It is manifested in the conversations in which one engages with others as a responsible person.

The first person indexes our discourse with at least three aspects of Self 1, spatial location of embodiment, continuity of personal history and certain moral relations to other persons. In each context the Self 1 is a singularity. The default position for the first indexical marking is that one perceives the world from the spatial location of one's body, unless otherwise argued for. The default position for the autobiographical indexical marking is that a person has a continuous history unless otherwise argued against. We create our minds *ad hoc* in the course of carrying on our lives. Stabilities and unities in these creations create the illusion of inner selves, but they have no more independent existence than the selves we produce *ad hoc* for others, which they may or may not confirm, and so bring more concretely into existence. At most this array of selves has the status of a vortex in the flow of the river.

In setting out the indexical thesis I have shown, I hope, how Wittgenstein's insight that there is a radical distinction between expressive and descriptive uses of language solves the methodological problem of entering in a robust manner, worthy to be subsumed under the strict umbrella of 'mental science', into the private experience of others. Underlying this insight is Wittgenstein's thesis of the holism of expression and experience, in such cases as feeling and the sense of self.

We have also solved our ontological problem – what is the self? Taking this question as if it invited a hunt for a special kind of entity has generated an ocean of metaphysics, the Cartesian ego and its rich crop of variations. By paying attention to the forms of the expression of the sense of self we have condensed this ocean into a drop of grammar. In the ontology of the human world the basic particulars are persons. Attempting to explain the sense of self by borrowing the hypothetico-deductive methods from the physical sciences and postulating unobservable entities, be it the ego or be it generic traits, just populates the ontology of psychology with a class of redundant and mythical beings, snarks, which, if *per impossible* were finally cornered would probably turn out to be boojums. Nonsense objects, as Lewis Carroll well knew, can have only nonsense properties!

All we need to do is to describe the manifold ways that we use personal concepts from the standard model in making sense of our lives to ourselves and to others. These reflect the complex patterns of experience I have called our senses of self. It is a basic and fundamental aspect of our psychology that characterizes the human form of life: it forms part of the framework in which we bring about all our thoughts and actions. It is one of the conditions that make human life possible.

Notes

1 There are people who believe that they are reincarnations of someone from the past.

2 Among the most perceptive descriptions of learning new Selves 2 and 3 is the marvellous account of emigration by E. Hoffman (1989), called *Lost in translation*.

3 Sabat has shown how inadequate attention to the overall structure of the discourse of Alzheimer's sufferers can induce a false sense in the interlocutor that the Self 1 of the sufferer has been disrupted (Sabat and Harré, 1995).

4 It is curious that at this time when life in the United States displays more cultural uniformity than it has done since the war between the states there has appeared a stream of writings about the predicaments of those who have to adapt to a variety of cultural roles (Gergen, 1991). Writings such as these must make strange reading for polyglot Europeans or Indians, moving freely about their respective complex social worlds.

5 Ruth Benedict never set foot in Japan!

References

Ackrill, J. R. (1987) *A new Aristotle reader.* Oxford: Clarendon Press.

Adams, L. (1990) *Journal of the self.* New York: Warner.

Adshead, G. (1997) 'Commentary on "pathological autobiographies"', *Philosophical, Psychiatry and Psychology,* 4(2): 111–13.

Aldridge-Lewis, R. (1990) *Multiple personality: an exercise in deception.* New York: Lawrence Earlbaum.

American Psychiatric Association (1987) *Diagnostic and statistical manual of mental disorders,* 3rd edn rev. (DSM-III-R). Washington, DC. APA p. 272.

Anderson, J. A. and Schoenig, G. T. (1996) 'The nature of the individual in communication research', in D. Grodin and T. R. Lindlof (eds), *Constructing the self in a mediated world.* Thousand Oaks, CA: Sage. pp. 206–25.

Anthony, A. J. (1993) *Total self-confidence.* New York: Berkeley.

Apter, M. (1989) 'Negativism and the sense of identity', in G. Breakwell (ed.), *Threatened identities.* London: Wiley.

Armstrong, D. (1968) *A materialist theory of the mind.* London: Routledge and Kegan Paul.

Aronson, J. R., Harré, R. and Way, E. C. (1995) *Realism rescued.* London: Duckworth.

Austin, J.L. (1961) *Philosophical papers.* Oxford: Oxford University Press.

Bachnik, J. (1982) 'Deixis and self/other reference in Japanese discourse', *Sociolinguistic Working Paper 99,* Southwest Educational Development Library, Austin, Texas.

Backman, C. (1977) 'Explorations in psycho-ethics', in R. Harré (ed.), *Life sentences.* Chichester: Wiley. pp. 99–108.

Bakhtin, M. M. (1986) *Speech genres and other essays,* eds C. Emerson and M. Holquiest, trans. V. McGee. Austin, TX: University of Texas Press.

Baumeister, R. (1984) *Self-esteem: the puzzle of low self-regard.* New York: Plenum.

Becker, A.L. and Oka, I. (1974) 'Person in Kawi', *Oceanic Linguistics,* 13(2): 229–55.

Benedict, R. (1946) *The chrysanthemum and the sword.* Boston: Houghton Mifflin.

Berman, L. A. (1992) 'First person identities in Indonesian conversational narratives', *Journal of Asiatic Pacific Communication,* 3: 3–14.

Bourdieu, P. (1977) *Outline of a theory of practice.* Cambridge and New York: Cambridge University Press.

Bourdieu, P. and Wacquant, L. J. D. (1992) *An invitation to reflexive sociology.* Chicago: University of Chicago Press.

Breakwell, G. M. (1992) *Social psychology of identity and the self concept.* London: Surrey University Press.

Brown, G. (1996) 'Centering the self', in D. Grodin and T.R. Lindlof (eds), *Constructing the self in a mediating world.* Thousand Oaks, CA: Sage. pp. 55–67.

Brown, R.W. and Gillman, A. (1970) 'Pronouns of power and solidarity', in R. Brown (ed.), *Psycholinguistics.* New York: Free Press. Chapter 1.

Bruner, J.S. (1986) *Actual minds, possible worlds*. Cambridge, MA: Harvard University Press.

Bruner, J. S. (1991) 'The narrative construction of reality', *Critical Inquiry*, Autumn: 1–21.

Bruner, J. S. (1993) 'The autobiographical process', in R. Folkenflik (ed.), *The culture of autobiography*. Stanford, CA: Stanford University Press. pp. 38–56.

Bruner, J.S. and Sherwood, V. (1977) 'Early rule structure', in R. Harré (ed.), *Life sentences*. Chichester: Wiley. pp. 55–62.

Bruner, J.S. and Watson, R. (1983) *Child's talk*. New York: Norton.

Butler, J. (1736) 'Dissertation I: Of personal identity', in W. E. Gladstone (ed.), *The Works of Joseph Butler*. Oxford: Clarendon Press (1897).

Castaneda, C. (1968) *The teachings of Don Juan*. Berkeley, CA: University of California Press.

Cattell, R. B. (1965) *The scientific analysis of personality*. London: Penguin Books.

Classen, C., Howes, D. and Synnott, A. (1994) *Aroma: the cultural history of smell*. London and New York: Routledge.

Cleghorn, P. (1996) *The secrets of self-esteem*. Shaftesbury: Element Books.

Cohen, A. and Eisdoríer, C. (1986). *The loss of self*. New York: Norton.

Cole, M. (1996) *Cultural psychology: a once and future discipline*. Cambridge, MA: Harvard University Press.

Coulter, J. (1983) *Rethinking cognitive theory*. New York: St Martin's Press.

Crapanzano, V. (1980) *Tuhami*. Chicago: Chicago University Press.

Crick, F. (1994) *The astonishing hypothesis: the scientific search for the soul*. New York: Scribners.

Crocker, J. and Luhtanen, R. (1990) 'Collective self-esteem and ingroup bias', *Journal of Personality and Social Psychology*. 58: 60–7.

Crocker, J., Luhtanen, R., Blaine, B. and Broadmax, S. (1994) 'Collective self-esteem and psychological well-being among white, black and asian college students', *Personality and Social Psychology Bulletin*, 20: 503–13.

Crystal, D., Watanabe, H., Wu Chin and Weinfurt, K. (in press) 'Concepts of human differences: a comparison between American, Japanese, and Chinese children and adolescents', *Developmental Psychology*.

Dennett, D. C. (1984) *Elbow room*. Cambridge, MA: MIT Press.

Dennett, D. C. (1991) *Consciousness explained*. Boston: Little Brown.

Deutsch, W., Wagner, A., Burchardt, R., Schulz, N. and Nakath, J. (1997) 'Person in the language of singletons, siblings and twins', in S. Levinson and M. Bowerman (eds), *Language acquisition and conceptual development*. Cambridge: Cambridge University Press.

Edwards, D. and Potter, J. (1992) *Discursive psychology*. Thousand Oaks, CA and London: Sage.

Elbaz, R. (1988) *The changing nature of the self: a critical study of the autobiographic discourse*. London: Croom Helm.

Erchak, G. M. (1992) *The anthropology of self and behavior*. New Brunswick, NJ: Rutgers University Press.

Evreinov, N. N. (1923) *The theatre in life*. London: Harrap.

Eysenck, H. J. and Eysenck, S. B. G. (1969) *Personality structure and measurement*. London: Routledge and Kegan Paul.

Fajans, J. (1985) 'The person in social context', in G.M.White and J. Kirkpatrick (eds), *Person, self and experience*. Berkeley, CA: University of California Press.

Field, L. (1997) *Self-esteem for women*. Shaftesbury: Element Books.

Fingarette, H. (1969) *Self-deception*. New York: Humanities Press.

Fodor, J. A. (1981) *Representing*. Brighton: Harvester.

Fraiberg, S. and Adelson, E. (1973) 'Self-representation in language and play: observations of blind children', *Psychoanalytic Quarterly*, 42: 539–62.

Gaines, A. D. (1996) 'Cultural definitions, behavior and the person', in D. Grodin and T. R. Lindlof (eds), *Constructing the self in a mediating world*. Thousand Oaks, CA: Sage. p. 177.

Geertz, C. (1977) *The interpretation of cultures*. New York: Basic Books.

Gergen, K. J. (1991) *The saturated self*. New York: Basic Books.

Gibson, J. J. (1979) *The ecological approach to visual perception*. Boston: Houghton Mifflin.

Gilbert, W. (1600) *De magnete*. London.

Glock, H.-J. and Hacker, P. M. S. (1996) 'Reference and first person pronouns', *Language and Communication*, 16: 95–105.

Glover, J. (1988) *I: the philosophy and psychology of personal identity*. London: Allen Lane.

Goddard, C. and Wierzbicka, A. (1995) 'Key words, culture and cognition', *Philosophica*, 55: 37–67.

Goffman, E. (1959) *The presentation of self in everyday life*. Garden City, NY: Doubleday.

Goffman, E. (1963) *Stigma*. Englewood Cliffs, NJ: Prentice-Hall.

Goffman, E. (1981) *Forms of talk*. Philadelphia: University of Pennsylvania Press.

Grodin, D. and Lindlof, T. R. (1996) *Constructing the self in a mediating world*. Thousand Oaks, CA: Sage.

Hacking, I. (1995) *Rewriting the soul*. Princeton: Princeton University Press.

Hammerle, C. (1995) *Plurality and individuality: autobiographical cultures of Europe*. Vienna: IFK.

Harré, R. (1983) *Personal being*. Oxford: Blackwell. Cambridge, MA: Harvard University Press.

Harré, R. and Madden, E. H. (1975) *Causal powers*. Oxford: Blackwell.

Harré, R. and Parrott, W. G. (1997) *The emotions*. London and Los Angeles: Sage.

Hawkins, H. (1990) *Classics and trash*. New York and London: Harvester/Wheatsheaf.

Heelan, P. (1988) *Spatial perception and the philosophy of science*. Berkeley, CA: University of California Press.

Heidegger, M. (1962) *Being and time*, trans. J. McQuarrie and E. Robinson. New York: Harper and Row.

Hoffman, E. (1989) *Lost in translation*. New York: Dutton.

Hong, M. K. (1975) *The woman warrior*. New York: Random House.

Hume, D. (1746) *A treatise of human nature*, ed. L. Selby-Bigge. New York: Dover (1965).

Humphrey, N. (1983) *Consciousness regained*. Oxford: Oxford University Press.

Husserl, E. (1960) *Cartesian meditations*, trans. D. Cairns. The Hague: Nijhoff.

Husserl, E. (1967) *Ideas* (original 1913). New York: Collier.

Husserl, E. (1970) *Logical investigations* (original 1900), trans. J. N. Findley. London: Routledge and Kegan Paul.

Jakobson, R. (1957) *Shifters, verbal categories and the Russian verb*. Cambridge, MA: Harvard University Russian Language Department.

James, W. (1977) *The writings of William James*. Chicago: Chicago University Press.

Jansz, J. (1991) *Reason, self and moral demands*. Leiden: DSWO Press.

Johnson, F. (1985) 'The Western concept of self', in A. J. Marsella, G. DeVos and F. L. K. Hsu (eds), *Culture and self: Asian and Western perspectives*. New York: Tavistock. pp. 91–138.

Jones, E. E. and Pittman, T. (1982) 'Toward a general theory of strategic self-presentation', in J. Suls (ed.), *Psychological perspectives on the self*. Hillsdale, NJ: Lawrence Erlbaum.

Kellerman, J. (1997) Lecture in 'Infancy' series, Spring Semester, Georgetown University, Washington DC.

Kenny, A. J. P. (1975) *Will, freedom and power*. Oxford: Blackwell.

Killen, M. (in press) 'Culture, self, and development: are cultural templates stereotypes?', *Developmental Review*.

Kitwood, T. M. (1980) *Disclosures to a stranger*. London: Routledge and Kegan Paul.

Kohut, H. (1977) *The analysis of the self*. New York: International Universities Press.

Lakoff, G. (1987) *Women, fire and dangerous things*. Chicago: Chicago University Press.

Lamiell, J. T. (1987) *The psychology of personality: an epistemological inquiry*. New York: Columbia University Press.

Lamiell, J. T. (1997) 'Individuals and the differences between them', in R. Hogan, J. A. Johnson and S. R. Briggs (eds), *Handbook of personality psychology*. New York: Academic Press. pp. 117–41.

Lee, B. (1979) *Psychosocial theories of the self*. New York and London: Plenum.

Lewis, M. and Ramsay, D. S. (1997) Lecture in 'Infancy' series, Spring Semester, Psychology Department, Georgetown University.

Liberman, K. (1989) 'Decentering the self: two perspectives from philosophical anthropology', in A. B. Dallery and C. E. Scott (eds), *The question of the other*. Albany, NY: State University of New York Press.

Locke, J. (1686) *An essay concerning human understanding*, ed. J. Yolton. London: Dent (1961).

Logan, R.D. (1987) 'Historical change in prevailing sense of self', in K. Yardley and T. Honess (eds), *Self and identity: psychosocial perspectives*. Chichester : Wiley.

Lutz, C. (1985) 'Ethnopsychology compared to what?' in G.M. White and J. Kirkpatrick (eds), *Person, self and experience*. Berkeley, CA: University of California Press. pp. 35–79.

McAdams, D.P. (1996) 'Personality, modernity, and the storied self: a contemporary framework for studying persons', *Psychological Inquiry*, 7: 295–321.

McAdams, D.P. (1997a) *The stories we live by*, 2nd edn. New York: Guilford.

McAdams, D.P. (1997b) 'Stories of commitment: the psychosocial construction of generative lives', *Journal of Personality and Social Psychology*, 72: 678–94.

McCrae, R.R. and Costa, P.T. (1995) 'Trait explanations in personality psychology', *European Journal of Personality*, 9: 231–52.

MacIntyre A. (1981) *After virtue*. Notre Dame: Notre Dame University Press.

Markova, I. and Foppa, K. (eds) (1990) *The dynamics of dialogue*. New York: Harvester.

Markus, H.R. and Kitayama, S. (1991) 'Culture and the self', *Psychological Review* 98: 224–53.

Markus, H.R. and Wurf, E. (1987) 'The dynamic self-concept: a social psychological perspective', *Annual Review of Psychology*, 38: 299–337.

Mead, G.H. (1934) *Mind, self and society*. Chicago: Chicago University Press.

Merleau-Ponty, M. (1962) *The phenomenology of perception*. London: Routledge and Kegan Paul.

Metzoff, A. (1997) Lecture to 'Infancy' series, Spring Semester, Psychology Department, Georgetown University, Washington DC.

Middleton, D. and Edwards, D. (1990) *Collective remembering*. London: Sage.

Midgley, M. (1996) 'One world, but a big one', *Journal of Consciousness Studies*, 3: 500–14.

Morgan, J., O'Neill, C. and Harré, R. (1977) *Nicknames*. London: Routledge and Kegan Paul.

Mühlhäusler, P. and Harré, R. (1993) *Pronouns and people*. Oxford: Blackwell.

Nash, C. (ed.) (1994) *Narrative in culture*. London and New York: Routledge. Chapters 1–5.

Neisser, U. and Fuvish, R. (1994) *The remembering self*. New York: Cambridge University Press.

Nicholson, L. (1997) 'Emotions in post-modern public space', in G. Hoffman and A. Hornung (eds), *Postmodernism and the emotions*. Heidelberg: Heidelberg Universitäts Verlag.

Norrie, A. (1997) 'Commentary on "pathological autobiographies"', *Philosophy, Psychiatry and Psychology*, 4(2): 115–18.

O'Connor, P. (1997) *Discourse and silencing*. New York: Longmans.

Parfitt, D. (1984) *Reasons and persons*. Oxford: Clarendon Press.

Peevers, B.H. and Secord, P.F. (1972) 'The development of person concepts in children'. Manuscript. University of Nevada.

Pierce, W. B. and Cronen, V. (1980) *Action, communication and meaning*. New York: Praeger.

Pinker, S. (1994) *The language instinct*. London: Allen Lane.

Prince, M. (1905) *The dissociation of personality*. London: Longmans Green (1968).

Propp, V. (1924) *The morphology of the folktale*. Austin: University of Texas Press.

Raeff, C. (1997) 'Individuals in relationship', *Developmental Review*, 10: 30–47.

Reid, T. (1788) *Essays on the active powers of the human mind*. Cambridge, MA: MIT Press (1969).

Robinson, D.N. (1989) *Aristotle's psychology*. New York: Columbia University Press.

Rosenberger, N. (1992) *Japanese sense of self*. Cambridge: Cambridge University Press.

Ryle, G. (1947) *The concept of mind*. London: Hutchinson.

Sabat, S.R. (1994) 'Excess disability and malignant social psychology: a case study of Alzheimer's disease', *Journal of Community and Applied Social Psychology*, 4: 157–66.

Sabat, S.R. and Harré, R. (1995) 'The Alzheimer's disease sufferer as semiotic subject', *Philosophy, Psychiatry and Psychology*, 1: 146–60.

Sapir, E. (1956) *Culture, language and personality*. Berkeley: University of California Press.

Sarbin, T. (1993) 'The narrative as the root metaphor for contextualism', in S. Hayes, L.P. Hayes, H. Reese and T.R. Sarbin (eds), *Varieties of scientific contextualism*. Reno: Context Press. pp. 51–66.

Schafer, R. (1992) *Retelling a life: narration and dialogue in psychoanalysis*. New York: Basic Books.

Searle, J. R. (1995) *The construction of social reality*. London: Allen Lane.

Shakur, A. (1987) *Assata: an autobiography*. London: Zed.

Shakur, S. (1993) *Monster: the autobiography of an LA gang member*. New York: Penguin.

Sherif, M. and Cantril, H. (1947) *The psychology of ego involvements*. New York: Wiley.

Shotter, J. (1971) 'Natural and acquired powers', *Journal of the Theory of Social Behaviour*, 1: 1–15.

Shotter, J. (1993) *Conversational realities*. London: Sage.

Shweder, R.A. (1991) *Thinking through cultures*. Cambridge, MA: Harvard University Press.

Siever, L.J. and Frucht, W. (1997) *The new view of self*. New York: Macmillan.

Smith, D. (1987) *The everyday world as problematic*. Boston: Northeastern University Press.

Spencer, H. (1896) *The principles of psychology*. New York: Appleton Century Crofts.

Spiro, M. (1993) 'Is the Western conception of "self" peculiar within the context of the world's cultures?', *Ethos*, 21: 107–53.

Stern, W. (1938) *General psychology from the personalistic standpoint*, trans. H.D. Spencer. New York: Macmillan.

Strawson, P.F. (1959) *Individuals*. London: Methuen.

Tafarodi, R.W. and Swann, W.B. (1995) 'Self-liking and self-competence as dimensions of global self-esteem', *Journal of Personality Assessment*, 65: 322–42.

Tajfel, H. (1981) *Human groups and social categories*. Cambridge: Cambridge University Press.

Tannen, D. (1989) *Talking voices*. Cambridge: Cambridge University Press.

Taylor, C. (1985) 'The person', in M. Carruthers, S. Collins and S. Lukes (eds), *The category of the person*. Cambridge: Cambridge University Press.

Taylor, C. (1989) *Sources of the self*. Cambridge, MA: Harvard University Press.

Taylor, C. (1991) 'The dialogical self', in J. Bohman, D. Hiley and R. Schusterman (eds), *The interpretative turn*. Ithaca, NY: Cornell University Press. pp. 304–14.

Taylor, D. and Harrison, R.M. (1977) 'On being categorized in the speech of others', in R. Harré (ed.), *Life sentences*. Chichester, Wiley. pp. 21–30.

Thigpen, C. H. and Cleckley, H. M. (1957) *The three faces of Eve*. New York: McGraw Hill.

van Langenhove, L. and Harré, R. (1991) 'Varieties of positioning', *Journal for the Theory of Social Behaviour*, 21: 393–407.

van Langenhove, L. and Harré, R. (1996) 'Telling your life', in N. Coupland and J.P. Nussbaum (eds), *Discourse and life-span identity*. Newbury Park, CA and London: Sage. pp. 81–99.

ver Eecke, W. (1989) 'Seeing and saying no within the theories of Spitz and Lacan', *Psychoanalysis and Contemporary Thought*, 12: 383–431.

Vygotsky, L.S. (1962) *Thought and language*. Cambridge, MA: MIT Press.

Vygotsky, L.S. (1978) *Mind in society*. Cambridge, MA: Harvard University Press.

Warner, C. T. (1986) 'Anger and other illusions', in R. Harré (ed.), *The social construction of emotions*. Oxford: Blackwell.

Wessley, S. (1993) 'Who is speaking?' *The Times*, 30 December.

Westcott, M. (1988) *The psychology of human freedom*. New York and London: Springer-Verlag.

Whorf, B.L. (1956) *Language, thought and reality*. Cambridge, MA: MIT Press.

Wierzbicka, A. (1992) *Semiotics, culture, and cognition*. Oxford: Oxford University Press.

Wittgenstein, L. (1953) *Philosophical investigations*, trans. G.E.M. Anscombe. Oxford: Blackwell.

Wittgenstein, L. (1969) *On certainty*, trans. D. Paul and G.E.M. Anscombe. Oxford: Blackwell.

Wittgenstein, L. (1979) *Remarks on Frazer's golden bough*, trans. A.C. Miles. Retford: Brymill.

Young-Eisendrath, P. and Hall, J. A. (1987) *The book of the self*. New York and London: New York University Press.

Subject Index

Name Index

Names of authors appearing only as authors of cited works appear in the bibliographical references only